WILDLIFE AND ECOTOURISM
Trends, Issues & Challenges

Wildlife and Ecotourism

Trends, Issues & Challenges

Edited by

R. Chandra

AKANSHA PUBLISHING HOUSE
NEW DELHI - 110 059 (INDIA)

AKANSHA PUBLISHING HOUSE
R-37B, Vani Vihar, Uttam Nagar
New Delhi - 10 059
E-mail: ektabooks@yahoo.com

Showroom
4649/21-B
Daryaganj, New Delhi - 110 002
Phones: 23263193, 9811582579

Wildlife and Ecotourism

First Published. 2005
Reprint : 2015
ISBN 81-8370-010-1

PRINTED IN INDIA

Published by M.P. Misra for Akansha Publishing House, New Delhi - 110 059 and Printed a Mehra Offset Press, New Delhi.

Contents

Contents

Preface

If seriously pondered over, 'Sustainability' is a fashionable topic, but coordinated and consistent efforts to achieve it in the face of soaring tourism are rare indeed. Nations desperate to promote international tourism are not especially susceptible to concepts of tourist carrying capacity, managed growth, or similar environmental niceties. Even areas where the main attractions are flora and fauna, and where 'ecotourism' is the buzzword, still allow shortcuts in environmentally sensitive development and permit far too many to visit fragile nesting, hatching or other endangered habitats. Ecotourism can make a virtue of small numbers of tourists, but unfortunately pressures to expand the scale and type of tourism grow with the industry's importance to the economy. For example, in the Galapagos Islands, the once pristine environment now hosts more than 300% of the number of visitors originally allowed. Another example is Costa Rica, renowned for its biodiversity and its commitment to make over 20% of its land mass a series of national parks. For years, growth in tourism was slowed by civil wars in neighbouring Central American nations, and promotion rather than control of tourism was the priority. However, since peace developed in neighbouring states, Costa Rican tourism has skyrocketed and the nation has become seduced by the money that tourism has brought. Lavish beach resorts without sewage systems have been developed and harsh and thoughtless logging practices near national parks threaten mudslides.

Generally, most discussions on sustainability focus on natural attractions, but it is also related to the growth, pace and type of tourist and the accompanying infrastructure. None of these factors can be taken for granted in developing nations. In some, accustomed to a high level of contact with outsiders, trading traditions have led to an entrepreneurial lifestyle that easily accommodates tourism, but elsewhere this is not the case and the potential for conflict can be high. Similarly, the adaptability and types of tourists may be an issue.

Because of the rapid increase in tourism, and its expansion to virtually every part of the world, modern tourists are inadequately prepared for visits to areas that seldom if ever saw colonial administrators. As a result, in some countries — notably India, Pakistan, Uganda, Algeria and Guatemala — opposition to tourists in general, and to certain nationalities and religions in particular, has grown. Other governments (e.g., Afghanistan, Iran, Iraq and Saudi Arabia) have moved to isolate their people from the allegedly pernicious effects of tourism, especially those emanating from Western women, by restricting or discouraging tourism.

With highly sophisticated tourism industries in developing countries, the issue of sustainability is becoming salient, especially as religious conservatives become more influential. As a consequence, some developed countries have discouraged their citizens from travelling to such destinations. At any given time, for example, the US State Department issues advisories on about 40 nations, ranging from simple cautionary statements, to warnings, to 'Don't Go' advisories. These may be based on probable political dangers, but just as often refer to crime and health hazards and, according to some critics, may also reflect political bias.

Especially, in the context of developing nations, then, sustainability has several facets. First, even in the absence of tourists, a nation must decide how to allocate scarce resources to nurture and sustain the natural and man-made heritage for its own citizens. Borabadur, Angkor Wat, Dubrovnik, the Amazon and the Galapagos Islands also have a value that should be supported by non-citizens as well. This is why the

United Nations Educational, Scientific and Cultural Organization (UNESCO) World Heritage List is critical for reinforcing the political will and helping developing nations to resist development that threatens world treasures. In essence, the allocation of resources to protecting sites, restoring habitats and promoting domestic and international tourism is a political rather than a technical decision. Similarly, the degree to which national culture is exhibited, modified, of influenced by visitors should not be a function of the advertising budgets of tour operators, the venture capital of investors, or the incapacity of government to know its own needs and those of its citizens.

It is general notion that tourists visit developing nations for sun, sand, sea and sex, and such motivations will continue, and will be facilitated by the Internet's ability to market anything, including child prostitution. But to these 'four Ss' must be added four more: a preoccupation with security, sanitation, safe transport, and the sensible protection of the built and natural heritage.

Currently, at the international level, several branches of the UN take tourism seriously. These include the WHO, the World Tourism Organization, the World Heritage programmes of the UNESCO, and the United Nations Development Programme (UNDP). Among their activities is help for developing nations in protecting their environment, their heritage and their health. In one instance, after decades of organizational lethargy, WHO, through WHONET, is accelerating its efforts to detect and prevent the spread of drug-resistant microbes. However, member nations still need to utilize WHO as an enforcement mechanism for meaningful health regulations — a function that will become increasingly critical as international tourism increases.

Obviously, it is observed over the years that developing nations suffered most due to tourism. Famous Dal Lake of Srinagar, Naini Lake in Nainital, Valley of Flowers, Sariska,

Rajaji National Park and other wildlife sanctuaries, Ladakh region, in India and Mt. Everest in Nepal etc. are facing the acute problem of ecological inbalance. Increased tourism activities are causing glaciers recede and fauna and flora extinction.

This book highlights all salient features of wildlife and ecotourism in modern perspective. The information is organised under eleven chapters, namely—Wildlife Tourism: An Introduction; Ecotourism and Wildlife Conservation in India; Growth of Ecotourism; Wildlife Ecology; Development and Sustainable Tourism Planning; Ecotourism Management; Sustainable Tourism in Protected Areas; Wildlife Tourism: A Case of Central Himalaya; Ecotourism in Eastern Europe; Case Studies on Ecotourism Development; and Wildlife Legislation and Administration etc. An extensive Bibliography at the end adds to its reference value.

Hopefully, the reading contained herein will benefit the academics as well as policy planners, activists, administrators, environmental and nature scientists etc. The source of data are all secondary, e.g. books, abstracts, journals, magazines, reports and notes. In strict moral sense the entire credit for this ought go to them all.

We owe a sincere gratitude to all the scholars of repute both from India and abroad, whose findings and views are shared here. We are thankful to all those who have rendered valuable help in the course of compiling relevant materials. In equal spirit we thank our collegues and friends also. Finally, Shri M.P. Misra of Akansha Publishing House, New Delhi deserves all appreciation for bringing out this volume.

—Editor

1

Wildlife Tourism: An Introduction

As per laid down by the environmentalists and naturalists there should be at least 33 per cent area of forest in a country. For ideal ecological balance there should be 60 per cent forests on the hilly mountainous terrain and 20 per cent forest cover on plains. In India, the data shows we have 22.8 per cent area under forest; but the recent satellite pictures show that we have hardly 10 per cent to 11 per cent forest area. These forests are natural habitat for the wild animals. So the number and variety of wildlife is affected by the expansion and shrinking of natural habitat.

Indian subcontinent has very important place on the wildlife map of the world. All representative animals are found in India. Hardly any faunal species is there, which is found in neighborhood, and not in India. There are transition zones, e.g., the fauna of Indian Thar desert is also common in Pakistan. The animals of Ladakh are common in India and Tibet and Nepal. Other Himalaya and Terai animals are common in India, Nepal, and Bhutan. The wild animals of Ganga-Brahmaputra plain and delta are common in India as well as Bangladesh. There are about five hundred species of mammals, over two thousand species of birds (avians), many species of fish, reptiles, amphibians and more than 30,000 forms of insects found in this subcontinent. The Astatic lion, the armored one horned great Indian rhinoceros, the magnificent Royal Bengal tiger, the massive Indian elephant and the large Indian gaur are the big five of Indian forests.

They are comparable only with their counterpart animals of Africa where heavy Ethiopian lion, big eared Elephant, two horned rhinoceros, etc. are found. India is the only country in the world where lion and, tiger both are found. The three species of cats including the spotted, marbled, fishing, desert, golden, jungle, pallas, the caracal types of cats and the lynx are found. The white tiger is very unique to India. India has twelve species of bats including the flying fox or fruit bat, the flying lemur, which is neither a lemur nor bat, but bears the same relationship to the shrews as the flying squirrel does to tile squirrels. There are four species of apes in the world, among them mighty gorilla are intelligent. Chimpanzees are found in Africa, orangutan, and gibbon are found in Asia; India has the noisiest ape the hoolock. There are 5 species of monkeys- the rhesus, the bonnest, the lion-tailed, the Assamese and the pigtailed. There are two species of lemurs-the slow Loris and the slender Loris found in Sikkim and Bhutan. The long tailed monkeys—Hanuman, the golden langur, the capped and Nilgiri langur are peculiar features of peninsula. Hares and rabbits are widely distributed in subcontinent. They are found from desert to snowcapped hills and from open to thick forests. There are about 1729 species of rodents in the world; they are also widely distributed in South Asian countries. They are squirrels, antelopes rats etc.

Up to Mughal period wild flora as well as fauna was abundant. But after the arrival of Britishers, due to expansion of their various economic and commercial activities like mining, plantation, roads-railways construction, etc. and later in on the world wars, a large tract of forests were swept away and the wild animals were killed in very massive number. In 20th century many species, which were abundant, came in the verge of extinction. So the need of having some law to protect them was felt. It was also thought that there would be some areas where the animals can refuge themselves in their natural environment. So the concepts of many categories of forests developed such as National Parks, Sanctuary, protected area, reserves etc. The Indian Board of Wildlife, which is responsible for the management, preservation and development of wild fauna and flora, has defined four areas where wildlife receives some kind of protection. Under the provision of Wildlife (Protection) Act, 1972, any area can be declared by the State government as a sanctuary or national park in case the concerned area needs protection and conservation for its ecological, faunal, floral, geomorphological and zoological significance. The Central government can establish a sanctuary or national park with the consent of the State governments concerned.

In the most countries of the world, the national, central or federal government of the country can only create a National Park. But in India a State government can constitute a National Park in its State Legislature—preferably subject to certain standards, which are now being drawn by the Indian Board of Wildlife. The history of National parks in India begins in 1936 when the Hailey (now Corbett) national parks of United Provinces (now Uttaranchal) was created. The definition of national parks evolved in 1933 at the London Conference of African Fauna, according to which a national park is an area placed under public control, the boundaries of which shall not be altered except by competent legislative authority. The area is declared for the protection and preservation for all time of wild animals life and wild vegetation for the benefit and advantage and enjoyment of the general public. Hunting of fauna or collection of flora is prohibited except under the direction of park authority in this area.

The Indian Board for Wildlife has defined a sanctuary as, An "area where killing, hunting, shooting or capturing of any species of bird or animals is prohibited except by or under the control of highest authority in the department responsible for the management of the sanctuary and whose boundaries and character should be sacrosanct as far as possible'. The Board has further clarified the position by stating that while the management of sanctuaries does not involve suspension or restriction of normal forest operation, it is desirable to aside a completely sacrosanct area within a sanctuary to be known as 'Abhyaranya'. It has also indicated that sanctuaries should be made accessible to the public.

In India sanctuary in usually created by an order or gazette notification of State government. So the weakness of a sanctuary is that it can be desanctuarised merely by another order or gazette notification of a State government because it is not safeguarded by any proper legislation. The idea behind a wildlife sanctuary and a national park is same, i.e., maximum protection, preservation and conservation of wild animals. But the fundamental difference between the two is that a sanctuary is created by order of a competent authority, who can be the Chief Conservator of forests or minister of a State, while a national park can be formed, abolished or changed only by the legislation of a State. Therefore, the status and degree of permanency and protection is much higher in a national park than in a sanctuary. In a wildlife sanctuary private ownership rights may continue and forestry and other usages also may continue so long as wildlife conservation is not adversely affected. However, in a national park all private ownership rights are extinguished and all forestry and other usages are prohibited. Every national park should have the minimum requisites of fauna, flora and scenery etc. There should be sufficient means of management and protection in a sanctuary to be upgraded as national park. Before declaring any forest as a national park, it must be confirmed that the area is of sufficient importance and status to deserve the appellation. Administration of such area must be improved and illegalities such as poaching and unauthorised gazing should be avoided.

The size of the park must be adequate, the boundaries should be well chosen and buffer zones should be provided against shooting, grazing and cultivation. Both sanctuaries and national parks may be formed out of reserved or protected forests and wherever forest products extraction is unavoidable, there must be an inner sanctuary or Abhayaranya, where no disturbances should be allowed. Central government provides assistance to the State governments for sanctuaries as well as for national parks.

Gee has clarified that protection of wildlife does not necessarily imply the protection of vermin. Those wild animals and birds etc. which are injurious to other animals, or to the man in short or long term, can be kept under the control or even destroyed altogether in extreme case in certain places. In November 1972 the Indian Wildlife Board chose the tiger as the national animal of India. A national scheme called the 'Project Tiger' was launched to protect the tiger population. At present there are 16 tiger reserves in India, of these 4 are wildlife sanctuaries and 12 are national parks. In India there were 63 national parks and 363 wildlife sanctuaries in 1987. 13 Indian subcontinents has grown with British legacy. They did the formation of many of national parks and sanctuaries. After Independence Government of India made some plans for the development of forests and their natural habitats. National forest policy was the first step in this direction in which one third of geographic area was aimed to achieve as forest areas (60 per cent in plains and 20 per cent in hill areas) for ecological balance and preservation of wildlife. Government of India is conscious for the preservation and development of wildlife and has taken many steps in the direction. Among these steps the most important is the financial assistance to States for the development of sanctuaries and national parks.

There was a total outlay of Rs. 360 lakh for the seventh plan period under the centrally sponsored schemes 'Assistance to States for development of sanctuaries Financial assistance is given to the States after scrutiny of their proposals on 100 per cent basis for items on non-recurring expenditure and on the condition that the wildlife sanctuary being financed is under the complete control of that State's wildlife wing. The budget provision for the development of 105 sanctuaries in 1987-88 was Rs 200 lakhs, which increased up to Rs. 275

lakhs for the year 1988-89 and further to Rs. 625 lakhs in 2000-01.

During sixth plan there was an allocation of only Rs. 99 lakh for the development of national parks, which was raised to Rs. 260 lakhs in Seventh plan period. Under the central scheme of assistance to States for development of national parks' given to States after scrutiny of their proposal, on 100 per cent basis for items of recurring expenditure and on 50 per cent basis for items of recurring expenditure. The budget provision for the development of 32 national parks in 1987-88 was Rs. 199 lakh and during 1988-89 it is Rs. 192 lakh. In November 1972 the Indian Wildlife Board chose the tiger as the national animal of India. A national scheme called the 'Project Tiger' was launched to protect the dangerously depleting species. There are " 16 tiger projects in India of which four are wildlife sanctuaries and 12 are national parks. These tiger reserves get special attention and allocated from center. In present plan Namdapha, Palamu, Nagarjun Sagar etc. are important reserves that have got special attention.

The Directorate of Wildlife under the Ministry of Environment and Forest was set up in pursuance of guidelines were given by the National Wildlife Action Plan to assist the State government in the proper management of the national parks and sanctuaries. The Directorate is also responsible for assigning the assistance to States. Its efforts to enlarge the network of wildlife-protected areas to adequately represent country's biological diversity were continued during 1988. By the end of 1988 there were 68 national parks and 366 sanctuaries in the country. The Wildlife Institute of India has completed a project for preparation of the biogeographic classification suitable for conservation, planning and has submitted a report entitled 'Planning a Wildlife Protected Area Network in India'. The report recommended that at least 4.6 per cent of geographic area of the country should be under national parks/ sanctuaries. At present it is 4.07 per cent. The Indian Board for Wildlife, the apex statutory advisory body for formulating policies on wildlife, the management of various national parks had been evaluated by a committee appointed by the Board. The Indian Board for Wildlife has played an important role in encouraging and growing consciousness among the people for wildlife. It organises various programmes, functions, seminars and workshops for conservation of wildlife during wildlife week, which is celebrated in first week of October every year.

Mainly the British were responsible for the large-scale deforestation and mass destruction of the wildlife. But they were also the people who became aware of their preservation and tried to regulate various laws. During that period British administrators passed various acts. The Indian Forest Act (1879, 1927, 1950) and its adaptations in States was administered by the forest departments and gave basic protection to wildlife in reserved and protected forests as follows:

(i) Prohibition of shooting, fishing and poisoning water, setting of traps and snares; Section 26(i) Reserved forests. Section 32(j) Protected forests.

(ii) Prohibition of killing or capturing of elephants in areas where the Elephant Preservation Act of 1879 is not in force. Section 32(j) Reserved forests. Section 33 (j) Protected forests.

"Wild Birds and Animals Protection Act' as it became in 1912 was applicable to all types of areas and in areas outside the reserves, which was administered by the civil and police departments of the States to which it has been extended, though in reality it was a dead letter. The act was applied to few specified wild birds and animals from time to time. Close reasons were declared for them. At that the penalties were fine up to Rs. 50 and for every subsequent conviction, imprisonment up to one month or fine up to Rs. 100 or both. Besides these acts, certain legislations applicable to certain places and time were also in existence, such as the Elephant Preservation Act of 1879, the Indian Fisheries Act 1897, the

Assam Rhinoceros Preservation Act and the Bengal Rhinoceros Protection Act.

After Independence the Bombay State (Maharashtra) Wild Birds and Animals Protection Act of 1951 was first step and was also recommended as a model for other States. This Act brought all types of areas; whether government forests or waste lands under the same law and the same set of rules, and this undoubtedly makes for simplicity of administration and control. The conservator of forests was empowered as special wildlife preservation officer, assisted by Game wardens (Divisional forest officers or Deputy collectors). The main machinery of enforcement is the forest department itself or revenue patel in the absence of forest staff. All forms of shooting and trapping of wildlife were licenced. Penalty and imprisonment for offence was also fixed. Many other States also modified their acts in more or less same manner.

Wildlife (Protection) Act 1972 is the recent and most scientific protection measures taken to preserve the vanishing species. Under the provision of this act, any area can be declared as a wildlife sanctuary or a national park in case the area concerned needs protection and conservation for its ecological, faunal, floral, geomorphological and zoological significance. The Central government can establish a wildlife sanctuary or national park with the consent of the concerned State government.

Attempts to control poaching and illegal trade in wildlife by strict implementation of this act were stepped up through the four regional offices. Financial assistance to twelve States to the tune of Rs. 30 lakh is being provided to tackle the problem of illegal killing of wild animals, particularly elephant in the southern States and has had a marked impact. To gather timely and correct intelligence about poachers and illegal traders, a system of cash awards both under the central sector and centrally sponsored schemes was introduced. In the cases of offences relating to species included in Schedule

I and Schedule II, Part II of the act, or to hunting in national park or sanctuary, the offender shall be liable for punishment for a term which shall not be less than six months, can be extended to six years and also with fine which shall not be less than five hundred rupees. In case of a subsequent offence the term of imprisonment shall not be less than one year and the fine shall not be less than one thousand rupees. The causes are compoundable. Officers not below the rank of Deputy Conservator of Forests are empowered to accept a sum up to Rs. 2000/ by way of compensation of such offences. In this act it is also mentioned that the wild animals, meat trophy, uncured trophy, animal article in respect to which an offence has been committed under this act shall be property of the government.

Surprisingly, till 1970s no serious attempt was made to exploit tourism potentialities in national parks and sanctuaries. But the enactment of Wildlife (Protection) Act, 1972 was significant step in the encouragement of tourism. Before this law wildlife tourism was disorganised and haphazard. The tourists were not enthusiastic to visit the forest knowing that poachers and other elements, might have wiped out or driven away the wild animals. After enforcement of the new measures, the strict restriction on hunting and building of infrastructures through financial aid by central government the tourism began to develop. They were not only encouraged for seeing wild animals, but natural flora also. Wildlife tourism has made people more conscious of nature conservation. Though it has also been alleged that tourism has led to the degradation of fauna of sanctuaries and parks.

However, the wildlife tourism could not grow substantially in India. Only in the case of Sariska and Periyer a marginal growth is recorded. Our wildlife tourism constitutes hardly 5 to 10 per cent foreign tourists. There many reasons behind this that lack of infrastructure like all season roads, hotel accommodations, vehicles and lack of properly trained guides. Public consciousness and enthusiasm about wildlife and nature has not grown so much, which can boost wildlife tourism. Other parks and sanctuaries, which are far from important places, have yet to do a lot for development. So, the impact of tourism on tribal community is also not countrywide but limited to few places.

The decade of 1975 was most favorable for wild animals when these silent creatures were protected under the umbrella or various laws and acts plans and projects. In 1970 tiger hunting was banned when Kailash Sankla a forest officer and former director of Project Tiger, drew attention to the plight of tigers in International Union for Conservation of Nature and Natural Resources Congress (New Delhi 1969). Tiger was included in *Red Data Book.* The result was the setting up the Project Tiger. The next important step was the Wildlife (Protection) Act of 1972. Thereafter the state-central governments tried to pay proper attention on the preservation of wildlife. Due to such efforts many species survived for example tiger. black buck crocodile, various types of monkeys etc. Though many cases of offences have also been reported were wild creatures were hunted by poachers.

A new problem has emerged now, that is the increasing/ increased numbers of many species of animals have created problems to the people living in nearby area. This problem was highlighted in the Conference of State Forest Ministers (May'89, New Delhi). S.N. Medhi, the forest- minister of Assam was too annoyed because the elephants have killed hundreds of people. They raid the crops and killed people if they come in the way. At present Assam has largest elephant population around 5,000 elephants in 5,000 sq. km. area. Crocodiles create other headache. In 1975 project crocodiles was launched to save this reptile from extinction. The project was successful and they grew three times. One third of them were released into rivers, but there are still above 7,000 in 32 farms of the country. The fisherman of those areas where these crocodiles attacked them and absorbed the fish population. In desperation many States proposed that they would sell crocodile skins in lucrative prices abroad. Initially the Environment Ministry agreed for it and even set up a Pilot Project for 'farming Crocodiles' in Tamil Nadu, but the ecologists opposed it and the government was compelled to stop this project.

Similar was the case with other well-known projects. The Project Tiger succeeded in increasing the population reported that more than 450 people have been killed by tigers since 1978 in Dudhwa (U.P.). Cattle lifting is a common phenomena. The people of Sunderban Ranthambhor and other reserves are always afraid of these animals. The Lions, though not much in number are also wandering out of reserve area. The most unfortunate situation is that the people who traditionally protected these animals are turning against them. The Bishnoi community around Jodhpur has protected black door population for centuries. Now they are in large numbers (around 12,000) and damage their crops.

Similar is the case of Nilgai of Rajasthan who became abundant and always raided the crops of villagers. Such incidents have caused the people around sanctuaries and parks to be 'anti-conservationists'. For instance, in Dudhwa, villagers who were fed up with their cattle being lifted regularly poisoned five tigers. Similar case of poisoning the lion in Gir has also come into light. The Director of the Project Tiger Dr. R.L. Singh has admitted that around 40,50 people became victims of tigers annually. The local people are raising their voices against this project because they are threatened with tigers and feel that land is encroached by tiger reserves where they are deprived of fodder.

Such dilemma has triggered of a nationwide debate about what to do with excessive numbers. Some are advocating for hunting also. But Dr. Ranjit Singh (Additional Secretary Ministry of Environment and Wildlife) a well known conservationist disagrees on this idea because if once their killing is allowed it would be very difficult to regulate it. It would lead to misuse and destruction of wildlife. H.S. Pawar, Director Wildlife Institute of India, Dehradun, has rightly pointed out that "local abundance of a species does not mean that it is out of danger. It means that it present habitat is insufficient." Real problem does not lie in the protection and conservation but in the management and planning of reserves. The original Project Tiger plan envisaged buffer zones around protected core, meant to take care of any pillover of tigers while allowing people from adjoining villages to forage. But so far the project officials have totally failed in preserving the buffer zones.

The grim reality is that most of India's wild animals are pushed into 363 plus 63 sanctuaries and parks, which account for barely 4 per cent of country's geographical area. These forest areas have also been encroached by villagers. Traditional corridors, which enabled the animals to move from one forest to next, have been cut off. That has led to very little gene mixing a vital part of natural regeneration. The Gir lions are living in an isolated small patch. They can be wiped out by just one epidemic. Even the protected parks and sanctuaries are not free from human intrusion and cattle grazing. A study done by Indian Institute of Public Administration found that about 50 per cent of parks and 70 per cent of the sanctuaries, the people are living inside the core zones. Most of buffer zones have disappeared and the fringes of these sanctuaries have turned into major battleground between man and animals.

The Ministry of Environment, Govt. of India has taken vital steps of identifying corridors between forests to enable movements of animals. The Wildlife Institute of India Dehradun has already submitted a blue print for developing corridors in all geographic regions in the country which will provide an additional 42 thousand sq, km protected area to animals. But it seems a difficult task to acquire land from villagers from these corridors and rehabilitating them elsewhere. The ecologists are also concentrating on the development of buffer zones. In the buffer zones areas for human use would be clearly demarcated. Here with the help of villagers in surroundings areas fuel and fodder would be grown to meet their needs and the remaining parts would be developed for animals to roam around freely.

Land Use

The modern world is faced with the twin problem of over population and poverty. The population of the world is increasing very rapidly and the existing resources of the earth are gradually getting depleted. The land and resources are limited but mouths to feed are innumerable and yet increasing. Under these, circumstances of stresses and strains we are striving for a place for the wildlife. Thus, if we realise the conditions and dimensions of the various sectors of our geography social, economic life, the concept of management of wildlife should strictly be guided by the doctrine of efficient and intensive land use. The fertility and texture of the soil is the main criteria of land classification and for proper distribution of land for various sectors such as agriculture, horticulture, flower culture etc. We must divide the land into several categories depending upon the quality of land and its use. The last type of land, which is unfertile, degraded and where the land cannot be used otherwise for any other purpose should be exclusively earmarked for wildlife. By applying modern management techniques, we can turn the economics of such kinds of lands by providing huge profit through tourism, trade and commercial business deals. It will serve the twin purpose of conservation of rare and threatened species, soil and water conservation and strengthing of our economy to a large extent.

Developed countries have already taken steps in this direction and wildlife is viewed as a land use and most of the wildlife in these countries is seen in the individual farms, trade centers and national parks, zoos and sanctuaries. In the world, about more than 75 million tons of food is produced in the forms of marine fisheries, which constitute a significant percentage of the world's animal protein content. A full-fledged Fish industry is thriving on it, throughout the world over.

The trade in animals and animal's product is continuing since times immemorial and there are several instances of animai trade in the chapters of ancient history of all countries. Kings and emperors raised Elephant armies. Again fur-bearing animals are supporting the fur trade, an industry in itself, and which has threatened some species. Many people may be found engaged in live animals trade.

Indian handicrafts have been famous world over and Indian Ivory-carvers are recognised everywhere in the world. Jaipur, Delhi, Mysore are some of the traditional centers of ivory-carving. Similarly the prices of musk and horn of Rhinoceros are skyrocketing. In 1978-80 the black market prices of musk fetched upto Rs. 50,000 per kg. On an average about 3 to 4 gram of musk is obtained from a musk deer. A single horn of Rhinoceros, on an average, weighs about 1 kg. In the Middle East it was selling for Rs. 51,000 in 1979 to be used as handles for dagger, which is treated a sign of masculine power. Further the skin trade is the other important item of trade and skin of crocodiles and alligators are highly priced for leather goods and bags. Most animals yielding the above items of trade had been hunted very badly and reduced almost to the level of extinction.

In U.S.A. in 1964, revenue of 1,120,000 Dollar was obtained in the trade of meat of wildlife. In Texas black buck harvesting is done and number of farms surpass the total number of these animals scattered in whole of India. It shows the outlook of developed countries towards the wildlife.

Similar sectors of economic activities can be identified in each area of the country depending upon land use pattern. The selection also depends upon the potential and type of wild fauna present in that particular area. For example, Jungle fowl breeding should be encouraged in certain areas, which should be closed for a certain period and then opened up so that people may be allowed hunting and Govt. may get revenue. Similarly trade can be carried through in silk, lac, feathers, wool, fats and oils, wild meat etc. if individual farms are created.

It involves a tremendous task of wildlife resource mobilisation, efficient land use and integration of wildlife economics with the basis planning process. All this and the prospective exploitation should form a part of our overall developmental strategy of every nation.

Wildlife Values

Wildlife is an important renewable natural resource at the hand of man with diverse use. The colourful and magnificent wildlife bestowed upon us by the nature had made tremendous contribution towards our culture, religion, courage and discipline, customs and traditions, education and economy, entertainment and aesthetic sense, maintaining balance of nature; the list is still longer making life on this planet full of joy and enjoyment, peace and prosperity. Certain negative aspects of wildlife are there, which should also be listed.

Positive Values

1. Ethical Value: There are three distinguished features, viz. human capacity of distinguishing between right and wrong, sense of reasoning, love and appreciation of beauty on the basis of which we human beings proclaim ourselves as superior to beasts, who totally out class us in ferocity, power, shape and size of the body, adaptability and swiftness. It may be mentioned here that our ancient philosophers, rulers and religious priests, books and scriptures, contributed significantly in the direction of protection, conservation and control of wildlife and in spreading and inculcating the sense of love and co-existence to wild creature among the masses. Throughout India, edicts carved on rocks and iron pillars are reminders that 22 centuries ago, the emperor Ashoka defined a kings duty as not merely to protect citizens and punish the guilty but also to protect and preserve animal life and, forest trees. In the Hindu pantheon, wild creatures enjoyed privileged positions of protection through large number of religious myths, and sentiments. The stories of Panchatantra are full of love for wild animals and made an indelible impact on the masses. Kautilya in his 'Arthshastra' has given a vivid and comprehensive coverage to the "Abhayaranya" or Forest sanctuary, where animals, could roam about without any fear. Hanuman helping Rama against the Ravana, the symbol of injustice. India's elephant guarding the light celestial points of the campus. Even Christianity had Francis of Assisi who lived and spoke to wild animals. In almost every religion it is wrong to take the life of an animal.

More scientifically Aldo Leopard in his book "A Sand Country Almaric" has stressed that "lȁnd ethic does not prevent the management and use of animal but it does affirm their right to continued existence". "The land ethics implies that human being should change from land conqueror to a plain member and citizen. It implies respect for his fellow members and also respect for the community as such."

2. *Ecological Value:* All animals, mammals, reptiles, birds and all aquatic as well as amphibians play their role in the maintenance of balance of nature-an intangible role, but real. Ecology may be defined as "the relationship between the living things with their environment". Wild animals are the part of nature and form a complex relationship with it through the dynamic ecosystem.

3. *Cultural Value:* Wildlife forms a part of our national heritage and glorious traditions, which we have inherited from our ancestors. Therefore, human being are duty bound to preserve, enrich and then handover it to the next generations. Mankind had learned many arts of living from the wild animals. These animals have been a source of inspirations for mankind. If, Lion and Tiger are to vanish from this planet, it

is possible that no body will be giving the example of acts of bravery by comparing it with lion and tiger. Thus the various wild creatures of our country and world over, whether animals, birds, reptiles, amphibians, fishes or insects, should be preserved because the knowledge which we have about these animals is the part of our culture.

In an ecosystem there are two components.

(i) *Biotic*—Includes all the living things of the nature, plants as well as animals. Animals may be herbivorous, who are called primary consumer; carnivorous, they are called secondary consumers and tertiary consumer, as the case may be and the last decomposers include bacteria and other micro organisms.

(ii) *Abiotic*—Includes all minerals, gases, nitrogen, oxygen, carbon dioxide, phosphorus, potassium, water etc. All the biotic and biotic components of the ecosystem are closely inter-linked with each other and there is continuous flow of energy from the biotic to biotic components through the different tropic levels, which are represented by a pyramid. If, any component of the ecosystem is disturbed deliberately or otherwise, it results in the disturbance of work of the ecosystem, which is generally called as natural imbalance resulting in many disastrous and calamitous situations for nature and for man, who is part of the overall ecosystem. The life in nature depends upon the dynamism,' structure and, stability of the ecosystem. There are several units of ecosystem. It may be a pond ecosystem, grassland ecosystem and a forest I ecosystem, all are surviving on the same principles and comprising all the components of ecosystem, though forming different communities. Wildlife occupies the position of consumer in this cycle of ecosystem. Wild animals feed upon plants, which produce food in nature from sunlight and carbon dioxide through the process of photosynthesis, these plants are known as producers of the ecosystem. These animals are called as primary consumers such as Deer, Rabbit, Nilgai, and Rat etc. The second category of wild animals prey upon these primary consumers, as secondary consumer, such as Tiger feeding on deer and snake on rat and this chain continued ill it reaches top level consumers which are then decomposed by bacteria into the abiotic components and thus again continuing the cycle. This is known as food chain.

Eenlisting the beneficial activities of wild animals is a very difficult task as the list is very long. However, a few examples are sufficient to illustrate their status, wild animals and bird's seasonal migration, help in the development of the vegetation and in the dispersal of the seeds, which they eat and defecate. Selective feeding habit of certain species is an important factor in plant dispersal and survival. Birds spread sandal in South India, likewise Emblica *officinal* is by deer. Other important acts of wild animal are noticed in cross-pollination. Most of the insects and birds perform this job. It increases the diversity of genetic recombination and viability of the plant vegetation, the producer component of the ecosystem. Not only this, some wild animals and birds are natural scavengers and thereby help in clearing the countryside and keeping it hygienic. The common kite, the crow, the vulture, the hated jackal and hyena all scavengers. Hyena also acts as "natural regulator" as it attacks the weak animals when they lack the power of resistance. Wildlife also acts as biological controlling agent for controlling various disease carrying agents.

4. Scientific Value: Whenever any drug for any disease is invented, the research on its effects is first carried on the wild animals, before it is used for human consumption and treatment. And for this, every year thousands of monkeys sacrifice themselves for our cause. Thousands of research workers are engaged all over the world in conducting scientific studies on the animals so as to achieve different scientific goals. Nobody would have known about Rh factor in human blood, had Rhesus monkey not been there. Chimpanzee had helped us in conducting serological protein tests. Many studies on the animal behaviours have unfolded many knots for the psychiatrist, making easier for them to study the human mind. Some of the wild plants and animals are of medicinal importance and have benefited us directly or indirectly or through the sale of their products. Musk pod of musk deer is valued as medicine. Snake venom is also used for preparing anti-venom for snakebite. If the scientifically important species are preserved and increased, it can help in earning goodwill of humanity, as well as can also generate valuable foreign exchange through the export of these specific animals.

5. *Game Value:* Wildlife has a greater value for those who hunt for sport. Our kings, emperors were famous for creating special reserves for hunting, such as Dachigam reserve now converted as Dachigam Sanctuary, was the exclusive hunting reserve of Maharaja of Kashmir. Bharatpur bird sanctuary formed the reserve of Maharaja Bharatpur. Likewise many European hunters have created stories all over the world. In India Zim Corbett had become a legendary figure for hunting the man-eaters of the Uttaranchal hills, for his love to this sport and wild animals. People have won large number of trophies by killing the wild animals. This resulted in the mass killing of some of the majestic wildlife. In U.S.A. and other countries many people spend millions of rupees in hunting or fishing in pursuit of their sport. Many people are getting livelihood through hunting and fishing industry by producing firearms, fishing tackle, camping materials and by providing accommodation and food and drink. These people are also contributing a lot by providing donation in the form of purchase of licenses, towards the conservation of animals. Hunting and fishing clubs have been created in many countries like U.S.A. All this adds to the recreational aspect of wildlife. In India hunting of big games cannot be

encouraged however, small game hunting can be permitted under strict control in certain areas for keeping a check on the population of these animals. Fishing can be encouraged as a sport, as it has still got wide scope in India.

6. *Aesthetic Value:* Some of the wild animals are simple and beautiful, some are majestic and powerful, some others are magnificent and colourful; this sheer beauty of the wildlife has a direct appeal to human spirit and humanity would like to preserve this splendid form of beauty of the nature at all costs. In the midst of capitalistic and industrial world where city life has became a typical stereotype and where pollution is gradually cutting at the availability of free air, wildlife in the quite and calm forests. National parks and sanctuaries provide relaxation and refreshing air. We forget every thing to see a Blue Black jump and to get a sight of moving Tiger or a Lion kill its prey. Wild animals, in the developed countries, have become a source of tremendous economic gain, through the integration of wildlife, with the tourism industry. Recreational forestry as it is known is becoming' fast popular in all countries of the world. People in these countries would like to find time, from the busy schedule of their modern life, to share some moments of pleasure and mental happiness with wildlife. Special facilities have been created for meeting the various demands of the people and modern concept of national parks and zoos have been evolved. In developing countries where adequate wasteland is available and in countries like India, which are very rich in the variety of wildlife the wildlife tourism can be a big source of income, as well as, principal source of foreign exchange. Large number of tourists will flock to the country, to see its rich and colourful wildlife. In India there are still about more than 350 species of mammals and 1200 species of birds in about 2000 forms. Throughout the world, especially in United States and other developed countries, the value of wildlife is measured in economic yardstick and it has become important and the creation of more and more reserves, national parks and zoos is justified on economic grounds.

7. Commercial or Economic Value: Throughout world many people are earning their livelihood by carrying trade in wildlife and their products. Many industries such as fish are as big as any other modern industry as far employment generation, output and income is concerned. Similarly, fur and skin trade has also developed into a industry. Trade in certain items like musk, ivory, rhinoceros horn, crocodile skin, fur from monkey, rabbit and bear etc. has threatened these animals on account of merciless hunting so much so that most of these animals are now on the verge of extinction. The trade in wildlife and wildlife products is very lucrative and previously there has been no uniform regulation of the trade throughout the country and no legislation existed to control and enforce uniform law all over the country till 1972, when Wildlife (Protection) Act 1972 was enacted. Studies in Africa and some other countries have shown that in marginal lands and those which are unsuited as pasture wild animals are proving to be more productive and economically profitable than the domesticated animals. Dasmann (1964) opined that many wild animal species would prove more profitable, if domesticated and more useful than rearing many other domestic animals in the same environment.

Negative Values

Wildlife has got certain negative values also which includes destruction of properties, predation and their potential role as reservoir or carriers of various diseases. Wildlife such as deer and other herbivorous animals destroy the crops in the field and the intensity is felt most by those countries whose agriculture is in the primitive stages and living standard is very poor. Carnivores like panther, tiger and lion sometime lift domestic animals and create hardships for the rural population.

There are many instances when loss of human life has been up to a great extent at the hand of man-eater carnivores. Some of the wild animals act as carriers or reservoirs of certain disease for example African Antelopes serve as reservoir for the African sleeping sickness caused by protozoan parasite hyprozona.

However, the positive values of wildlife far outweigh the negative ones. And it is in the interest of man that wildlife must be protected and preserved. With emergence of tourism as flourishing industry, wildlife tourism can contribute a lot to state exchequer. In recent years, wildlife tourism is gaining popularity. India can exploit its potential to a lot on one hand and preserve environmental and ecological balance on the other. This the demand of the time.

2

Ecotourism and Wildlife Conservation in India

Wildlife Conservation in India in Historical Perspective

Till 1952 the management of wildlife in India consisted of no more than regulation of *hunting*. Although a few protected areas had been declared before this (notably Hailey National Park in 1932), it was with the formation of the Indian Board for Wildlife in Mysore in 1952 that wildlife preservation and management began on a serious footing in India. The Board was given the task of devising ways and means of wildlife conservation through various legislative and practical methods, including the closure of shooting of several species. The Wildlife (Protection) Act was passed in 1972. This was the first unified national act for wildlife protection and deals with hunting, creation of protected areas, and control of trade in wildlife products. The act also provides for the appointment of wildlife preservation staff and lists several specified animals in four schedules. Animals in Schedule 1 are completely protected throughout India. Following the passage and adoption of the Wildlife (Protection) Act in 1972 came Project Tiger in 1973 and several special programmes aimed at preserving endangered species, for example, the Gir Lion Sanctuary Project, Himalayan Musk Deer Project, Crocodile Breeding Project, Project Hangul, Rhino Reintroduction Programme, and Manipur Brow-Antlered Deer Conservation Project. These projects have been highly successful in achieving their limited objectives. While the focal species have benefited greatly, so has the habitat, and this in turn, has benefited other species as well. The reserves under the administration of Project Tiger are afforded the best protection in the country and include the following 17 areas in 12 states Bandipur, Corbett, Kanha, Manas, Melghat, Palamau, Ranthambhor, Simlipal, Sunderbans, Periyar, Sariska, Buxa, Indravati, Nagarjunasagar, Namdapha, Dudhwa, and Kalakad. Improved protection of tiger in these areas has correspondingly helped the prey species and associated mammals such as elephants and rhinos. A significant step towards wildlife conservation was taken in 1982 with the drawing up of the National Wildlife Action Plan (NWAP). This Plan lists 12 aims for the implementation of a sound strategy of wildlife conservation for India:

(a) The establishment of a network of protected areas such as national parks, sanctuaries and biosphere Reserves. To cover representative samples of all major ecosystems and with adequate distribution.

(b) The restoration of degraded habitats to their natural state, within these protected areas.

(c) The rehabilitation of endangered and threatened species and the restoration of protected portions of their former habitats, in a manner, which provides some reflection of their original distribution.

(d) The provision of adequate protection to wildlife in multiple use areas (such as production forests and pasture lands) so as to form 'corridors' linking up the protected areas and providing for genetic continuity between them.

(e) Support for the management of botanical and zoological parks and gardens and undertaking captive breeding programmes for the threatened species of plants and animals.

(f) The development of appropriate management systems for protected areas, including a professional cadre of personnel fully trained in all aspects of wildlife and sanctuary management as well as the provision of proper orientation to all officers concerned with wildlife.

(g) The development of research and monitoring facilities, which will provide a scientific understanding of wildlife populations and habitats essential to their proper management.

(h) Support for wildlife education and interpretation aimed at a wider public appreciation of the importance of wildlife to human betterment.

(i) The review and updating of statutory provisions providing protection to wildlife and regulating all forms of trade, so as to ensure their current effectiveness.

(j) Assistance in the formulation and adoption of National Conservation Strategy for all living natural resources on the lines of the World Conservation Strategy launched in 1980.

- Participation in international conventions designed to prevent the depletion of the wildlife resources and to provide protection to migratory species.
- Long-term conservation of wildlife based on the scientific principles of evolution and genetics.

The sections pertinent to the management of human conflict are Management of PAs and Habitat Restoration and Wildlife Protection in Multiple Use Areas. Under the former section the identification of Special Areas for Eco-development (SAEDs) was urged by the Task Force for Eliciting Public Support for Wildlife Conservation. The Taskforce proposed special, community development programmes with a conservation bias for the SAEDs surrounding wildlife reserves, to gain the support of local people in wildlife protection. These schemes are to be implemented by all government agencies influencing land use (forest, agriculture, pasture, irrigation) and executing rural development and tribal welfare programmes. It is proposed that higher per capita inputs of capital are assigned to the SAEDs in comparison with other areas, which is not an unreasonable proposal since areas adjacent to PAs are usually in the interior and less-developed areas.

Importance of Conservation

Why should we care about disappearing animals? The answer to such a question can be attributed to many, reasons. The following are some of the major reasons.

(i) Economic Value. Wild species of animals provide meat for food and skin for fur. The financial value of wild species is of major importance in the economics of many nations.

(ii) Survival Value. Every species plays an important role in maintaining an ecological balance among the living systems of the earth, these systems must continue to function if life is to survive. Loss of any species threatens the survival of several species inclusive of man. Man's own survival depends on his willingness and ability to cooperate with the living environment. Human beings turn to nature and wildlife for spiritual, psychological, physical and cultural benefits.

(iii) Scientific Value. The study of wildlife provides valuable knowledge about life processes which has helped scientists understand the functioning and behaviour of the human body. Scientists have also gained medical knowledge and discovered important medical products by studying wildlife. By studying the effects of environmental pollution on wildlife it is possible to learn how pollution may affect human life as well.

(iv) Nature's Beauty. Wildlife includes a diversity of species that contributes in a special way to the beauty of nature. Such beauty enriches life and increases the enjoyment of camping and outdoor amusement.

Now wildlife is becoming an increasingly important recreational asset and tourist attraction everywhere. They maintain the health of the living landscape and productivity of the ecosystem. Wildlife represents the result of many years of evolution and constitutes an environmental heritage to the past, a world which once surrounded our ancestors. Moreover, why should man deny that animals as species have the right to live and coexist with ourselves? We are accountable to the coming generation to leave an inheritance an unspoiled world with intact living beauty and richness.

Man in his zest for progress fails to realise that his own existence is being jeopardized. The so-called "Progress," has made him contaminate air, pollute streams, lakes and oceans, drain, swamps and wetlands, lowering the water table; rape prairies and forests; spray pesticides over water and land; kill animals excessively for immediate profit, or on false assumptions that they are noxious or for fashionable "sport." Man alone though often in combination with his livestock, is destroying the natural environment. Thus the civilisation is not just cities, industrial development, miles of highways, several airfields and numerous other technological conveniences. By destroying wildlife for civilisation and culture, we are only negating the meaning of the words. If he does have to change habits, then he must be able to manage them properly in order to maintain rich and varied wildlife. Man has to think of the dangerous trap he is setting up for himself by human overpopulation. It is man's ability to think that formulated the idea of conservation. Conservation is applied ecology and may also be regarded as bio-economy. In other words, conservation is defined as sound preservation, management and sensible use of the available renewable natural resources. This decision of conservation is in our hands and man seems to be going the right direction regarding this decision that holds the key to the future of our most valuable natural resources. Governments of several nations have passed laws and set aside national parks, sanctuaries and other wildlife reserves in an effort to save the dwindling wildlife. Such efforts have saved several species from becoming extinct.

Rare Wildlife

Three major categories of wildlife are there which are facing extinction for ever.

(i) Endangered Species. These species face the most severe threat of extinction and require direct human protection for survival.

(ii) Threatened Species. They are abundant in certain areas but face serious dangers nevertheless. Dangers being caused due to unfavourable environmental conditions, extensive hunting, fishing, trapping or even collecting by hobbyists.

(iii) Rare Species. These species have small populations. They live in protected environments and their numbers are not decreasing.

Wildlife Conservation Methods

In many cases, wildlife can be helped by ensuring that their environment is favourable with regards to availability of food, water and shelter. This method is called Habitat Management. It involves such action as soil conservation, good forestry practices and wildlife management. Several species have been threatened with extinction due to destruction of habitat by human activities like deforestation for farming, pollution of air, water, land, plants and animals etc. People must set aside separate areas like sanctuaries, wildlife reserves, parks etc. in which wildlife can survive. Hunting is another major cause for the dwindle in the wildlife and this can be prevented by enforcement of strict laws that forbid or regulate such killings. Excessive increase in the number of one species in a given area threatens not only its own endurance but also that of the other species by consuming major portion of the available food. Such numbers must be reduced by controlled hunting or by restoring its natural enemies where they have become scarce. Sometimes species find it extremely difficult to survive in their own once favourable environment. Breeding in captivity and releasing in a protected area that satisfies the conditions favourable for survival can protect such species. A species threatened with disease can be protected by sanitation measures in a habitat. The success of wildlife conservation depends on the knowledge of the ECOLOGY of the species, which involves an understanding of the way of life of the species and its relationship with its biotic and abiotic environment. The Indian Wildlife possesses a rich and diverse fauna and is unique in having immense natural beauty in its different ecosystems. Out of the 75,000 species known in India, there are 2,500 fishes, 150 amphibians, 450 reptiles, 2000 birds and 850 mammals. The remaining are the invertebrates, including protozoa, porifera, worms, insects, mollusks and crustaceans. Of these, 81 species of mammals, 47 of birds, 15 of reptiles, 3 of amphibians and a large number of butterflies, moths and beetles are listed as endangered: The animals that make up the Indian fauna are elephant, Rhinoceros, Musk deer (Kastura), Barking deer (Kotra), Spotted deer (Cheetal), Hog deer (Hoghirgn), Mouse deer (Indian chevrotain), Swamp deer (Barasingha), Dancing deer (Sambar), Thamin, Kashimir stag, Four horned antelope (Chausingha), Indian Gazelle (Chinkara), Blue Bull (Nilgai), Bison, Wild buffalo, Himalayan ibex or wild goat, Wild boar, Wild ass, Nilgiri tahr, Lion, Tiger, Leopard, Striped hyena, Nilgiri langur. Lion tailed macaque (Macaco silenus). Rhesus monkey (Macacamulatha), Hanuman monkey (semnopithecus entellus), Indian giant squirrel (Batufa indica). Porcupine, Pangolin, Peafowl (Pavocristatus), Jungle fowl, Patridge, Quali Great Indian Bustard (Choriotes nigriceps), Sand grouse, Duck pigeon, Stroks and Egrets, Pelicans, Eagle, Crane, Owl, Hornbill, Gharials, Lizards, Crocodiles and about 218 species snake.

Endangered Species of India

In order to protect these species from extinction we have to know about their habits and habitats. Once we are thorough with such facts, preservation of endangered species can be carried out successfully.

Lion Tailed Macque: Size—Head and Body-20-24 inches. Tail-10-15 inches (25-38 cms). Females slightly smaller. Distribution-Western Ghats from North Kamara, southwards to Kerala and Kanyakumari district, Tamilnadu. Distinctive Characters-Great mane of long dark grey or brownish grey hair from temple and cheek. Glossy black coat. *Habits*—It habitats lonelier evergreen tropical forest belt between 2000-3500 ft. (610-1070 m). They are dark coloured, shy and seclusive in habit. Macaques are gregarious. They live in herds of 12-20 or more. The call of the male resembles that of the human voice- "COYEH" or the "COO" of a pigeon. Their movement through the treetops is slow and deliberate. Newborns are seen in September in South India. Destruction of habitat and poaching has made this species an endangered species. Trees are the means of transport and form the habitat of this species. Hence afforestation and prevention of poaching are the methods to be adapted for protecting them.

Hispid Hare or Assam Rabbit. Not much is known about this species except that they are the same size of the hare with a shorter, dark-brown tail. The fur is coarse and made of dark-brown. Bristles which are paler on the under surface of the body. The outer side of the ear is brown. The eyes are small. Hind legs are short and stout. Their claws are long and teeth are large. They feed on bark and roots. Usually seen in Terai, Dooars and Himalayan foothills.

Tiger

Size—Average length-9ft.-9.6 ft. (275-290 cm). Female 8 ft. 6 in. (260 cms) *Average weight*—160-230 kgs Female 100 lbs less (45 kgs). *Distinctive Characters*—Tigers have a rich-coloured, well-striped, short coat. Individual variations are great. *Distribution*—They are found throughout India from the Himalayas to Cape Comorin except in the deserts of Punjab, Sind and Kutch. Also found in Burma. *Habits*—Tigers are found at 10,000 ft. in the Himalayas, humid evergreen forests in dry open jungle, grassy swamp of Terai, in Sunderbans leading an amphibious life, on trees, in mud and in water. Food, shade, and shelter are essential for their survival. Tigers hunt from sunset to dawn, when it is not too hot. Its prey comprises of elephant (female and young), nilgai, deer, wild pig, bears, porcupine, gaur, buffalo, panthers, other tigers and when extremely hungry feeds on fowl or fish. When game is not available, tigers attack cattle and even man. They climb trees and are excellent swimmers. Though they are heavy, they are athletic. Mating is usually after the rain. Young ones are born between February and May. Male-Female relationship ends when young are born; Gestation period is about 15-16 weeks. Tigresses give birth to 2 to 3 cubs per litter. The cubs begin to hunt when they are 6 months old and they stay with the tigress for 2 years. Sexual maturity is attained at the age of 3 years in the case of the tigress and 4 years in the case of the male. Tigers are essentially animals of the forest. Once deprived of their habitat they are doomed. Life span of a tiger is about 20 years. Hunting had greatly reduced their number in India. The Indian government, through the state forest and wildlife departments, and encouraged by the Indian Board for Wildlife and the World Wildlife Fund, conducted a, careful census in 1972 which revealed that only about 1826 Tigers survived in India. On 1st April 1973, the Indian Government launched its PROJECT TIGER,' a scheme set to achieve the following objectives.

- to ensure the maintenance of a viable population of the (tigers in India for scientific, economic, aesthetic, cultural and ecological values,
- to preserve for all times areas of such biological importance as a national heritage for the-benefit, education and enjoyment of the people.

To achieve these objectives 17 Tiger Reserves have so far been established in 13 states, covering an area of 26643 sq. kms. The 17th Tiger Reserve has been established in the state of Tamil Nadu during 1988-89, with Kalakad and Mundanthurai wildlife sanctuaries as its core area. The tigers in the now strictly protected reserves are thriving and their present number as on 15th June, 2002 was 5031.

Snow Leopard

Size—Smaller than a panther with a relatively longer tail. Head and body -3ft. 3in—3ft 8in. (100-110cm). Tail 3ft. (90in.) *Distinctive Characters*—The snow leopard has a short muzzle, high forehead with a vertical chin. The colour of the coat is soft grey palling to pure while on the underside. Grey is sometimes tinged with buff. Spots are unbroken and distinct on the head, nape, and lower parts of the limbs. On the body they break up into larger, paler rosettes. These rosetes are less pronounced in the luxuriant winter coat. The undersides are pale while except for a few black blotches and fur. Newly born cubs are darker than the adults. *Distribution*—In India, the range extends along the whole of the Himalayan chain from Kashmir to Bhutan northwards into Tibet, Central Asia. *Habits*—Not much is known about the snow leopard. Its home is the higher altitudes of Himalayas at heights of 12,000-13,000 ft. (3660-3965m.) above sea level, above the tree line where the rocks and cliffs form the mountain sides. Lying by day, snow leopards hunt at night preying on wild sheep and goats, musk deer, hares, mamots and other rodents, or even larger birds. In summer, when the upland pastures are open to grazing, they follow their prey to these higher reaches and finding opportunity feed on domestic animals like goats, sheep or ponies. They establish territory near human settlements and feed on domestic animals. In winter, they move down with the animals to about 600 ft. (1830m.). The gestation period is about 3 months. Snow leopards give birth to 2-4 young per litter. These are persistently hunted for their valuable fur.

Loin

The actual number of at present is far less. Recently the

Apex court directed a CBI inquiry about this. And the question was raised in parliamentary circles.

Local Name-Hindi-Sher Gujarat-Untiad Bagh, Malayayam-Simham, Tamil-Singham. Distinctive Characters—Mane is lesser than of African Lion, cost is fuller and longer tassel of hair at the end of it tail, more, pronounced tuft of hair at the elbow joints and fuller fringe of hairs on its belly. The mahe is light or dark, rarely, black. Cubs are spotted or striped. *Distribution*—Once found in the whole of Northwest and Central India as far south as Narmada. Now lions are restricted to the Gir, forest, Kathiawar, Gujarat. *Habits*—Gir forest in Junagadh district covers about 500 square miles of rugged country and is, composed of mainly stunted teak trees, palas, junbal, ber, patches of bamboo with an undergrowth of thorny shrubs and bushes. Lions hunt at dusk and rest during the day. Their roars are heard throughout the night. They prey on game and cattle. Lions do not have a particular breeding season. They are known to mate during October and November. Young ones are born during January and February. Gestation periods is about 116 days. The male stays with the family and helps to defend the young and to get food for the young. Young ones are produced at intervals of at least 18 months to 2 years. A lioness gives birth to its first litter when it is 2 1/2-3 year old. There may be 2,8 or even upto 5 cubs per litter.

Indus Dolphin

The Indus dolphin was considered a unique species. Now considered conspecific with Platanista gangetic. They are found in the Ganga, Brahmaputra, Indus and other large tributaries to the bases of hills. They are seen within tidal limits, but do not enter the sea. Its body oil is used for burning lamps and for various other purposes. Not much is known about this species.

Malabar Large Spotted Givet

This species was once very common in the coastal districts

of Malabar and Travancore. It lied in the wooded plains and in the adjoining hills slopes. At present they are scarcely seen and appears to be nearly extinct. Nothing else is known about this species.

Indian Wild Ass

Size—Height at shoulder 3ft. 8in. (110cms.) to 4 ft. (120cms.) *Distinctive Characters*—The colour of the coat varies from reddish grey to fawn or pale chestnut. The erect dark brown mane is continued as a dark brown stripe extending along the back to the root of the tail, the lower being white. *Distribution*—The Indian Wild Ass is found in the dense of the Rann of Cutch and Peninsular India. The present population is less than 2000. *Habits*—They roam in groups of 10-20, or in 2 or 3's or as individuals in the scorching sun. They are capable of remaining in the open for hours on end and run for a great distance at a speed of 30-32 miles per hour. The Indian wild ass mate in the months of August, September. The gestation period is about 11 months. Young ones appear in the month of July, August, September. They are readily tamed when young. They grow as vicious and untenable animals.

Asian Elephant

Size—Average height -Adult male 9ft., (2.75m.). Female-A foot lower 30cms. *Distinctive Characters*—The Asian elephant is smaller than the African elephant while the ears of the African elephant are enormous, that of the Asian elephant are smaller. The major distinctive feature is that of the hollow hack of the African elephant to that of the rounded back in the Asian counterpart. Generally only the males have tusks, while females have a protrusion of a few inches or nothing at all. *Distribution*—The Asian elephant in India is found in the Western Ghats, southwards from Mysore, Orissa, Bihar, Himalayan range, almost all over India. *Habits*—The asian elephant is found in areas covered with forests. They are extremely adaptable and live in steamy, humid jungle or in cool elevated forests. They live in herds of 5-60 (usually single families). When fodder is scarce heards break up into smaller parties. Big tuskers feed away from the herd. Bulls lead solitary life and joins a herd when he feels the urge to mate. Elephants sleep when it is hot and feed in the mornings and evenings and during nights invade open forests and raid crops. They raid and retire after midnight. They feed on various kinds of grasses and leaves stem and leaves of wild bamboo and plantain, all species of crops, barks of some kinds of trees. A full grown elephant eats about 600-700 lbs of fodder a day. The exact breeding-season is uncertain, but is estimated at the beginning of the rains. Young appear in Autumn. The gestation period is about 20 months. Elephants give birth too only one calf at a time. Elephants have poor sight but their sense of hearing and smell are excellent. Hunting and poaching for ivory has very greatly decreased the number of Indian elephants.

Great Indian Rhinoceros

Size—Average height of male-5ft. 8in. (170 cms.) with a girth of 11ft. (335cms.) behind the wither. *Distribution*—The Great Indian Rhinoceros was formerly extensively distributed throughout the Gangetic plain, but is now restricted to the Dooars and parts of West Bengal and Assam. *Distinctive Characters*—The skin is divided into shields by heavy folds before and behind the shoulder and in front of the things. The fold is not continued across the back which is a distinctive character in the Indian species. Another distinctive character is that the horn is smaller in the Indian Rhinoceros. *Habits*—Rhinos prefer swamps and grasslands but are also found in wood jungles and ravines of low hills. They lead a solitary life. Rhinos feed on grass. They breed throughout the year. Their gestation period is 16 months. The young one are born as heavy as 60 kgs. and are about 150 cms. in length. The female Rhino-acquires sexual maturity at the age of 4 years while the male takes 7 years to attain sexual maturity. The Indian Rhinoceros is a fast diminishing species. They, are hunted for sport and their skin is used for making leather products. Their horn is supposed to have medicinal value. They are found in majority only in the Kaziranga Sanctuary in Sibasagar/Nowgong district in Assam. The Bengal Rhinoceros Preservation Act of 1932 and the Assam Rhinoceros Preservation Act of 1954 were fruitful in protecting the animal and by the end of 1978 the population of the Rhino in the Kaziranga Sanctuary was estimated to be around 800.

Pygmy Hog

The pygmy hog is scarcely 10 inches high (25 cms.). They inhabit the forests of the Himalayas in Sikkim, Nepal, Bhutan and Assam. Their habits are similar to that of the wild boar. They live in herds of 5-20 in number. They are nocturnal by nature and rarely seen. Hence nothing much is known about this species.

Swamp Deer

Size—Average height 54 in (135 cms.) at the shoulder, average weight 170-180 kg), Average length of the horn-30 in. (75 cms.) with a girth of 5 in. (13cms) at mid-beam. *Distinctive characters*—The coat is almost woolly and has colour shades from brown to yellowish brown. Stags are manned and darker in colour. Younger ones are spotted. The size and shape of antlers vary. *Distribution*—Swamp deer are found in Terai, Uttar Pradesh, Assam, Sunderbans, and Madhya Pradesh. *Habits*—They live on Marsh land, seldom out of water. They are also found on grassy maidans. They are highly gregarious by nature and less nocturnal. Swamp deers feed till late morning and in the evenings, taking rest during most of the hot day. Their eye sight and hearing are moderate, with excellent sense of smell. They are an endangered species and strict protection is necessary to prevent their total extinction. The total number in Central India is estimated less than 200.

Hangul

Size—Average height 40-50 inches (120-125 cms.) at withers. Average weight 180 kgs. Average length of herein

40 inches (100 cms.). *Distinctive Characters*—The coat is light to dark brown fading to a dinghy white on the lips, chin, under parts and buttocks. The white rump patch is divided by broad median stripe extending to the base of the tail. Fawns are spotted. *Distribution*—Northern side of the Valley of Kashmir and some adjacent valleys. *Habits*—The Hangul is basically a forest animal and leads a solitary life or live in small parties. They roare around in search of food. They give birth to their young ones in late May. They spend their time in summer at heights of 900-12000 ft. (2750-3680 m.). They shed their antlers before they migrate and grow new ones. This is a very regular feature among this species. In winter they descend to lower levels and feed on fresh grass.

Manipur Brownanlered Deer

Size—Average height 4ft. (120 cms.) at withers, hindsare smaller. Average length of antler 42 inches (107 cms.). Average length of head-over 35 inches (90 cms.) *Distinctive Character*—The coat is coarse and sparse. The stags have a dark brown or black coat. Hinds are light brown or fawn. Young ones are spotted. Antlers are almost erect. *Distribution*—Manipur. *Habits*—The manipur Deer avoid hills and heavy forests. They prefer open scrub jungle or flat undulating land between rivers and hill ranges. They live in small herds. Their main food comprises of grass on which they feed in the mornings and evenings. Their speed and their sharp eye sight protect them from their predators. Young ones come in the month of October. Gestation period is about 239-250 days. The present number is only about 100 most of which are restricted to Keibal Lanjao Sanctuary on the shore of Loktal Lake in Manipur.

Wild Asiatic Water Buffalo

Size—Average height of Bull 6ft. 6in. (170 cms.) at shoulder to 6 ft. Average weight 900 kgs. or more. *Distinctive Character*—the wild buffalo is sleeker, heavier and more robust-looking than their tame counterpart. Their body is slaty black in colour. The newborn are light coloured, almost yellow in colour. Their horns are curve or spread outwards. The horns may be flat, triangular in cross-section, the horns of the cows are less massive and vary less in shape. *Distribution*—They are found in the grass jungles of Terai and the plains of Brahmaputra in Assam, Orissa and Bastar District of Madhya Pradesh. *Habits*—Tall grass jungles with food, shelter and water to lie in, form the natural habitat of the wild buffalo. They live in small herds. They feed chiefly on grass. Feeding is one only in the mornings and evenings and sometimes in the night. During the day they lie down in the shade. Wild Buffaloes are bold and most savage by nature. They invade cultivation in search of food. Bulls may attack without wanting or provocation. The chief enemies of this species are man and tiger. Their sense of smell is well developed and they possess good hearing. They have moderate eyesight. Calves appear in the months of March, April or May.

Wildlife Conservation Patterns in India

Many statutory measures such as laws have been passed and enacted in India and sanctuaries and national parks have been established for the protection of the dwindling wildlife. The Wild Birds and Animals Protection Act was passed in 1887 and repealed in 1912. For game protection in the states, in 1927, the Forest Act XVI was enacted. Indian Board for Wildlife was established in 1952 and this was followed by setting up of Wildlife Boards in different States in India. In 1972, a new Wildlife Protection Act was passed. Under this Act, possession, trapping, shooting of wild animals alive or dead, serving their meat in eating houses, their transport and export are all controlled and watched by special staff (Chief Wildlife Warden and authorised officers). This act prevents hunting of female and young ones. Under this Act the threatened species are absolutely protected and the rest afforded graded protection according to their state of population size. National Park is an area which is strictly reserved for the betterment of the wildlife. Forestry, grazing or cultivation like activities are not permitted there.

IMPORTANT NATIONAL PARTES AND SANCTUARIES

(1) Kanha National Park

Established in 1955 in former Banjar Valley Reserve (Madhya Pradesh), this park has an area of 939.94 sq.kms. and includes hilly terrain and streams. It is 175 kms. away from Jabalpur and has forests of sal trees. Its typical fauna includes animals like tiger, chital, panther, sambar, black buck and barasingha etc.

(2) Kalameru Bird Sanctuary

This is a small bird sanctuary near Tadepallegudam in Andhra Pradesh. It is a breeding place for pelicans, and many marine birds visit this place.

(3) Manas WildLife Sanctuary and Tiger Reserve

It is located in the Kamrup in Assam, covering an area 540 sq. kms. and is situated at an altitude of 80 meters. The river Manas runs through this sanctuary. It contains the following wild animals: tiger, panther, wild dog, wild boar, rhinoceros, gaur, wild buffalo, sambar, swamp deer and goiter langur.

(4) Cotigo Wild Life Sanctuary

It is located in South Goa and has an area of 105 sq. kms. It has wet evergreen forest of Elve and Beria trees and supports rich fauna of the following animals: gaur, sambar, chital, hog-deer, harking deer wild boar, hyaena, panther, leopard, jackal, otter, porcupine, and birds like parakeet lorokeet, woodpecker, kingfisher, bulbul jungle fowl, egret etc.

(5) Jaldapara Wildlife Sanctuary

It is situated in the Jalpaiguri district of West Bengal and covers an area of 65 sq.kms. of grassland. Wildlife fauna includes animals like rhinoceros, gaur, elephant, tiger, leopard, deer and a variety of birds and reptiles.

(6) Point Calimer Wildlife Sanctuary

This is situated at the southern tip of the Thanjavur district of Tamil Nadu abutting the Palk Strait. Its back water and lagoon is visited by flamingoes and pelicans. It is close to the Vedaranyam forests which has a fauna of numerous black bucks chitals and wild boars.

(7) Hazaribagh National Park

This national park has established in 1954 in Bihar. It has an area of 2750 sq.kms. of thick tropical forests. The typical fauna of this park includes wild boar, sambar, nilgai, tiger, leopard, sloth bear, hyena and gaur.

(8) Palamau National Park

It is situated in the Daltongunj district of Bihar and has an area of 345 sq.kms. The fauna of this includes tiger, panther, sloth bear, elephant, chital, gaur, nilgai, tiger, chinkara, chosingha and mouse deer. The Flora is thick tropical forest.

(9) Kaziranga Wildlife Sanctuary

It was established in 1926 in the district of Sibsagar, subdivision Jorhat (Assam) on the southern bank of the Brahmaputra river. It covers an area of 430 sq. kms. of forest grasslands and swamps and supports a fauna of 700 rhinoceros, besides elephant, wild buffalo, bison, tiger, leopard, sloth bear, sambar, swamp deer, hogdeer, barking deer, wild boar, gibbon and birds like pelican, stork and ring-tailed fishing eagles.

(10) Simplipal National Park

It is situated in the Mayurbhanj district in Orissa and an area of 2750 sq.kms. It is covered with dense sal forests and has been chosen for Project Tiger. Its typical fauna includes tiger, elephant, deer, pea fowl, talking mynas, chital, sambar, panther, gaur, hyena, and sloth bear.

(11) Vedanthangal Bird Century

This small-sized but very old sanctuary extends over a lake of about 0-30 sq.kms. 85 kms. from Chennai. Many migratory birds regularly visits this temporary lake. The regular visitors *of* this lake are birds like spoon bills, open billed storks, egrets, ibis, cormorant, darter, grey beron, pelicans, snipes and dab chicks.

(12) Chilka Lake

This largest inland lake has an area of 1000 sq.kms. and, is about 100 kms. from Bhubaneshwar. Its fauna includes waterfowl, duck, cranes, ospreys, golden plover, sandpiper, stone curlews, flamingos, etc.

(13) Periyar Wildlife Sanctuary

Situated in-the state of Kerala, this sanctuary covers an area of 777 sq.kms. It was established in 1949 around the artificial lake which arose behind the dam built across the "Periyar river in 1900. This sanctuary of great scenic beauty support a fauna of wild elephants, gaurs, leopards, sloth bear, sambars, barking deer, wild dogs, wild boars, black Nilgiri langur and water birds like grey hornbills, egrets.

(14) Mundatburai Sanctuary

It is situated in the Tirunelveli district of Tamil Nadu and was established in 1964. It covers an area of 520 sq. kms. The Tamaraparani river flows through the evergreen forests of the sanctuary. Panther, tiger, sambar and chital form the major fauna of this sanctuary.

(15) Guindy National Park

It is situated near Chennai city and has mainly chitals and black bucks. A few albinos of black buck are also found here.

(16) Bandipar Wildlife Sanctuary

This sanctuary was established in 1941 by the then ruler

of Mysore (Karnataka State). It is situated 80 kms. south of Mysore City enroute to Octacamund. It has an area of 874 sq.kms and is at an altitude of 1454.4 metres. Its forest is very thick and has plenty of rain fall. It wildlife fauna includes plenty of gaurs and animals like elephant, leopard, sloth bear, wild dog, chital, panther, barking deer, porcupine and langur.

(17) Ranganthitto Bird Sanctuary

It covers an area of 166 sq.kms. and includes a series of islands in the Cauvery river 15 kms of the Bangalore Mysore road, near Shrirangapatnam. Its avail fauna includes open bill stork, white ibis, egret, spoon bill, wild duck, pea fowl, night heron.

(18) Mundumalai Wildlife Sanctuary

This wildlife sanctuary was established in 1940 in North Western part of Nilgiris in Tamil Nadu. It is Known for its rich forests and diversity of fauna that includes wild elephants, gaur, sambar, chital, barking deer, mouse deer, four-horned antelope, tiger, panther, bonnet monkey, langur, gaint squirrel, flying squirrel, wild dog, jackal, wild cat, sloth beat, porcupine, pangolin, flying lizard, monitor lizard, rat snake, python and various birds.

(19) Tandoba National Park

It is located in Candrapur district (Maharashtra) and has, an area of 116 sq.kms. Its fauna include tiger, sambar, sloth bear, bison, chital, chinkara, barking deer, blue bull, four-horned deer, langur, peafowl and Cew crocodiles.

(20) Bhagwan Mahadeve Wildlife Sanctuary

It is located in North Goa and an area 240 sq.kms. and supports fauna almost similar to Cotigao Wildlife Sanctuary.

(21) Sasan Gir

This famous wildlife sanctuary for the Asiatic lion is situated in Gujarat state, 468 kms from Ahmedabad and 43 kms from Veraval. It has an area of 1295 sq.km. of semi-arid country with patches ofthom scrub and deciduous trees. Its fauna include Asiatic lion, spotted, deer, blue bull (nilgai), fur-horned antelope, chinkara, striped hyena, wildboar, porcupine, langur, python, crocodiles and birds like green pigeon, partridge, rock-grouse etc.

(22) Bharatpur Bird Sanctuary (Keoladeo Ghana)

It is located in Bharatpur district in Rajasthan, has an area of 29 sq.kms. and harbours all kinds of indigenous birds like nesting water birds, water birds and migratory birds. More than 328 varieties of birds including cormorants. Spoonbills, white ibis, Indian darters, egrets, painted storks, open billed storkes, great black necked storks, etc. Many migratory birds like ducks, geese, Siberian cranes, etc. regularly visit this sanctuary. Drier parts of this marshy sanctuary have animals like spotted deer, black buck, sambar, wild boar and python. To provide the basic needs for the wildlife the following steps may be taken as far as, possible for conservational purposes.

(23) Sariska

It is one of the most beautiful sanctuaries situated in the state of Rajasthan near Alwar. It has an area of 800 sq. kms and has dense Dohokara and Solar forests. Its fauna include tiger, leopard, spotted deer jungle cat, four-horned antelope, langur, porcupine, hedgehog, peafowl etc.

- The forest inside the sanctuary/national park should be left unexploited as far as possible. It would be an ideal environment for the wildlife to get the fullest measure of protection, and in such preserved conditions of life they can multiply freely.

- If total check on exploitation is not possible, the cutting operations of the forest should be in small units, well-distributed over the forest. Frequent light cut are generally better for wildlife than infrequent heavy cuts.
- Poaching needs to be ruthlessly prohibited in the sanctuaries in particular and generally in other areas outside them, where wildlife still exists mobile armed units should be attached to all sanctuaries to patrol regularly the entire sanctuary to stop illegal activities.
- Provision for dust bath for animals should also be made by leaving some exposed soil for their dusting. These spots may be prepared in the form of small mounds elevated a few inches from the forest floor to allow for drainage and to dry quickly in wet months.
- The water holes and stream sides should be managed and guarded carefully for the benefit of wildlife. Such critical areas may be of small size, but their importance is disproportionately great because they supply important elements in wildlife ecology-forlargerareas during hot months of the year.
- The forest should not be planted with or allowed to grow only a single species of plant. Further, fruit-bearing shrubs and trees should be encouraged wherever possible and the natural openings of the forests should be preserved.
- Annual burning of the grassland in most ot our sanctuaries has become an integral part of management, since not burning these might bring about a lack of suitable fodder during the hotter months. Controlled burning has been found to increase forage and to preserve organic material in the soil. Such burning may be done in blocks with unburned

areas in between, so that areas are burnt in rotation. The burning is to be confined to definite blocks by means of fivebreaks. Burning at night is favoured unless it is likely to extend the fire beyond the desired limits.

- Cultivation near the sanctuary should be avoided as a rule as it may have an indirect effect on the wildlife. The chemical control of certain pests is often desirable for better yield in agriculture, but these pesticides can present ecological hazards for wildlife.
- Some artificial salt-licks are also be provided in the sanctuaries since the wildlife need them at regular intervals for their normal health. Such salt-licks are necessary for animals especially in areas where natural salted clay is scanty.
- Scientific studies or the sanctuary-wildlife particularly of threatened species, by qualified persons, should encouraged in order or improve the status of the animals even by breeding them in captivity to rehabilitate them in suitable habitats.
- Concentrated grazing by domestic livestock is to be prevented as wildlife can never compete with domestic stock under ordinary circumstances and domestic animals may be responsible for transmitting diseases like foot and mouth diseases, rinderpest, heamorrhagic sepicaemia, arthrax etc.

Most wildlife could be saved by sufficiently rigid protection of their natural habitat, combined with controlled exploitation of species which are of economic importance. Some of wildlife may be driven away from their natural habitats so that their requirements are not in conflict with human interests. The only possible cause for maintaining their viable number is in national parks, sanctuaries, game reserves, where they could thrive unharmed. In the case of the most endangered species which have reached a point of extinction in their favourable habitat, their survival may be ensured through the maintenance of breeding stock in zoological parks in suitable parts of the country.

Activities and Restraints Suggested for Agencies Working in Special Areas for Ecodevelopment

(i) Forestry

- Strictly wildlife-oriented forestry operations in buffer zones.
- Restricted community uses of forests in buffer zones.
- Soil conservation in eroded areas.
- Pasture development and afforestation of denuded areas so to meet the pasture and firewood needs of local communities.
- Monocultures to be discouraged and efforts made to preserve and regenerate diversity in forests.

(ii) Soil Conservation

- Contour bunding and soil conservation works in village areas.

(iii) Agriculture

- Develop and apply improved dry farming techniques for marginal lands. Develop improved seeds and fertilizer regimes.
- Introduce cash crops where they are likely to be more profitable in preference to cereals.

(iv) Animal Husbandry

- Gradually reduce cattle population and improve the breeds through castration of scrub bulls and controlled fertilization of cows and female buffaloes in proper health and age with bulls of good breed.

- Establish fodder farms where feasible.
- Discourage goat keeping in SAEDs.

(v) Irrigation

- Take up diversion or- diversion-cum-storage or minor irrigation schemes.
- Support soil conservation of forest and agricultural lands as a part of catchments treatment for major irrigation projects in lower reaches.

(vi) Tribal Welfare and Rural Development

- Activities when sponsored through special programmes must conform to above items listed for various sectors.
- Promotion of local art and handicraft with sale outlets in tourist complexes of well-visited wildlife reserves.

(vii) All Agencies

- Preference in employment to local people.

The aforementioned special programmes are to be coupled with strict wildlife protection and the establishment of the "core-buffer- multiple use surrounds" structure. Section 4 of the NWAP seeks to provide for protection of wildlife in production forests and pasture lands to preserve corridors between protected-forests for the movement of animals such as elephants. Over seven years after the adoption of the NWAP no action has been taken on either of these sections, though there are proposals to connect several PAs in India by means of viable, corridors as described in Rodgers (1988). Section I of the NWAP called for the establishment of a Representative Network of Protected Areas. A major contribution to this effort to review the status of an protected areas and suggest new ones to represent all 10 major biogeographic zones and 25 biotic provinces of India, has been the compilation of the Biogeographic Report by the Wildlife Institute of India—*Planning a Protected Area Network in India*. This report recommends the addition of 148 parks comprising 50,797 sq km and 503 sanctuaries comprising 100,545 sq km to the existing network of 426 PAs covering 3.3 per cent of the country. The biogeographic report underscores the necessity for the final notification of the Rajaji National Park, and declares it a task of national importance to give protection to the Upper Gangetic Plain Biogeographic Province 7A. It is suggested that Kanjilal proposed the Golathappar swamp is also incorporated into the park to include the unique swamp type of vegetation, as at the turn of the century. In addition to the Wildlife (Protection) Act of 1972, there is also the Forest (Conservation) Act of 1980, which governs forestlands. This Act lays down that no forest area can be dereserved or diverted to any non-forest purpose without prior approval of the Central Government. Since the passage of the Act the forest area dereserved annually has declined.

Wildlife Conservation and the Eighth Five-year Plan

The Report and proposals of the Sub-Group on Wildlife and Nature Conservation clearly stress the need and commitment for wildlife conservation. A target area of 5 per cent of the land area of the country is suggested for wildlife protection. Only about 2 per cent of the total land area is to be afforded complete protection, while the remaining 3 per cent may be managed for multiple usage. The report includes a list of 10 problems facing wildlife conservation caused by resource dependencies of local people. The report goes on to mention, as a consequence of these problems, "conservation success in multiple use areas will depend on eco-development measures that can bring about higher productivity for the use of the local people". The list squarely recognises the paramount problems of wildlife conservation in India-livestock pressure, firewood demand from urban centers, ecologically unsound rural development, poaching, habitat fragmentation, and so on.

Problems of Wildlife Conservation in India

By far the largest problems common to forest and wildlife conservation are the resource dependencies of local people. Some key problems are enumerated below.

1. Pressures of demand of firewood, small timber and other forest products from forest side people and urban settlements.
2. Pasturing of unsustainably high populations of scrub livestock by forest side rural people and by communities respectively dependent upon livestock raising e.g. Gurjars, Maldharis, Ahirs etc.
3. Commercial poaching of a few species, e.g. elephant, rhino, musk deer, and common fur bearing species like jackal.
4. Restoration of critically endangered species because in many cases *'in situ'* amelipration of habitats is problematic and populations are on the verge of genetic threshold.
5. Interface conflicts arising from above pressures and from crop and livestock raiding by wild animals.
6. Habitat fragmentation and jeopardizing of crucial movement corridors
7. Lack of fiscal and manpower resources to devise scientific wildlife, management plans for protected areas and to implement them, including also enforcement aspects.
8. Habitat degradation because of such overuse manifest in accelerated erosion, desiccation, impoverishment of water regime, Proliferation of weeds and lack of regeneration of fodder plants and forest trees.
9. Inadequacy of biogeographic representation and geographic networking in the existing protected area system,

10. Lack of appreciation in agencies responsible for rural development, that not only forest and wildlife conservation, but also the welfare of the forest living people is substantially dependent upon restoration of degraded rural ecosystems and adjacent forest environments, which in turn is possible only if the resource dependencies of such people are rationalised. Also, that is possible through ecologically sound development inputs that address area-specific problems rather than the usual individual beneficiary oriented approach applicable to plains.

The report identifies the major deficiencies in the national efforts towards wildlife conservation. One of the major flaws is the very poor allocation towards wildlife conservation in the five-year plans. The other flaw pointed out has been the lack of effort to mitigate interface conflicts, which alone can make wildlife conservation acceptable to the people living in the forested region. The report proposes the relocation' of 300 villages inside 50 national parks at a cost of Rs 10 lakhs each and the removal of 500 villages from 200 sanctuaries at the same unit cost. The relocation of insular villages is also a directive of the Wildlife (Protection) Act. However, in a marked departure from previous strategies in wildlife management in India, the report stresses the necessity of managing human pressures on forests and forest resources. The need to improve the lot of the forest side poor is repeated several times. With this in mind the authors make the following proposals:

> Therefore a land use strategy which stresses the need for both a framework of inviolate areas to protect key water, wildlife, and forest resources and concomitant development of buffer and multiple use forests and pastures for people's use is the only solution. Rural development inputs should be area specific and aim at enhancing the economic productivity of marginal farmland

through soil conservation, micro-minor irrigation schemes, improved dry farming techniques and crop alternatives. Likewise they should be directed towards improving productivity of pastures as well as to gradual reduction in population and concomitant improvement of breed and productivity of the excessive scrub livestock.

This innovative land use strategy is recommended for immediate implementation in the areas surrounding a few key PA's. Even if only a few schemes are implemented they will act as models for rural development schemes which mitigates pressures on the PA's. To make this strategy successfully reduce pressures and animosity against conservation, it is suggested that these schemes be taken up by the PA managers themselves in accordance with systematic management plans involving eco-development. For eco-development around important PA's, the report has proposed a central outlay of Rs. 150 crores for the Eighth Plan. This is to be distributed among 100 national parks, sanctuaries, and Tiger reserves. One or two model schemes are suggested for each Park costing Rs 1.50 crore each. Various details on central nodal coordination, the various types of schemes, and means for designing eco-development programmes to reduce people/park conflict have also been submitted. The total outlay proposed for the eighth plan is Rs 315 crores. Only an allocation of like magnitude around 15 per cent of the proposed forestry allocation, will significantly improve wildlife conservation in India, and in turn improve the quality of life of people.

Management of National Parks and Sanctuaries in India

While India has today a fairly extensive set of PAs, and with the adoption of the recommendations of the Biogeographic Report, should eventually have a comprehensive network of PAs merely the identification and notification of areas to be protected doesn't necessarily lead to enhanced conservation.

There are many pressures associated with the management of most PAs, the most important of which is obtaining the cooperation of the rural population, which is usually dependent on forest resources. Presently, a number of the country's PAs exist only in name and do not actively manage and control the level of resource utilisation by local communities. Accommodating and controlling the resource dependencies of local people on park resources often requires sacrifices on the part of the local people who have traditionally enjoyed rights in the protected forests. Forests and associated resources have continued to be buffers for emergencies such as droughts and famines for the poorest people living near forest areas. Similarly for people who live in forest areas, once these are declared as protected, a whole new set of problems arise which require the provision of alternative resources, and often alternative lifestyles, as these people may have to be resettled outside these PAs. On the part of the government authorities, to make conservation beneficial to local people for their development, or at the very least to avoid the type of conflicts and confrontations that have characterised wildlife protection in India over the last decade, requires the provision of special developmental inputs for local people, and often modification of conservation strategies.

The two basic wildlife protection units in India are national parks and sanctuaries. These apply to all states except Jammu and Kashmir. The concept of biosphere reserves has been accepted by India and several PAs have been identified as biosphere reserves but so far this idea arising from the Man and Biosphere Programme of UNESCO has not been implemented in India. People and human settlement: are included in biosphere reserves and changes in land use not normally considered in the designation of biosphere reserves. Harmonious relationships between indigenous people and the environment are sought to be retained in biosphere reserves. If would be apparent to all except the most purblind that these considerations would have to be substantially reworked in Indian conditions. The highest protection status in India is that of a national park, as described by the Wildlife (Protection) Act. E.P.Gee, one of the founding members of the Indian Board for Wildlife, describes a national park as "an area dedicated to conserve the scenery and natural and historical objects of national significance, to conserve wildlife therein and to provide for the enjoyment of the same in such manner and by such means as will leave them unimpaired for the enjoyment of future generations, with such modifications as local conditions may demand". National parks are free from rights such, as landholding or grazing. These rights may be accepted in the case of wildlife sanctuaries under the Act. Under the aegis, of the Act, wildlife is defined to include "any animal, bees, butterflies, crustacea, fish and moths and aquatic or land vegetation which forms part of any habitat". There are set procedures for the notification and declaration of National Park and Sanctuaries under the Wildlife Act.

Human Activities

(a) There has long been an interaction between human populations and forest and wildlife resources. Human activities have exploited these resources from time immemorial. In recent time the advent of new resource intensive activities and the tremendous pressure exerted even by traditional activities because of an increased human population have contributed to the extensive destruction of wildlife,

(b) Some salient features of human activities in and around India's PA's are listed below:

56% of the 32 National Parks and 72 % of 138 Sanctuaries responding reported human populations within their boundaries.

83% of the 23 National Parks and 87 of the Sanctuaries reported populations in their adjacent areas.

43% of the 44 National Parks and 68% of the 187

sanctuaries responding reported the existence of rights and leases. The majority of these were for grazing and fuel wood collection. Sariska Sanctuary reported eight types of rights. The low since only a fraction of the PAs have completed their legal procedures.

Of the 36 national parks and 138 sanctuaries responding, 39 per cent and 73 per cent respectively reported the grazing of livestock within their boundaries. For several of these PAs the animals grazed exceeded, the national density.

(c) The extraction of fodder, timber, and minor forestry produce are significant for those PAs responding. Compared with the adjacent populations there is discrepancy since population living within and adjacent to forest areas in India invariably uses the local resources to meet some of their needs.

(d) Of the 36 national parks and 176 sanctuaries responding, 8 per cent and 46 per cent respectively reported the incidence of illegal occupation or use. Encroachment was the common form of occupation and cultivation and grazing of use. The most common offenders were villagers.

(e) Seven per cent of the 44 national parks and 20 per cent of the 160 sanctuaries responding reported encroachment.

(f) Of the 45 national parks and 172 sanctuaries responding 69 per cent and 56 per cent respectively reported the incidence of one or more type of offences. The most common were destruction of habitat, illegal grazing causing fire hazards, illegal hunting, and so on.

(g) Of the 39 national parks and 167 sanctuaries responding, 36 per cent and 29 per cent respectively reported incidents of injury or death of human beings due to attacks by wild animals, either inside or adjacent to them. Of the 629 cases reported for the period of 1979-84, 77 per cent were fatal.

(h) And finally, 37% per cent of the 43 national parks and 17% of the 179 sanctuaries responding reported incidence of confrontations or clashes between local people and authorities. These clashes were reported over illicit felling of trees, poaching, illegal grazing, a, encroachments, and so on. The compulsions of the local people were not recorded.

Management is designed to improve the protection of the habitat and the wildlife to let populations reach natural population densities." Some salient features of management in India's PAs, which have a bearing on the emerging situation at Rajaji, are as follows:

(a) 38% per cent of the 48 national parks surveyed and 9 per cent of 221 sanctuaries report the existence of zoning.

(b) Of the 16 national parks and 88 sanctuaries surveyed which have human population inside them and have responded to the IIPA questionnaire, 31 per cent of the national parks and 5 per cent of the sanctuaries had proposed to relocate apart or whole of their population- prior to 1984. Actual relocation till 1984 has been done in 25 per cent of the national parks and 3 per cent of the sanctuaries responding.

(c) Twenty per cent of the 45 national parks and 25 per cent of the sanctuaries responding have reported that compensation is paid for injury or killing of livestock by wild animals both within and outside the PA.

(d) Twelve per cent of the 43 national parks and 14 per cent of the 188 sanctuaries responding reported that compensation is payable for crop damage by wildlife in adjacent areas.

(e) Twenty per cent of the 44 national parks and 121 per cent of the 197 sanctuaries responding reported educational programmes for villagers. However it was found that the frequency of these programmes was low and not regularly scheduled.

3

Growth of Ecotourism

At an operational level, though, the interest in ecotourism does not appear to have translated into the emergence of a vibrant, profitable business sector. With the exception of the accommodation sector and some ecotourism businesses with mass market appeal, most ecotourism enterprises are finding it difficult to identify and reach viable market segments. The failure to translate apparent demand into profitable business ventures is driven by two flawed assumptions made by government agencies, academics and many potential operators. The first is the misinterpretation of statistics that confuse visitation to natural areas with demand for commercial ecotourism products (Blarney, 1996a, b). Most people can consume an ecotourism experience without the need to purchase a product from a commercial operator. The real market demand for ecotourism activities is, therefore, only a small fraction of the apparent market interest (McKercher, 1998). The second reason is based more on ideological hope than commercial reality. Ecotourism is recognised widely as an ecologically, morally and ethically preferred form of tourism that, if done correctly, optimizes social, cultural and ecological benefits, while providing the tourist with an uplifting experience. Further, it is recognised that eco-tourism can only he sustainable if it is profitable for ecotourism operators. Thus, it is felt that because this activity is so morally, ecologically and ethically sound, amass market must exist for such activities. What little empirical research that has been conducted examining the profitability of this sector, suggests that many businesses are under-performing. Indeed, the challenges of running a nature-based tourism business are similar to the generic types of challenges faced by all small businesses which, typically, have a 90% plus failure rate. These issues include: the failure to identify real market opportunities, lack of business planning, under-capitalisation, little or no marketing skills and poor financial management skills. Much of this is explained by the fact that many people apparently enter this sector out of their love for certain non-commercial recreation activities. Their motives are driven by a desire to play, rather than to develop a quality tourism product. Many new operators often find it difficult to adjust from the low pressure situation of leading friends on tour to the greater expectations and demands of fee-paying clients.

Marketing Issues

Amazingly in many people entering the ecotourism sectors have a remarkable lack of business skills and, of more concern, do not appear to have considered their lack of skills as a problem. Most will bring strong operational skills, based on their many years of participation in their respected activity. Many people choose to enter the field for lifestyle reasons, thinking that they can get paid to play. Few have ever run a business before and few seem concerned about business issues. But unless they learn about running a business, the lifestyle dream can turn into a night mare, poverty is not an attractive lifestyle for an aspiring ecotourism. The, following discussion summarizes the key findings of a study conducted of the business planning and marketing needs of the ecotourism sector as identified by successful Australian ecotourism businesses.

Business Plans

Entering business with a clear business plan, is or should be one of the first tasks completed by prospective operators. Business plans serve two main purposes. The first is that they force prospective operators to work through the fine detail of their proposed venture prior to its establishment. By following a logical and rigorous process, operators can test their idea to see if a real business opportunity exists. The goal of the exercise prior to operation becomes one of demonstrating that a true market opportunity exists or aborting a non-viable idea prior to start-up. While a business plan will not guarantee success, it has been shown to reduce failure by 60% or more. The second key role played by business plans begins once the business starts. Business plans outline a desired growth path for the enterprise and, importantly; establish benchmarks by which to monitor the performance of the business. Operators can then adjust their business plans, or alter their operations if the business does not seem to match the projections.

As a result, they fail to identify clear goals and objectives for their business or, alternatively, identify unrealistic goals. Many do not know if a viable market opportunity exists for their idea and do not have a realistic assessment of the costs involved in starting and incubating a business. Typically, they assume unrealistically high sales and profit figures and budget unrealistically low cost figures. The result is that many businesses are under-capitalised and because revenue is not what was hoped for, cannot thrive. Successful operators appreciate that it takes many years for a business to establish itself. To succeed, and the resources required to survive during those fragile early years.

Financial Management Skills

It is significant to note that financial management is a significant issue for most new operators. It is not surprising considering that many come from an operational background and have never had to manage an organisation's finances before. Slower than expected growth, coupled with higher than anticipated costs cause many operators to face financial crises in the formative years of the business. A lack of resources will affect all areas of a business, from marketing and advertising to equipment purchases and the ability to hire staff. A serious miscalculation of thereal costs of running a business cans effectively strangle growth for many years. In addition, many operators do not understand the concept of cash flow. Businesses run on cash, just as a car runs on petrol. No matter how expensive a car is, if it does not have any petrol in the tank, it won't work. The same applies to a business.

In a similar manner, there is a general lack of marketing knowledge among many new entrants. A request for marketing help often belies a deeper problem in the business, namely the failure to identify a commercially viable business opportunity right from the start. Regardless, many ecotourism operators do not understand what marketing is or how marketing works. Given that most have limited resources, one would think that they would adopt a targeted marketing approach, allocating those scarce resources in such a way that they optimize the chance to reach their desired markets. Instead, many adopt what is known in the trade as a shotgun marketing approach, squandering their resources and hoping that by chance they will find a desired client. This occurs usually as a function of not knowing who the target market is, not understanding its habits and buying power and not having a clear idea of how to reach that market. Many operators are also quite ignorant of how the tourism distribution system works and also appear wary of having to pay between a 10 and 35% commission to someone else to sell their product.

A complex system of retail travel agents, wholesale tour operators and inbound tour operators has evolved over the past 150 years to act as the conduit between the provider of the product and the marketplace. This system works on a commission basis. If anyone is interested in gaining international distribution for their product, or of even gaining broad national distribution, they must work through the travel trade. Failure to cost products so that they are attractive to the travel trade, coupled with a failure to take advantage of these networks, constrains the ability of most businesses to achieve wide market penetration of their products. Price is an interesting issue for this sector for many operators does not understand what they are really selling and, therefore, are reluctant to charge what the product is worth. At one level, price is an accounting concept: you must charge enough to cover your costs and to provide you with an acceptable profit. At another level, though, price is an important marketing concept for the price charged reflects the value the product. Many operators adopt a cost plus approach to pricing by adding up the component costs of the trip (food, guide, vehicle, accommodation, etc.) and then adding a profit component. These operators invariably under-price their product. In reality, the true worth of a product and, therefore, the price that can be charged conies not from the component costs, but from the value-adding made by the operator, often brought about by the ease of access provided by the product and the quality of the personalised service offered. The more unique the product being offered, the higher the price that can be charged. Ironically, charging a low price, especially if all around you are charging a higher price for the same product, may be counter-productive. Ecotourism is all about selling experiences. Good operators have come to realise that good ecotourism practices begin with good customer service. Staff must be both professional and approachable. Further, staff must engender a sense of confidence, especially if the experience involves, or is perceived to involve some risk. Effective communication skills are a vital ingredient of good customer satisfaction.

Operators must possess a number of personal attributes. Prospective operators must have patience, determination, drive, enthusiasm, a love of hard work, be willing to work long hours, genuinely enjoy meeting and being with new people, have a friendly disposition and be able to act in a clear, concise and professional manner. Moreover stress and the risk of personal hurt-out in this sector is especially, during, those critical early years of the business. New operators are faced with long hours and often low rewards. In most cases, the business will become all consuming, becoming an extension of the operator and not just his or her job. To survive, operators must, therefore, ensure that they have a healthy balance between their work and non-work lives.

Identifying Viable Business Opportunities

They highlight that most ecotourism businesses fail to identify a viable business opportunity. Should they be lucky enough to do so, many operators do not know how to capitalize on that opportunity, either because of a failure to plan or for a lack of marketing skills. In this author's opinion, the single greatest problem facing this sector is the failure of prospective operators to identify a commercially viable market and to deliver products that satisfy the needs, wants and desires of that market. Instead, they try to push inappropriate products onto an undifferentiated market that is really not very interested in what they are trying to sell. The key to any successful ecotourism business is predicated on developing a deep knowledge of who the market is and why it wants to purchase an operator's product. It is only from this knowledge that an operator can develop products that meet the needs of the market and can plan to position them attractively for the right markets.

How large is the market for commercial ecotourism products? No one knows for sure, but it is fair to say it is only a small fraction of the total number of people who have been labeled as 'ecotourists'. Indeed, phantom demand seems to be driving much of the unrealistic expectations of the sector. On the surface, ecotourism seems to be a booming activity, which would imply the existence of substantial business opportunities. The Australian Bureau of Tourism Research, for example, suggests that up to 50% of the more than 4 million international tourists to that country engaged in what could loosely be described as an ecotourism experience during their visit. Similarly, the aforementioned comment by WTO suggests that ecotourists now account for 20% of world travel.

But these figures are misleading, for most of these 'ecotourists' are labeled thus based on a visit they made to a protected area sometime during their trip. But, as Acott (1998) argue, visiting an ecotourism site does not make one an ecotourist. Whether or not you agree with their assertion, it is true that visiting an ecotourism site certainly does not make one a prospective commercial ecotourism client. A deeper examination of Australian tourism statistics reveals that only 5% of international visitors indicated that experiencing outdoor or nature-based activities particularly influenced their decision to travel to Australia (Blarney, 1996a). It is likely that an even smaller percentage purchased ecotourism goods and services. In reality, the commercial ecotourism market is a true niche market; small, specialised and discrete.

Commercial Ecotourists

To a large extent, the legitimacy of ecotourism rests primarily in its ability to achieve sustainable land uses rather than as a product category (Lawrence, 1997). Using this supply-side definition, any visitor to land managed along sustainable ecotourism principles can be labeled an ecotourist, regardless of the activity the person pursued. In addition, a lack of clarity over the use of the term in a tourism context has further confused the issue. There is no doubt that the term 'ecotourism' has been misused by tourism marketers and tourism promotion agencies alike, to the extent that almost any form of non-urban tourism can be labeled as ecotourism. But even when used legitimately, ecotourism can simultaneously describe destinations, experiences and products (parks, attractions, accommodation and tours). Many ecotourism destinations and experiences can be consumed at little or no cost, especially when one remembers that most land use management agencies have legislative obligation to provide recreational opportunities at minimal cost to the public. Further ecotourism destinations may not provide business opportunities for commercial ecotourism operators, especially if the ecotourism attraction is a protected area.

Many national parks, for example, preclude the provision of commercial activities inside park boundaries. The result is a disparity between the number of people who visit ecotourism areas and the actual number of 'real' ecotourists. At an operational level, the commercial realities of running ecotourism businesses further limit the number of people who are willing or able to pay for services. Why would anyone purchase a commercial product if they could participate in exactly the same experience at little or no cost?

The answer is few would, unless the ecotourism product offered something of added value that the consumer could not otherwise get. Many recreational ecotourists are philosophically opposed to what they see as the commercial exploitation of protected areas and eschew commercial operators. Many former operators have made the fatal mistake of looking at participation rates in conservation/recreational clubs and associations (bird watching, bush walking, etc.) and assumed that a ready market was available to them. What they failed to appreciate is that one of the reasons why people join these organisations is to gain inexpensive access to high quality experiences. Many of these people are exactly the wrong market for the commercial ecotourism sector for they have substitute products that provide an experience of equal or greater quality at a fraction of the cost.

The most successful ecotourism businesses fill the need-satisfaction gap that the traveler would otherwise not have. For example, ecotourism operators that visit the Great Barrier Reef in far North Queens land, Australia, provide their clients with access that most would not be able to provide themselves.

In a similar manner, fly-in wilderness fishing lodges in the Canadian Shield area of North America provide access that would otherwise not be available to all but the hardiest wilderness traveler. Many marginally viable businesses feel their unique selling point is the quality of the information they impart to the consumer, when the consumer clearly feels this is not essential to their being able to enjoy the experience. Finally, it is expensive to operate an ecotourism business, and these expenses must be passed on to the clients in the form of relatively high prices. This financial reality further limits the market by pricing ecotourism as an exclusive activity.

Ecotourism businesses rarely enjoy the economies of scale of mass-tourism ventures, and as such, have relatively high fixed costs per client. In addition, these ventures often must overcome small group sizes, seasonality issues, higher per capital marketing costs, in-built volatility in the marketplace and a whole host of other factors that drive tip their costs and consequently their prices.

Commercial ecotourists are affluent, well travelled, well educated, independent, have a high disposable income, eschew normal packaged tours aimed at the mass market and seek an alternative vacation experience. Their age can vary, with two dominant age groups evident: older experienced travellers who are prepared to purchase up- market products and younger travellers who are seeking innovative experiences (Pearce and Wilson, 1996). Most are women and many travel on their own. They are very active and belong to environmental organisations more than the general populations as a whole. Their involvement in environmental and public interest group organisations means that not only do they have a keen interest in environmental issues, they also tend to have a greater knowledge of environmental issues. They choose ecotourism experiences because they want to be active, meet people with similar interests, learn new skills and optimize their time use.

That fact that most ecotourists are women is something that many in the industry seem to recognise, but at the same time seem to overlook in their product design and promotional activities. It has been estimated that women constitute up to 75% of the nature-based and cultural tourism market. Most of these women do not want to travel in women-only travel parties. While in private conversation, operators acknowledge that women constitute their dominant market, few operators appear to target their promotional activities, or tailor their trips specifically to suit the demands of women. Women and men respond differently to promotional activities and read different media. Moreover, women participate in nature based tourism trips for a variety of reasons that operators do not seem to appreciate fully.

Research into the nature-based tourism industry in the Australian state of Victoria showed that women purchased commercial nature-based tourism products for the following reasons ease and convenience of participation, safety and security provided by a guided trip; and the opportunity to travel with others, especially if the woman was traveling by herself. The industry, on the other hand, thought that women purchased their products because of the trip attributes, such as route selection, equipment provision and the area being visited. Dissonance between this markets real needs and the operator's perception of these needs may explain low participation rates in some businesses.

Types of Ecotourists

It is a mistake to assume that the nature based tourism market is a single, unified market. Instead, different types of people are attracted to different activities. This overview lesson does not permit a detailed examination of each sub market; however, it is important to appreciate that a continuum of ecotourists exists that can be defined based on the traveler's commitment to ecotourism and the centrality of an ecotourism experience in their vacation choice. These different market segments have been labeled alternatively as specialist and generalist ecotourists, or have been placed on a continuum front 'hard core' to casual ecotourists, or deep to shallow. Specialist or hard core ecotourists are committed the experience because it provides them with an intense, nature-based tourism activity. They are likely to participate in longer trips, be knowledgeable about the experience offered and be experienced travellers. The nature-based tourism experience is the main purpose of the trip for these people. Specialist nature based tourists are prepared to make sacrifices to participate in their tourism experience. They are prepared to travel long distances to participate in the activity and do not want nor do they expect luxurious accommodation, food and night life (Long et al., 1996).

This market is quite small and is seeking exclusive activities. 'Generalist' or 'casual' ecotourists, on the other hand, participate in ecotourism as one of many activities they will do while on holiday. Their decision to participate is convenience based. They are likely to take short duration trips, have limited knowledge about the area being visited, book at the last minute and may only have a casual interest in the activity. These people are less likely to travel large distances explicitly for the nature-based tourism experience, but may be prodigious consumers if an experience is easy to consume in close proximity to their current destination. Depending on the activity, this market is large, and in fact, more closely approximates the mass tourism market, especially for easy to consume discretionary ecotourism experiences provided in main stream destinations.

Anyone entering the 'hard' ecotourism market must appreciate that the absolute market for their activities is small. To succeed, operators must provide truly unique experiences that offer exceptional quality experiences. These businesses will most likely be small scale, with high prices being charged. Location is a critical factor in their success, for the area must be recognised as an important ecotourism destination. It will be difficult to run a successful ecotourism venture if the market considers the location as not having the necessary qualities it wants in an eco-product. One of the factors mitigating against the success of eco-resorts in Finland, for example, is that it is not perceived to have high quality environmental assets needed to sustain such businesses.

Conversely, recreation, fun, activity and ease of access seem to drive demand for soft ecotourism experiences. In these cases, the thrill of the experience plays a stronger role in attracting visitors than the skill or desired learning outcomes.

Products that provide an enjoyable, recreational and, dare say, an escapist and commodified, outdoor-oriented tourism experience are desired by this market. While this assertion may be an anathema to committed, hardcore ecotourists, it none the less represents the reality of the desires of a market that consumes an eco-experience as one of many experiences they might consume during a holiday. Further, to be able to compete, such experiences must be seen as being attractive alternatives to other recreational experiences. Emanuel de Kadft (1979) said some 20 years ago 'the normal tourist is not to be confused with an anthropologist or other researcher. Tourists are pleasure seekers, temporarily unemployed and above all, consumers; they are taking their trip to get away from everyday cares'. To a large extent, this maxim still holds true today for the vast majority of tourists who may be interested in eco-experience.

What is it that ecotourists buy when they purchase a commercial product? What does anyone buy when he or she buys a holiday? Do you buy airfare, accommodation and transfers or are you really buying something else? You may pay for air fare, accommodation and transfers, but in reality you are buying something that will provide you with an intrinsic or personal benefit. Far too many operators look at their product from the perspective of what they are selling to the tourist and not from the perspective of what the tourist is buying. As such, they tend to focus on the tangible elements that make up the product. In fact, these features are simply elements that facilitate consumption of an experience. What the ecotourist, and indeed any consumer purchases when he or she buys a product is personal needs satisfaction. Products are defined as anything that can be offered to a market for attention, acquisition, use or consumption that might satisfy a need or a want. The key words are 'satisfying need or want'. It is difficult to do, but operators must always think of their product from the perspective of the person who is buying the good or service. When consumers buy nature-based tourism products, they are buying a range of personal benefits (Hawkins, 1994).

Increasingly, tourists are buying products that satisfy their lifestyle preferences, with the quest for adventure or the desire to see nature becoming increasingly important aspects of many people's lifestyles.

The key questions to consider when examining any ecotourism product are what needs are being satisfied by purchasing this product? and 'why would anyone prefer any product to someone else's? These questions are so basic that many people fail to ask them, let alone answer them effectively, is the decision to establish an ecotourism business in a certain location based on the ability to satisfy customer needs effectively, or is made simply because that is where the operator lives?.

Products exist on three levels: core, tangible and augmented. The core product represents the most fundamental level of any product and answers the question of what needs, wants or desires are being satisfied by buying the product. Someone purchasing a hotel room is buying the need satisfaction of sleep. The bed, color TV and decor are the tangible components that facilitate this need satisfaction. Someone buying a computer may be purchasing the need satisfaction of being able to communicate with the world via the Internet and email. The components that go into the computer, the RAM and ROM and the like, only serve to facilitate this need satisfaction. The same is true with any ecotourism product. It is only once the core benefit has been identified that the rest of the product can be tailored to deliver the need satisfaction. The tangible aspect of a product represents the elements that are assembled to facilitate need satisfaction. In the ecotourism industry, these are usually features like accommodation, transport, food, guides and the like. There is a challenge in developing the tangible component of the product when the good being sold is experiential or ethereal in nature, for the consumer cannot inspect the product and assess its value. Augmented product elements are those additional features and service that make the product complete. Augmented products for the tourism industry might include easy reservation services, credit or cancellation policies, the provision of travel insurance the inclusion of wildlife manuals while on tour or the sale of film.

Belatedly, a number of operators have come to realise that success in the nature based tourism business comes not from as ales approach of pushing products on to clients, but from a marketing approach of delivering products that satisfy the clients' needs, wants and desires. As a result, many operators have had to modify their products substantially over the years. One operator related to me, for example, that his clients were upper-middle-class residents, and as such they were not happy being provided with a barbecue every night. They would rough it but really appreciated some attempt to lift catering standards. A tag-along four-wheel drive operator (four wheel drive tours where the clients bring their own vehicles and 'tag-along' with the guide) expected his clients to be satisfied with simple guiding and support services, but soon realised that they also wanted meals and equipment. Many operators do not fully appreciate the core need that their product is satisfying. Indeed, it may have less to do with the eco-experience and may have more to do with the ease with which the experience can be consumed. The appeal of purchasing a commercial package lies not in the provision of access to an area that everyone can access, nor is it necessarily the quality of the interpretation, unless the product is targeted at hard ecotourists. Instead, the appeal is that the consumer is offered an one-stop shopping experience.

With one phone call, an extremely busy professional woman can overcome all the problems associated with negotiating departure dates, researching the trip route, booking all accommodation, food and services, obtaining the equipment needed, overcoming, safety and security concerns and in many cases, finding suitable travel partners. The opportunity/ cost savings provided by a relatively low-involvement purchasing decision enables clients to overcome real or perceived time barriers that would have otherwise blocked their participation. This is not to suggest for an instant that the tangible product is not important in the successful delivery of tourism products. In fact the opposite is true. If the tangible product is substandard or deficient in any way, clients will not be satisfied because their core needs are not being met. The tangible product becomes a reflection of the core product and, as such, should be developed to satisfy fully core needs. Further, tangible products have a quality or value adding level that makes the product as a whole more valuable than the sum of the individual component parts.

They have distinctive features that distinguish them from other similar products. They have some styling that usually reflects the personality of the owner/operator. Further, as a separate entity, they can be branded. Finally, tangible products have some level of packaging that can be used to make the product attractive.

Product-Market Nexus

Obviously, the former is preferred, but in far too many instances, the latter is what is delivered. It is true that all great businesses begin with great ideas. It is equally true that not all great ideas lead to viable business prospects.

Basic Tenets

- Any successful business delivers products that satisfy the needs, wants and desires of its clients.

— This objective can only be achieved if a business knows who its clients are and understands their motives.
— Successful businesses must be able to target their products at market segments that are large enough to be profitable, have growth potential, are interested in the products on offer, have unique characteristics that identify them as discrete segments, are easy to access in a cost-effective manner and are willing to pay the price being asked.
— The products must be seen as being preferred products by the target market.

The first law is predicated on a basic understanding of why products exist. The second tenet recognises the assumption of understanding the motives that drive the decision making process of the market. It is only through a deep understanding of what influences a market that anyone can deliver products to satisfy their needs. The third tenet identifies the features of attractive markets. They must be sufficiently large to support the business, yet at the same time share common characteristics that enable the operator to identify potential consumers, isolate them from the broader market place and reach them in a cost-effective manner. 'The 'fourth recognise that competition is intense. Successful products must somehow offer something to their target audience that makes them preferred over the noise in the marketplace. In essence, these rules argue that successful businesses in general, and successful small businesses in particular, must develop specialised products-targeted tightly at defined markets. Most operators are faced with a number of challenges. They have limited resources that must be allocated effectively and efficiently.

Further, they are forced to compete in a crowded marketplace where, in some cases, operators have literally dozens of potential competitors. Understanding the premise behind the product-market nexus, also allows the operator to understand the basic concept of strategic marketing management. Strategic marketing argues that no organisation, not even the largest global companies, can be all things to all consumers. In order to survive, businesses must make a number of strategic decisions about what they want to be, and who they want to target.

They must further differentiate their product offerings in a way that is meaningful to the consumer in order to gain a preferred place in the consumer's mind.

Strategic marketing is all about defining an organisation's product-market nexus by defining:

— the competitors it chooses to compete with
— the products it chooses not to offer
— the markets it chooses not to target
— the markets it chooses to target
— the competitors it chooses to avoid
— the products it chooses to offer.

The act of defining the products offered and the markets targeted dictates the types of business the operator will compete against. To succeed, one must know exactly what products it is offering at what markets and who its competitors are. It is only in this manner that one can develop business and marketing strategies to position the product as the preferred choice for its target markets. By the same token, it is equally important to know what the business does not do, which markets it does not target and which businesses it does not choose to compete with. This is especially true for small businesses with limited budgets that must allocatescant resources wisely. Too many tourism businesses try to do too many things. As a result, they lose their focus, and in doing so forget, what their core product is and who their core markets are. Moreover, the features of the product usually have to be compromised in order to broaden the appeal of the product to as wide'a market as possible. As a result, the quality and uniqueness of the product is diminished. A true recipe for failure is to assume that any business must compete against all other tourism businesses worldwide.

There are little chances of success or its likelihood in Ecotourism like all other small businesses. However, the failure rate and under-performance of many existing businesses can be reduced dramatically if prospective operators see their venture for what it is. It is a business whose success will depend on how well it is planned, financed, managed and marketed as a business. It is not a lifestyle, nor is it a means of getting paid to play. The future development and, indeed, the future existence of commercial ecotourism rely on the development of appropriate business skills. Hence there is need of perfect professionalism—in outlook, trends and action. And sustainability will sustain for long.

4

Wildlife Ecology

Ecology is a Greek word, which means the study of the habitation of living organism (vices-habitation or home and logos= discourse or study). Some define it as "Scientific natural history or the study of biotic communities". The most comprehensive and popular definition of the ecology is "the study of animals and plants in their relations to each other and to their environment". The environment includes both physical and abiotic and the living or biotic environment. The abiotic environment includes the medium of life and the climate. This medium and climatic condition regulate and considerably affects the behaviour and the activities of the organism. The biotic environment refers to the relationship existing among different organisms.

The physical environment or condition that surrounds a single species, a group of species or a large community is termed as—habitat. The available space on the earth containing' living organism is known as "biosphere". The physical portion of the biosphere consists of: i) Hydrosphere including the water component such as ocean, lake, river and on land, ii) Lithosphere, comprising the solid land mass and iii) Atmosphere-the gaseous mantle around the hydrosphere and lithosphere. The ultimate division of the biosphere is the microhabitat, which is the most intimately local and immediate, set of conditions surrounding a single individual. Thus the territory of a tiger and nest of are the microhabitats of a tiger and a bird. Other individuals or species are considered as part of the community but not part of its habitat.

All animals and plants are not isolated, they are in intimate relationship with each other as well as with the environment. Both of them are surrounded by a host of abiotic or non-living factors. These factors are measured in terms of chemical composition, texture, pressure, temperature, humidity etc. And in a community of plants or animals different members develop various sorts of inter-relationship concerning food, shelter and reproduction etc. Thus animals may have relations with other animals, plants with other plants, animals with plants and some plants are dependent upon animals. Wild animals also perform the pollination and dispersal mechanism for reproduction and distribution respectively in plants. Inter-dependence may exist between the same species or between species of widely different kinds and sizes as between mighty redwood trees and microscopic bacteria or between elephants and fleas. The interaction or inter-dependence or relationship among the individuals of the same species is known as intra-specific relationship and among the organisms of different species is termed as inter-specific relationship.

Environmental Factors

Obviously, environmental factors fall into two categories, viz. abiotic or physical and biotic or living.

1. Abiotic or Physical Factors: The physical environment, which affected the animal and plants of an ecosystem, includes medium and the climate. For a better understanding of the importance of wildlife in the ecosystem, it is a must that scientific knowledge of environmental factor is attained.

Medium: There are four types of media in which plants and animals live, i.e., Soil, Water, air and Bodies of other organism (only in case of parasites).

Soil contains a variety of elements, chemical compounds and minerals such as calcium, magnesium, sodium, silicon, iron, chloride, sulphate, oxygen, iodine, zinc, barium etc. and other organic, matters like bodies of plants and animals.

The health, size and vigor of any wild animal depend upon the presence and absence of minerals in the soil. Soil that have a proper balance of these minerals needed for adequate nutrition will support more wildlife than soils that are deficient in any minerals. Animals do not inhabit peaty soils because they are poorly aerated and are more acidic. Land snails are found on the soils that are rich in calcium salts as it is required for their shell. In the Chaparral region of California the soils are shallow, water holding capacity is less and the fertility is low. When deer from this region have access to, food grown on more fertile alluvial soils, they grow to larger size, have larger anhans and mature fast. Deer placed in pens and fed on an optimum diet can reach a larger size the very first year than some of the adults in the wild can attain ill the whole of lifetime. Soil may be three kinds viz. neutral, acidic or alkaline, depending upon the pH value. The soils, which are slightly acidic or neutral, are generally considered to be well suited for most of the plant and animal life.

There is a direct relationship between the status and kind of wildlife and the soil condition of an area. On good soils the vegetation is luxuriant, protein and carbohydrate components are more. It results in the increase in size and population of the herbivorous animals and consequent upon this the carnivorous animals find themselves concentrated in that particular area, and ultimately a viable and dynamic forest ecosystem is established. The soil and its nutritive potential also affect the behaviour and characteristic of the wild animals. If the" growth of a particular kind of vegetation is increased it will help survive the herbivorous animals like deer, sambhar etc. and ultimately the tiger and leopard.

Light: Another important factor, which influences the growth, distribution and behavioural characteristic of the plants and animals, is the light. With the help of sunlight the plants manufacture the food material for the ecosystem, through the complex mechanism of photosynthesis in which the solar energy is transformed into chemical energy and stored in the form of carbohydrate. The intensity of the light falling on the earth depends upon the angle of incidence and the absorption of the light rays by the different layers of the atmosphere. The presence of clouds, moisture and dust in the atmosphere also affects the intensity of tight. In the forests, the intensity of light is reduced to the presence of forest vegetation. The total amount of light received by an organism is determined by the intensity and duration of light. The duration of light for which an organism is exposed to light is called photoperiodism. The effect of light on the living plants and animals is composite of various factors, which are generated due to the presence, absence or intensity of the light.

Temperature

Temperature controls the distribution and behaviour characteristics of the living organism and it is one of the important environmental factors. It also acts as a limiting factor and influence and controls reproduction, pace of embryonic development, migration of birds and animals and other metabolic processes of the body. The range of temperature varies greatly in different environments such as freshwater bodies, marine and terrestrial. In the marine water the temperature never falls below -2.5°C and in open water lakes and ponds it never falls below 0°C. The maximum temperature in marine water has been recorded at 36°C in Persian Gulf. On land lowest temperature of -70°C has been recorded in Siberia in U.S.S.R. and highest of 60°C in desert areas. In hot springs the temperature may rise up to 100°C. During daytime the temperature on land surface is 17°C higher than at night and in desert areas the difference is as much as 40°C. The difference in temperatures between day and night in water bodies like lakes and ponds is generally less than 1°C whereas in marine environment it may be around 4°C.

The temperature changes in the lakes and marine water

are much less and much slower than in the terrestrial environment. Even if there is a high or low change in the temperature the animals can easily avoid it by a short journey into the deeper water. The seasonal changes or thermal stratification in temperature can be best studied in large deep Jakes of the temperate region. The maximum density of the fresh water is 4°C and therefore any warmer or colder water will not as top of water of the temperature. During winter, the temperature falls and the water surface freezes into ice and it prevent the cooling of water below it. This ice is melt during the onset of spring and the temperature again rises to 4°C and the whole water body requires the same temperature. During summer the temperature, of upper surface of water may go up to 20 to 25°C but the below it, it remains only up to 4 or 5°C. The upper warm water is called as Epilimnion and the bottom as Hypolimnion whereas the intermediate zone where the temperature may vary from 9 to 20°C is called as Thermocline, This is the zone of rapid vertical temperature change with the thermal gradient of 1 °C per -meter.

Water: Water constitutes about 85% or the body parts of any animal and is a very vital requirement of the life. Water is essential for all kinds of metabolic and chemical reactions that are going on in the body of any plant or animal. It acts as major controlling factor of the organism. Animals of aquatic and terrestrial mediums have adopted themselves separately to that mode of environment; aquatic animals are commonly adopted to live within a specific range of salt concentration. The limitation of these adaptive characteristics generally restricts the animals either to fresh or salt water. These animals, which can tolerate narrow fluctuation in the salt concentration, are known as Sterohyline. But the animals, which can tolerate a wide range of salt concentration, are known as Euryhaline. All animals require water and terrestrial animals are no exception. These animals have evolved various ways of conserving water and getting adapted a particular mode of life. Lower animals such as earthworms who are soft skinned and moist are found in the vicinity of pond or river. These animals drink water for maintaining the balance. The internal physiology or the urinary system is so modified that a proper concentration is maintained between the body and outside environment. The structure of glomerulus in the kidney is so modified as to excrete more water (as in case of fresh water fishes) or reduce water loss (as in most terrestrial vertebrates). In Elasmobranch fishes the urea concentration in blood is so maintained that a proper balance is ensured. The birds need more water to fly in the air and they excrete solid urea. Similarly most of the desert animals also dispose off their urine in the form of solid state. Animals like kangaroo, rat, jack, rabbit and mountain goat satisfy their water requirements from their food. Predatory animals like lion, tiger and other carnivorous derive water from the blood of their prey. Animals differ widely from each other in their requirement of water. The kangaroo, rats can live on dry seeds in desert areas and will not drink water. It has evolved to suit this environment through changes in kidney function that cut down on water loss from excretion, by an ability to obtain water through the metabolism of starch; and by adapting nocturnal habit and by avoiding the desiccating heat of the day in underground burrows. Many other desert species have developed adaptation that permits survival without free water through an evolved ability to obtain water from their food.

Among large animals the addax antelopes of the Sahara do not drink. When a species requires drinking water its home area must include a permanent water supply or it must develop a pattern of migrating to water during the dry months. Animals occupying areas in which water sources are some distance away may develop a pattern of movement that result in their occupying larger tracts of grounds than animals of the same species occupying areas which are plenty in water. Areas too far from water will not be utilised even if food and other factors are in abundance. This also depend upon the frequency of water taking as species of the animal that need to drink only once in several days can use areas further from water than those that drink, water daily. Birds can use far from water supplies. The distribution of water points in area also determine carrying capacity of all area. If there is only one water source no matter how big is it will support only a limited number of animals.

The actual limitation will often be imposed by the food supply within the area near water. By providing more water points, we can increase the carrying capacity of any area, provided that adequate food sources are available. But it is disputable to say that increasing the water point will help in better management of wildlife. Too much water points will attracts large numbers of animals around that point and due to this there is risk of habitat destruction and in the long run the population increase will again affect the carrying capacity. In America water development has become a technique frequently used in wildlife management. Here using the devices such as the "gallinaceous guzzler" which are developed Fish and Game Department of California University has increased wildlife. This guzzler collect the water during the rainy season, as a concrete or plastic apron and holds it in underground storage, there the birds and quail reach during the dry seasons. For mammals, deer and other animals big game guzzlers are used. It has already been stated that most of the aquatic or semi aquatic animals are concentrated to the watery areas Id their number is linked with the distribution of ponds, lakes, rivers, tributaries and marshy places.

The habitat of lese animals have been affected due to human interference, pollution and siltation resulting from overgrazing, deforestation and other agricultural devices. Due to this many good species of fishes in different parts of the world are facing extinction and every year a heavy casualties occur in different lakes. Relative humidity determine the occurrence of a particular kind of vegetation and also the distribution and presence of animals. Relative humidity is the percentage of the amount of Water vapour that all could hold at saturation at the existing temperature.

Juspis Liebig in 1840, a chemist, while studying the relationship between plants and available amount of nutrition, devised the concept of the "law of minimum". According to him "the growth of the plant is dependent on the amount of food stuff which is present to it in minimum quantity". This concept also holds true regarding the growth of animals. If an environmental factor exceeds the maximum tolerable level or it comes down the minimum tolerance in any given area it becomes a limiting factor presenting the distribution of the particular organism or group of organisms in that area. If all other requirements are present in adequate amounts but Water is scarce, water will be the limiting factor for wildlife.

Several environmental factors like temperature, atmospheric gases, and humidity digest as well as other abiotic and biotic factors are able to act as limiting factors with respect to that organism. F.F. Blackman incorporated the law of minimum with the law of limiting factors. The level of the factor that is operating at a limiting intensity governs Blackman while studying the factors affecting the rate of photosynthesis discovered that rate of photosynthesis. The amount of a substance below or above certain limits may also limits the abundance or distribution of a species. Small increase in its concentration increases the rate of plant growth. But if the concentration of carbon dioxide is increased significantly it becomes toxic. Shelford introduced this idea that a factor could have a limiting effect at its maximum and minimum value in 1913. The postulation was described as "Law of Tolerance". According to Shelford all environmental factors have a tolerable limit, the critical minimum and critical maximum. The range between the critical minimum and critical maximum is known as limits of tolerance. If, for a particular species the telerance elceeds its limit, the species will disappear from that particular area, as long as such condition exists. But, before this range is crossed on either side and the limits of tolerance are reached there is a zone of physiological stress.

Mostly it is difficult to identify a single limiting factor because an entire complex of conditions are involved. In one area a lack of escape cover may prevent population from maintaining themselves above a certain limit. If in this area predators are removed and hunting is stopped, the cover would no longer be limiting. If more food and water are available within the existing cover, higher population could also be supported. Anyone of these factors could be called limiting and if factor improved, population might increase. However, further analysis of the situation might reveals that soil nutrients were limited the growth of food or cover Plants. Thus it is complex problem and it is not easy to single out any one of the factor as limiting factor; while searching limiting factor for wildlife management we have to follow the concept of whole ecosystem and all the intricacies functional aspect of it should be involved, single species and simplified approach to wildlife will not produce desirable results.

The presence and absence of an organism or a group of organisms in an ecosystem depends upon a complex of factors. Any factor, which approaches or exceeds the limits of tolerance is said to be limiting. According to Odium- (1959), the organism in nature are controlled by (1) the quantity and variability of materials for which there is a minimum requirement and the physical factors which are critical and (2) the limits of tolerance of the organism to these and other components of the environment. Suppose if one organism has a wide range of tolerance for a particular factor and if the factor is relatively constant than that does not act as a limiting factor but if an animal or plant has a limited tolerance for a particular factor than that acts as a limiting factor.

Animal Distribution

Animals are found everywhere in the world. But the species of the animals on land as well as water are confined to a particular range and that range is the area of distribution of the species. The horizontal distribution of animals on land

and water in different continents and in islands is known as geographical distribution. The study of geographical distribution of animals is known as zoogeography and these realms are called as Zoogeographical realms.

(1) Continuous Distribution

Those animals, which are found in the every part of the world, are said to be cosmopolitan or continuous in distribution. These animals are able to adjust themselves to a wide range of climatic variability and are successfully adapted to different types of habitat. Animals like rats, bats, cuckoos, hawks are worldwide and represent the extreme of continuous distribution, and less extensive in the range though still continuous is the crow family. These animals are very active and agile and can migrate over long distances and overcome natural barriers. Cosmopolitan animals found uniformly distributed are referred to as eurytopic while those, which are restricted, are called as stenotopic. The former One can cope with all kinds of environments and exhibits generalised adaptive characteristics whereas the later stenotopic have developed specialised adaptive features for a particular environment.

(2) Bipolar Distribution

In the polar regions number of species are found to inhabit only the arctic and Antarctic waters with no representation in the intermediate oceans, and such interesting partner of distribution is known as Bipolar distribution. It is mostly exhibited by invertebrates and lower vertebrates like Shark fishes.

The factors, which guide distribution of animals in diverce habitats in different areas and localities and control the movement, migration and dispersal of these animals are, known as Barriers. Animal exhibits complicated pattern of distribution due to barriers. For example Britain and Japan are separated thousands of miles have almost identical fauna, whereas Lambok and Bali are very close to each other but have totally different faunal life. Barriers, which prevent the normal distribution of the animals, can be divided into three categories viz. physical barriers, climatic barriers and biological barriers.

(3) Discontinuous Distribution

When the animals of die same species or closely related species are found to be present in particular localised area widely separated and with or without any continuity. These animals are said to have discontinuous distribution. Among invertebrates Peripatus is the interesting connecting link between arthropoda and annelida and found present in tropical America, tropical Africa, New Zealand, and East India and Indo-Malaya region. There are numerous examples of discontinuous distribution among the vertebrates: The lungfishes of the Clars Dipris are the classic example of discontinuous distribution. Its genera Protopterus are found in Africa, Lepidosiren in marshes of South America and Neoceratodus in the rivers of Australia. Among birds, the flightless birds Ratifoe exhibits discontinuous distribution. The groups consists of five genera each of which is confined to an isolated island having no interconnection. The Kiwis are restricted to the damp forests of New Zealand, Emus in the grassy plains and open forests of Australian region, Rheas are confined to plains of Argentina and South Brazil, whereas Ostriches are restricted in burning deserts of Africa and Arabia. Most notable discontinuous distribution is exemplified by the marsupial mammals, which are exclusively confined to South America and North America, kangaroo in Australia and New Zealand. Among marsupial opossum is the sole exemption.

Causes of Discontinuous Distribution: Discontinuous distribution can be explained on the basis of the fact that the animal forms, which present a discontinuous distribution at present, might have been uniformly, evenly, and continuously distributed within a wide range previously. The present status may be the results of changes in the earth crust, or in the environmental condition or by the invasion of the animals of different varieties Due to all these activities barriers were created which prevented the intermingling and migration of some species or the some group of animals. Gradually some of the groups perished and the population got divided into isolated groups.

The topographical features like high mountain ranges the barriers for terrestrial animals. Their effectiveness increase if the range run parallel to the equator, as Himalayan range in India and Alps in Europe. On the north side of the Himalaya are the snow covered mountain peaks while southern side are the hot plains of India. The fauna in these two zones are quite different. The fauna, which are north of Himalaya, are similar with that of Europe, and contain Gibbons while the fauna to south of Himalayas are similar to Africa and contain tiger and elephant. The difference is explained on the basis of Himalayan barriers. When the mountain range run north to south, the influence on animal is less, such as North and South America, where the mountain run at right angle to equator (_north to south). The Sahara and great other deserts also act as barriers for terrestrial flora and fauna. Due to the presence of Sahara desert between the North and South Africa the plants and animals life is totally different from each other.

The big rivers, giant streams of and oceans act as most important barriers in the distribution of terrestrial animals. The big rivers like Brahmaputra and Ganga with their many tributaries hinder the distribution of wild animals in India. The land mass act barriers for the aquatic form of life and likewise _he great bodies of water act as a barrier for the land animals. Further the salt concentration in the water and land also act as obstacle in migration and dispersal. Small areas of salt water act as absolute barriers for fishes and amphibians. For example, at the Pacific Coast many freshwater streams flow parallel to each other and end in the sea, but each stream has its species or subspecies of fishes. Similarly snake, though good swimmer, fail to cross-large bodies of salt water with the exception of sea snake.

The extremes of temperature, light and moisture act as barrier for the animals together with other abiotic ecological factors. The extremes of temperature act as limiting factor for the distribution of animals, particularly cold-blooded animals. In warm-blooded animals like tiger, lion, elephant, antelope, deer etc. the effect is not significant but it has its slight effect. Tigers are generally found in abundance in the warmer parts of the country but are also seen in cold hilly tracts of Himalaya. Generally the vegetation is different in different temperature zones and it controls the distribution of animals that feed on a particular kind of diet. For example, red tree mouse, Phenacomys *longicandus* lives on a diet of fir needles and rests in fir trees, which are found only in cold temperate zones, and therefore the mouse is restricted to that particular area only.

The excess as well as lack of humidity acts as a barrier for the dispersal of animals. In the excessive moisture prone areas, where due to moisture heavy and thick forests are, developed only a particular kind of animals are found. Similarly in desert areas only those types of animals can survive' which are adapted for the drier climatic conditions through water retaining devices such as tough and thick hide, thorns, water bags and hygroscopic skin etc.

The biological barriers are created due to the liking of some animals for special kind of food and shelter. If the particular food is not present in any area, the area will be a barrier for that species. Further presence and absence of predators and other enemies and competitor may also act as a barrier. The sedentary habitat of some animals makes them confined to a particular area.

Zoogeographical Distribution of Animals

The first attempt to depict the biological communities of animals on the map and describe their distribution was made by P.L. Sclater in 1858. A.R. Wallace further developed this attempt. Wallace recognised that animal distribution was characterised by marked differences between regions whose boundaries were sometime well defined but more often blended gradually between adjoining regions. Thus the fauna of North America and Northern Eurasia were more similar than Northern and Southern Asia. Wallace opined that there must have been a center of origin for all the species and similarities in between the two regions are the results of inter change of the species through land bridges or waterways. Gradually the bridges perished and tae landmasses got separated. Major differences between regions are due to the long period of isolation. For example Australia, represent the most distinctive and unique fauna in the world and it is because it was cut off from the rest of the world by ocean barriers over millions of years. The native mammals of Australia are mostly marsupials such as kangaroos, possiums. Echidna and Platypus. The oriental and African regions have many similarities and both have lion, leopards, elephants and rhinos but each group is represented by different kind of species, which is because they were separated long ago. Udvardy in 1975 had modified the faunal region of the Wallace by taking into account both the plants and animals life.

(1) Palaearctic Region

The entire Europe, China, Japan, Africa, North Sahara, Siberia, Mediterranean, Manchuria, Asia north of Himalaya and north of Arabia fall within the limits of this area. The region is surrounded by sea from three sides, viz. West, North and East, on the southern side by Sahara and. Himalayas. It has got a continuous connecting link with its two neighboring region of Ethiopia and Oriental.

The climate is chiefly temperate with arctic tinge in it. It includes wet forests lands and dry open steppe land, large area of coniferous forest and some tundra. Thus great degree of climatic variability is exhibited and this is also exhibited by the variation in the fauna. The fauna is dominant and rich in warmer areas and diminishes northward and ultimately in arctic area, only some fresh water fishes or Rana sp. (frog) is found. The fauna of palaearctic region exhibits similarity with Nearctic fauna and a number of genera and families are common to both regions. It supports that there might existed some land bridge in between the two region during earlier times. Palaearctic region possess 33 families of mammals, 68 of birds, 24 of reptiles and 10 of amphibians and 13 families of fresh water fishes.

Fishes: The freshwater fishes include many species of cyprinids, a few localised catfishes, cobitridis, choundis etc.

Amphibians: It is varied and rich and includes Rana, Toad, Hyla, Necturus, Proteus, and Siren etc. The Giant salamanders are found both in Palaearctic as well as Nearctic regions.

Reptiles: The region is poor in reptilian stock and there are a few lizards, tortoises and a few species of snakes. True vipers and Asian pit vipers and colubirds are the only snakes found in Palaearctic region: In northern portion however, Trionyx and Tertudo, *Alligator* of China, noranus, Chamdan and sand Boas etc. are found.

Birds: The region represents about 53 families of birds and about 17 families are widely distributed and are also met in other regions of the world. The bird species found include Hawks, Herons, Storks, Ducks, Loons, Rails, Grebes, Wrenks, Cuckoos, King fishers. Woodpeckers, Shallows, Crows, Finches, Warblets, Old world flycatcher. Hedge sparrows are exclusively confined to this region, whereas Parrots are absent.

Mammals: Out of the 33 families of the mammals found, only two are endemic. The important mammalian fauna include

Moles, Shrews, Pandas Pigs, Rabbit, Squirrel, Deer, number of Dog and Cat families.

Palaearctic region has further been subdivided into:

— European sub region
— Mediterranean sub region
— Siberian sub region—the families of yak and musk deer and moles are exclusively confined to this sub region and
— Manchurian sub-division—the great panda, Tibetan langurs, Chinese water-deer are confined in this region only.

(2) Nearctic Region

The geographical limits of Nearctic region comprises of North America above tropics. New Found land and Mexican plateau and Greenland. It is connected by a very narrow strip with Central America and from all other sides is surrounded by the sea. The climatic conditions are varied and extreme and similar to palaearctic region. It has extensive mountain ranges in he west running north to south. There are coniferous belt, deciduous forests in the eastern part of North America and grasslands in the central part and also the arid zone in the southwest part of North America..

Fauna: Fauna of this region are transitional and represent the mixture of Palaeaictic and Neotropical region. There are about 26 families of mammals, 49 of birds, 21 of reptiles, 14 of amphibian and 24 of fishes.

Fishes: 13 genera of Cyprinidae, Catfishes, sturgeon etc.

Amphibians: Tailed amphibian such as Axolotal, Ambystoma and Siren are notable. Among toilers are Rana, Bufo and Hyla.

Reptiles: Quite varied and found in abundance having a mixture of tropical American groups and Palaearctic.

The common reptiles are musk turtle, crocodiles and alligators. Lizards include Geekas, Ophisaurus. Heloderma is found only in southwest Central America. Snake includes the pit vipers, cesal snakes and rattle snake. Snapping turtle Heloderma and musk turtle are endemic to this region.

Mammals: Most commonly found mammals are rabbits, shrews moles, squirrel, beavers, cats, bats, bears, deer, flying squirrels, tree porcupine, star nosed moles. Canadian porcupines, long legged bats and America badger are the exclusive form of mammals founding Nearctic region.

Avifauna: There are 49 families of birds, of which 32 are widely distributed fed and present mixture of Netropical and Palaearctic regions. The common birds are Pelican, grebes, vultures rails, cranes, cuckoos, gull, pigeons, owl, heron, hawks kingfisher, humming birds, wood peckers, wax-wings flycatchers.

(3) Neotropical Region

The geographical limits of this region are South America, Central America, tropical low land of South Mexico and West Indies. The general Climatic southern part of South America show temperate zone. Due to the tropical climate, extensive evergreen forests are found in Amazon Valley. In Argentina and Savanna tracts drier patches are found. In the western South America sub desert conditions are met.

Fauna: Out of the 155 families of terrestrial, vertebrates about 39 are absolutely endemic. The region is both distinctive and varied in fauna.

Fishes: Complete absence of Cyprinidae. Catfishes, gymnoitids and electric cells dominate the area. One genus of long fishes showing discontinuous distribution is present (Lepidosiren).

Amphibians: The most common of the tail-less are hyla, rana, bufo and pipa. There are 14 families of amphibia.

Reptiles: Variety of reptilian fauna is present and includes crocodiles, alligators, turtles and tortoises. There are 15 families of lizards and Helodermidae, Anadiadae, Chircocolidae', Cercosauridae and Iphisiadae are peculiar. But the families Varanidae and Agamidae are absent.

Mammals: The opossunus marsupials are present, sloths, armidallos, new world monkeys, rabbits, deers, squirrels and new world porcupines and II families of rodents are commonly found. The-re are about 32 families of mammals. Moles, hyenas and hedgehogs are absent.

Birds: South America is called as "Bird Continent" on account of the diverse presence of birds. There are about 67 families of the birds here of which about 23 families are restricted and two others are confined to this region only. American Ostrich (Rhea) and Tantalus are endemic to this region. The common birds are storkes, barets, kingfishers, herons, woodpeckers, ducks, pigeons and plovers.

(4) Ethiopian Region

It includes Africa, South of Sahara, Madagascar and South Arabia. All other sides are surrounded by sea except the land link with northern Palaearctic region. The climatic conditions of Ethiopian region are tropical and due to this there IS lush growth of evergreen tropical rain forests.

Fauna: Ethiopian region is very rich and colourful in its fauna. The birds and mammals present show great degree of affinity with the oriental region, while the fish, amphibian, reptiles resemble with new tropical and oriental region. There are about 161 families of terrestrial vertebrates in this region.

Fishes: Carps, catfishes, cyprinodants and cichlids, protopterus of lungfishes, archaic bichris and a few catfishes are exclusive of this zone.

Reptiles: It includes crocodiles, turtles, Lacertid and Agamid lizards. Chandeon is almost exclusive. Pythons, Colubrids,

Typhlops, Viperids and Leptotyphons represent snakes of the area.

Amphibians: The families Bufonids, Ranids, Rhaephonids and Caecillans represent only tail-less amphibia. Rana and Bufo are absent. Tailed amphibians are also absent.

Birds: The most exclusive birds of the region are ostriches. Helmet birds, hammer headed birds, pitta, mouse birds. The common birds are herons, hornbills, cuckoos, weavers, storks, goatsuckers, parrots, larks, pigeons, bee-eaters, finches, bustards etc. There are 67 families of the birds found in this region and out of which 53 are worldwide.

Mammals: There are about 38 families of mammals here out of which about 10 families are exclusive and the rest are shared with Palaearctic or oriental regions. Most widely distributed mammals are bats, shrews, rabbits, squirrels, dogs and cats. The oriental mammals present here are quite different from the oriental one and include limurs, loris, apes, elephants, rhinoceros etc. The exclusive families include hippopotamus giraffes and rodents. In addition, species of zebras and other large number of antelopes are unique to this region. The species of bear, deer, goats and sheep are entirely absent which are found in abundance in other regions.

(5) Oriental Region

This region comprised of the entire Indian sub-continent, Indo-China, Philippines and South China.

The region abounds varied climatic conditions. The region is represented by tropical rain forests in Burma, Indo-China and northeast Asia and southern parts of India, temperate climate in northern part of India.

Amphibians: Mostly tail-less amphibians such as bufo, rana, hyrids and Rhaeophosids are numerous. Salamanders and Caecilidus are also found.

Fauna: The fauna of oriental region exhibits considerable affinity with the Ethiopian region and the resemblance is so great that some zoogeographers have prefer to put both these regions into one region under the name Palaeotropical region. The families of the region are widely distributed.

Reptiles: All the important genera of snakes-python, vipers and pit vipers, colubrids, typhlops and leptotyphops are widely present. Among lizard chanebons, varanus, Agamids are present. *Crocodililus* polusfris and *Gavialis gangeticus* are found in India. Trionychids Testudinius and Bumydine turtles represent turtles.

Fishes: Dominated by carps and catfishes. Other fish families seen are Cobitidae, Osteoglossid, Notopteridae, Cypriniformis, Anabantidae.

Mammals: Mammals include four exclusive families of Hylobatiodae (gibbons), Tarsidae (tarsiers). Galeopithecidae (flying lemurs) and Tupaiidae (tree shrew). There are 30 mammalian families. The most common mammals are shrews, rabbits, squirrel; dogs, mustelids, cats, bovid, civets, hyenas, pigs and porcupine, apes, pangolin, elephant, rhinoceros, old world monkeys" moles, bears and deer are found widely distributed, though interestingly enough these animals are absent in Ethiopian region.

Avifauna: Pigeons and pheasants are very numerous. There are 66 families out of which 52 are widely distributed. Eurylaemidae (Peacock) is the only one exclusive bird family. Other birds found are peacock, the national bird of India, wood pickers, hornbills, parrots, honey guids, sunbirds and finches.

(1) The Himalayan Mountain System

The fauna of Himalayan region resemble of both the oriental and palaearctic regions and animals such as tiger, leopard, bear, wild pigs and snow leopard are found on both sides of Himalaya in the palaearctic and oriental regions. It is presumed that these animals might have migrated to India in the distant past when the Himalayan barrier was not formed. It may be mentioned here that the geological structure of Himalaya are of recent origin. The distribution of fauna is affected by the influence of altitudinal change and amount of rainfall. The Himalaya of eastern region receives heavy rainfall and practically no snowfall except in very high altitude, this has resulted in profuse growth of tropical flora and the fauna are also different, having similarities with the Chinese fauna of palaearctic. In the western Himalaya rainfall is less and climate is temperate with heavy snowfall. Therefore, the fauna of Himalayan system can be understood, by further dividing it into following sub region.

(i) The Himalayan Foot Hills: The Himalayan foothills consist of Tarai, Bhabar and Siwalik ranges of the geological formation. In the Bhabar area the tract consists of the boulders and due to this the water, table is very low but in Tarai region the geological structure consists of thick deposit of silt, where the water table is very high. This Tarai region characterised *by* the grassy meadows and savannah vegetation. Here Sal is the dominant species. This area is the richest in mammalian wildlife," elephants tigers, cheetal, nilgai, sambhar, barking deer, hog deer, wild boar, wild dog, jackal, hyaena, sloth bear etc. all are represented in this region along with the rhinoceros and bison in the Assam foot hills. The Gangetic gharial found elsewhere in the oriental region is also found in the tributaries of Ganga. The hispid hare, golden langur, discovered recently by E P. Gee in Assam are also found in this part.

(ii) Western Himalayan High Altitude Region: It consists of the higher altitudinal zone commencing (from 1500 m to 3000 m having coniferous forests at the lower level and alpine forests and alpine scrub at the higher level. It extends up to the cold desert area of Ladakh. The climate is temperate and rainfall low, with heavy snowfall. There are many species of

the goats here and they include the their, markhor and the ibex species. Among sheep there are the shapu, bharal and Dayan. These species are distributed throughout the higher altitudinal ranges of the Himalayas from Nepal to Sikkim and Kashmir. The other wildlife include the wild ass and yak in Ladakh and the hangul or Kashmir stag and the musk deer. The Kashmir stag is found only in Dachigam sanctuary area of J & K. Then there are marmots found above the tree line. Among the carnivores, the most beautiful is the snow leopard, found hunting in the night. The others are wolf, fox and other smaller cats, brown bear, black bear. Among birds peasants are more common with their beautiful plumage.

These are the Himalayan monal pheasant. The western tragopan. the satyr tragopan, cheers Pheasants and koklars. All the animal life found in this part of the Himalaya are adapted for the intense cold and harsh condition of the climate. The most interesting feature of these animals is the adaptation for climbing the rocks.

(iii) Eastern Himalayan Sub-Region: The forests of this region are dense semi-evergreen to evergreen. The wildlife present here includes the ghoral and serow of the antelopes, the red panda, hog badgers, ferret badgers and crestler porcupine.

(2) *The Peninsular Indian Sub-Region*

Most of the Indian wild animals are found in this part and it comprises of the Deccan plateau extending up to Indo-Gangetic plains in the north and great Thar Desert Rajasthan in the west. The wildlife of this area is somewhat akin In the Ethiopian region of North Africa and both share lion, leopard, hyena and many species of antelope.

The wildlife inhabiting these forests includes the elephants, sambhar, nilgai, barking deer, cheetal, hog deer, barasingha, black buck, chinkara and wild bear. The cheetal are not found in the tropical rain forests of eastern and northeastern India. The presence of ample number of herbivorous animals supports a good variety of carnivorous and predatory animals. The main predatory animals are the tiger, leopard and the wild dog. The other big cats include the cheetah and the lion. These animals had their origin in Ethiopian region and had migrated to India. The magnificent cheetah, the fastest land animal, which can run at a speed of 100 km/hour, is now extinct from the limits of our country and the Asiatic lion is reduced in the Gir forests of Gujarat. The Govt. of India has launched a specific project Gir sanctuary project. This graceful animal once abundant in the forests of India, now number only in Gir sanctuary, as per the census conducted in 1979. The other wildlife includes the jackal

The Indian Deserts

The Thar Desert of Rajasthan is the main desert of India and is linked with the deserts of Arabia through the land tracts of Sindh and Baluchistan. The plant and animal life faces the problem of water and its conservation and have been variously adapted to life under such condition. The wildlife include the burrowing mammals and rodents are in large number. Other includes the Asiatic wild ass in the Rann of Kutch, Black buck in semi-desert areas, red fox, caracal and desert cat. Among the reptiles a number of species of snakes, lizard and turtles are present. Among the birds is the famous and beautiful great Indian bustard.

(3) The Tropical Rain Forests

The areas in entire northeastern belt and the areas of Western Ghats and Malabar Coast in the South India are zones where due to heavy rain the tropical vegetation had developed. The Nilgiri's densely forested evergreen vegetation known as sholas, provide shelter to a variety of animals such as elephants, bison etc. The higher- altitude comprises of Nilgiri tahr, European otter and the pine marten. The dense rain forests of north-east and western ghats, where the vegetation supports a variety of wildlife, most of the herbivorous animals are tree dwellers except the bigger animals like elephants and deer. The tree dwellers include the rare species of hoolock, gibbon, the only ape found in India, golden langur, Assam macaque, leaf monkey and pig tailed macaque and slow loris in Assam and binturang a rare species is also found in northeast rain forests together with red panda, which also a rare species. In the southern rain forests, lion tailed macaque, Nilgiri langur and slender loris. The rain forests of India are so rich in its flora and fauna that these are considered as the richest gene pool available to us.

(4) Wildlife of Andman and Nicobar Islands

Andaman and Nicobar islands have a peculiar position in the forest map of India and have the flora and fauna, which are typical representative of the islands. There are 348 islands of various sizes covering an area of 8,136 sq. km. The forest of these islands is very dense and consists of giant trees of Dipterocarpus and Terminalia spp. The climate of the region is tropical and the islands receive both the southwest and northeast monsoons-thus the zone of heavy rainfall having an annual precipitation of 2550 to 4000 mm. The wildlife of Andaman is similar with the wildlife of Burma whereas the Nicobar fauna are similar to Malaysia. The main feature is preponderance of bats and rats, while ungulates, squirrels carnivores are completely absent. The other mammals found are the Andaman pig, the palm civet, crab-eating macaque, and introduced deer species of cheetal, barking deer, sambhar and hog deer. Among the aquatic marine mammals are the false killer whale, dolphin and dugong. Among reptiles salt-water crocodile a rare and threatened species is found. There are many species of marine turtle here of which the green turtle is very common. There are about 240 species of birds found here, such as fruit pejin, white bellied sea eagle including some endemic rare species like narcondum hornbili, Nicobar pigeon and the megapods. Among the many lizard the water monitor is very common. Almost all the Indian poison snakes like cobra, viper, ceral and sea snake are found along with the python.

(5) *Indian Sub Region*

The Indian sub region includes the whole of India, Pakistan, Nepal, Bhutan. Andaman and Nicobar Islands and Laccadive and Maldives Islands. Due to intense climatic variability Indian sub region has further been grouped into the ecological sub divisions. The other sub regions are Ceylonese, Indo-Chinese and Indo-Malayan.

(6) *Australian Region*

The Australian region comprised of Australia, New Zealand, Tasmania, New Guinea and other islands. The region is completely isolated and has no link with any other region of the world. In Australian region both tropical and temperate climatic conditions are found.

Fauna: The Australian region has unique faunal significance. The region is very poor in animal population and the most interesting thing is the absence of higher mammals. Marsupials and monotrems are found only in this part of the world.

Fishes: Osteoglossids and Neoceratodus.

Amphibian: Hyla and Rana, Tailed amphibian are absent.

Birds: About 58 families of the birds are found in Australian region of these about 44 are widely distributed.. Of these 12 families are exclusive of the region. The common birds are trogan, icing fishers, hawks, pigeons, cuckoos, and parrots. The families of parrots, cuckoos, loris and pigmy parrots, wood-swallows, Dower-peckers and megapodes are shared with oriental region.

Reptiles: Among snakes python and biting tiger snakes are in abundance. (Zither reptiles include crocodiles, turtle, geekos, varanus, typhops and colubrids.

5

Development and Sustainable Tourism Planning

The Manila Declaration (1980) of the World Tourism Organisation (WTO), the most comprehensive international statement adopted on the goals of modern tourism, emphasises the importance of both natural and cultural resources in tourism and the need for conservation of these resources for the benefit of both tourism and local residents of the tourism destinations. Following on from the Manila Declaration, the Joint Declaration of the WTO and United Nations Environment Programme (UNEP), which formalised inter-agency coordination on tourism and the environment, states:

> "The protection, enhancement and improvement of the various components of man's environment are among the fundamental conditions for the harmonious development of tourism. Similarly, rational management of tourism may contribute to a large extent to protecting and developing the physical environment and the cultural heritage, as well as improving the quality of life.."

Appropriate relationships between tourism and the natural and socio-cultural environments, which places responsibilities on both the tourist-receiving countries and the tourists themselves, were further specified by the WTO in 1985 during its Sixth General Assembly through its adoption of the Tourism Bill of Rights and Tourist Code. This statement contained the following provisions:

— In the interest of present and future generations, (States should) protect the tourist environment which, being at once human, natural, social and cultural, is the legacy of all mankind....

— The populations constituting host communities in places of transit and stay are entitled to free access to their own tourism resources...

— They are also entitled to expect from tourists, understanding of the respect for their customs, religions and other elements of their cultures which are part of human heritage.

— To facilitate such understanding and respect, the dissemination of appropriate information should be encouraged on:

(a) the customs of host communities, their traditional and religious practices, local taboos and sacred sites and shrines, which must be respected;

(b) their artistic, archaeological and cultural treasures, which must be preserved; and

(c) wildlife and other natural resources, which must be protected.

— Tourists should, by their behaviour, foster understanding and friendly relations among peoples, at both the national and international levels, and thus contribute to lasting peace.

— At places of transit and stay, tourists must respect the established political, social, moral and religious order and comply with legislation and regulations in force. In these places, tourists must also:

(a) show the greatest understanding for the customs, beliefs and behaviour of the host communities and the greatest respect for their natural and cultural heritage...; and

(b) refrain from exploiting others.....

Before the adoption of the Tourism Bill of Rights and Tourist Code by the WTO, WTO and the UNEP had held an earlier joint workshop in 1983 on the Environmental Aspects of Tourism. Among other conclusions reached by the Workshop participants, several statements touched on the social-cultural problems introduced by mass tourism:

— When tourists enter the host country, they do not just bring their purchasing power..... they also, and above all, bring a different type of society which profoundly transforms local social habits by removing and upsetting the basic and long-established values and patterns of behaviour of the host population.

— Tourism is indeed, therefore, a 'total social event' which leads to structural changes in all sectors of society and which becomes generalised by progressively being extended to all regions of the globe.

— During the tourist season, the resident population not only has to accept the effects of overcrowding, which do not exist for the remainder of the year, but they must often completely modify their way of life (increased work rhythm, dual activity, etc.) and live in close contact with a different type of population, mainly urban, who are there simply for leisure. However, this 'coexistence' is not always easy and often leads to social tension, xenophobia, particularly noticeable in very populous tourist areas or where the population, for psychological, cultural or social reasons, is not ready to be submitted to the 'the tourist invasion'.

Osaka Tourism Forum

Again the importance of environment was also recognised in the Osaka Tourism net. High-ranking officials and tourism ministers from 96 countries called for preservation of the natural environment and increased international co-operation during the Osaka World Tourist Forum, 94. The declaration, the first of its kind since the Manila Declaration of 1980, calls on tourists and the tourism industry to share the responsibility for protecting the environment and respecting cultural values. The salient features of the Osaka Tourism Declaration were as follows:

— tourism is the greatest producer of world gross domestic product and employment, accounting for one-tenth of each.

— the growth of international tourism contributes to the promotion of mutual understanding among countries and peoples.

— tourism is an effective means of income redistribution between countries and thus contributes to a more balanced development of world economies.

— tourism is essentially an act of being in touch with, appreciating and learning from bountiful nature and foreign societies and cultures. In that regard, tourists should possess humility and respectfulness in their journeys.

— the destruction of traditional cultures and lifestyles and exploitation of vulnerable groups caused by tourism development can lead to serious consequences and must be avoided. Tourists must also bear responsibility for discreet and desirable behaviour to avoid negatively influencing local society.

— tourism should never be the destroyer, rather, it should be the protector. If the tourism industry and tourists share responsibility for conservation of the environment and cultural heritage, it becomes possible to preserve their value and at the same time use them as tourism resources.

— governments need to have a greater awareness of the crucial role tourism plays in the formulation of policy and should formulate policies with an emphasis on tourism.

Sustainable conveys an integrated act in the environment, the "optimum" use of the resources, the involvement of the local population, the preservation and improvement of the surroundings, all of which allow a sustainable and therefore, lasting process as against the popular concept of the maximum use of space and time. But some tourist activities are not sustainable, and, therefore, scientific approach for sustainable development of tourism should be evolved which conserve and not consume the environment, establishing tourism environment capability. Such a development has to explore the relationship between the natural resources and the visitor community, with special regard to its conservation through sensitive planning and management. Sustainable tourism was defined by the Globe 90 Conference on Sustainable Development as the management of tourism resources in such a way that fulfill economic, social and aesthetic needs while maintaining cultural integrity, essential ecological processes, biological diversity and life support systems. In the words of Inskeep (1991) continuous maintenance of environmental resources and cultural integrity while still bringing equitably distributed socio-economic benefits of tourism to residents of the area is the essence of sustainable tourism development. According to the WTO (1993) 'Sustainability' is a more powerful concept of defining an appropriate approach to tourism development. It encompasses the requirements of all forms of tourism, from individuals travelling to the most sensitive environments to large groups visiting resort destination. Sustainable tourism development is development that has been carefully planned and is carefully managed. It is the antithesis of tourism that has developed for short run gains with the expectation that they will have a Product life cycle declining after some years of fashion. The most successful tourism development of the future will be sustainable that is they will not over consume the resources used to attract tourists. Sustainability is generally taken to mean the existence of the ecological conditions necessary 'to support human life at a specified level of well being through future generations (Lele 1991). According to Beaumont et al., (1993):

— not using renewable resources faster than they can be replenished;
— not using non-renewable resources faster than renewable substitutes can be found for them;
— not releasing pollutants faster than the biosphere can process them to be harmless.

Manning (1996), define it as a concept fundamental to the management of sustainable tourism is carrying capacity. It is founded on the experience of pastoral agriculture where it was observed that a pasture could support in perpetuity a particular number of cattle. If this threshold was exceeded, the supporting system was damaged, often to the point where it could no longer support grazing at all. In its simplest form, carrying capacity measures what level of use is sustainable. But originally it dealt with only one product-the number of cattle which could be fed by one pasture. In tourism, carrying capacity is much more complex, because a variety of products and services must come from the same environment. The environment becomes the supply side to support tourism and other types of economic activities, while the demand side of the ecosphere model is driven by human numbers. Population and consumption demands include such things as food shelter, security, education, culture and recreation. This wider approach helps planners to better focus on achieving optional results in the development process. Since the 1992 Earth Summit, the concept of sustainable development has been placed firmly on the global agenda. It calls for a fundamental reorientation in the way we do business, in order to place the environment at the key centre of the decision making process for governments and their regional authorities, for communities, for environmental groups, and for business and industry. But in recent years it is noticed that there has been little progress since the ambitious Rio Summit which was considered the blueprint for sustainable development. This situation at present is alarming: more than 50,000 square miles of forests are being stripped of their green cover every day, green house gases emission is at an all time high, and the number of people living on less than a dollar per day has risen to above 1.1 billion. Forest fires have become more common; around 200,000 hectors of Mediterranean forests are destroyed each year by fire. Over 500 Mediterranean plant species are threatened with extinction.

The U.S. along with China, Japan, Indonesia, Russia, Germany, Brazil and India have 56 per cent of the world's population and 53 per cent of its forest cover. But under no circumstances can all these countries be held equally responsible for the environment as they are in the various stages of development. In fact, it becomes incumbent upon the more industrialised countries and indeed funding agencies like the World Bank to ensure that aid to the developing World does not go to projects which have the potential to destroy natural ecosystems. Economic growth in any nation cannot be at the cost of sustainable development. Tourism industry, covers diverse activities such as transport, accommodation, entertainment, catering, handicrafts and souvenirs among many others. Some may have severe negative impacts on visiting destinations and population in the absence of proper checks and balances.

Tourism development puts pressure on all local resources; tourists consume energy, water, food and other raw materials, some of which may be in short supply locally. Tourists now go everywhere and on account of this, some of the destinations have come up very recently, some have achieved balanced position in Tourism business and a few of them have reached saturation point. Developing countries like India, where tourism as a business activity is a recent development have already started to realise repercussions at a number of tourist places. But due to haphazard development, some tourism destinations have lost their naturality and are likely to become the centres of garbage and litter very soon. 2.3 million foreign tourists is a much smaller number to cause great deal of damage who come into this vast country of 950 million people, but the much larger number of domestic tourists and pilgrims cause greater damage. According to a rough estimate of the Ministry of Tourism, Govt. of India the domestic tourists account to about 135 million. Besides this, there are visitors to special events where lakhs of people congregate at one place. They cannot be prevented to visit sacred holy places as it is linked to their religious sentiments. It is estimated that every year Indians are paying Rs. 34,000 crore due to the effects of massive environmental degradation which will eventually threaten our future generations. The economic loss due to environmental degradation has been grossly underestimated due to lack of adequate data. Ahmedabad, Mumbai, Kolcutta, Delhi, Kanpur and Nagpur, the major centres of business centres, have three times more suspended particulate matter than prescribed by the World Health Organisation (WHO). Carbon Monoxide emissions in many cities are 50 times higher than the WHO standards.

The Himalaya

The Himalaya range is spread in a total length of 2400 km., measuring along the arc; the width varies from 325 to 425 km. The actual Himalayan range commences at Naga Parbat (8126 m) in the north-west, passes through Pakistan, Kashmir, Himachal Pradesh, and ends at Namche Barwa (7825 m) in the east (Singh 1992). With the expansion of urbanisation, the Himalaya has started to receive increased number of visitors. The situation in the Himalaya needs careful monitoring so that unnecessary human interference may be curbed from causing serious problem. Sunderial Bahuguna (1996), stressed the need for banning human movements in the form of trekking and mountaineering on glaciers. Glaciers, along with forest, are the permanent storehouse, of water in the Himalaya and must be protected at all costs. The Govt. of India has recently made the area accessible for foreign tourists and it has further increased the overall number of international trekkers and nature lovers. The recession of the glaciers is causing a high level of ecological stress in the Himalayan region, according to a study by the Glaciological Survey of India. The Himalaya constitute one of the most important glacier systems in the world, covering a vast area. Nearly 15000 glaciers exist in the Himalaya and are an important source of fresh water of North India's perennial rivers. The Gangotri Glacier, in the Garhwal Himalaya, has been shrinking at an alarming rate and had receded at the rate of 7.31 metres annually during the last century, 18 metres a year until 1990 and of more than 20 metres per year after 1990. Over the last 50 years, the Gangotri Glacier has receded by 600 metres. Due to recession of glaciers, the unique plant wealth of the high altitude meadows in the Himalaya is also being affected. Some of the flowers locally known Brahma Kamal, Barmoola, Laljari, Neelkanthi, and Ratanjot—all medicinal and aromatic plants, are found in these meadows. Relentless killing of wild flowers has caused irreparable loss to the flowering species. As a result, many of them have vanished from forests and some are at the verge of extinction. A fairly large number of wild flower species are now on the verge of permanent extinction. A recent report published by the United Nations Environment Programme (UNEP) contains some bombshells as how man has maimed biodiversity. According to the report, 4000 plant species, most of them flowering plants, are currently threatened with extinction. The Himalaya is also known for a variety of wild flowers. The tourist places like Shimla, Kufri, Naldehra, Kasauli, Chail and Solan which were at one time famous wild bloom spots are loosing their natural set-up as wild flowers have eclipsed from the valleys of the State. One of the structures at Kufri near Shimla was named as Wild Flower

Hall. Now neither wild flowers nor the famous structure exist. Indiscreet cutting of trees are turning these forests into brown deserts and have led to hill erosion. Nainital is also no longer a green valley. The increasing influx of tourists has led to a host of problems. The problems of this town have turned out to be more acute because of its geographical limitations, concentration of building activity and tourist traffic in and around the natural lake. Excessive construction and a gradual depletion of the green cover, along with intensified demographic pressure on its limited resources has badly mutilated this once beautiful destination of tourists. This town has a population of 32,000. But during the peak tourist season, the figure rises to two lakh. According to forest department sources, between 1950 and 1975, approximately 40,000 trees were felled down in the town for different purposes, mainly for construction of hotel buildings.

To cite one more instance, a pastoral village Manali, with 650 households, was suddenly overwhelmed by outsiders emerging from Indian metropolises and from the West. The planned area increased from 47 to 194 hectres within the span of a decade. On account of political movement in U.P. hills, and problem of terrorism in J & K, tourist traffic to Manali had increased fourfold during the last seven years. To check the mushrooming growth of commercial units, a height restriction of 33 feet has been in place for about three years, but four storeyed hotels are a common sight. For the last 3 years, there has been a ban on construction of houses and hotels within 50 metres and 100 metres of the Beas river bank at different locations. But surprisingly, around fifty and twenty new hotels came up in 1995 and 1996 respectively. In Mussoorie, its inherent beauty has been spoilt because of the garbage and filth left behind by increased number of visitors. According to a Mussoorie-based voluntary organisation, Self-Help Environment Programme (SHEP) founded in 1994, due to excessive presence of non-biodegradable substances in the area, a variety of plants like moss are dying and the entire hydrological regime of Mussoorie has been altered leading to the drying of water channels. Similar problems have been noticed in the higher Himalaya where people go for mountaineering. As the Monsoon season comes to an end, thousands of our young people visit the Himalaya. A maximum number of trekkers go to Gangotri, Pindari Glacier, Milam Glacier, Amarnath, Rohtang Pass and Sikkim Himalaya, besides millions of tourists and pilgrims to hill stations and religious shrines respectively. An environmental time bomb is ticking beneath the simmering waters of the world famous Dal Lake in Srinagar, Kasmir and environmentalists fear that unless immediate steps are taken the lake would disappear in the next century. Once a star tourist attraction with its famed *Shiksras*, the lake appears to be facing a slow death due to increasing encroachment along its banks, dumping of wastes, mechanical deweeding and sluggish water movement. The lake has shrunk from 48 sq.kms, in 1947 to mere 12 sq.kms. or less today. The Comptroller and Auditor General of India (CAG), which had tabled the report on Dal Lake in 1997 in the state legislature said that human interference by way of settlement on the lake shores, construction of embankments within the lake, increase in number of house-boats for tourists, and denudation of the catchment area have been the cause of shrinkage and pollution of the lake. The area of the lake shrink from 24 sq.kms. in 1962 to 15 sq.kms. in 1982. The condition of Ladakh is also deteriorating. According to M.S. Kohli, former President of Indian Mountaineering Federation, when he first visited Ladakh on an expedition to Saser Kangri in 1956 not many from the outside world had visited the area. The age-old local habits and customs of the Ladakh were intact, and this in itself was a rewarding experience. At each village they were invited by the local people to their houses with folded hands. But the old culture and hospitality has vanished. By opening Ladakh for tourists, many of the historic monasteries have been stripped. In the words of the first Union Minister for Tourism and Civil Aviation, Govt. of India, Karan Singh, "The monasteries have just been stripped because if a person is sitting in a monastery for 500 years in a tradition and a tourist comes and offers US $ 100 for some work of art: $ 100 may be a very small amount for the tourist but for a poor person who is sitting in a monastery, $ 100 is something. And we know that they are very convinced about reincarnation. Therefore, a large number of tank has and other art treasures have disappeared." Increased number of Mountaineering expeditions have eroded the peaks of faith of the Himalaya since 1980. In case of the Mount Everest two people climbed the summit in 1970, ten in 1980 but there were 72 who reached the top in 1990. But the increase in the number of successful climbers has been matched by an equal rise in mortality figures. There were only 44 death between 1921 and 1970 but in 1992, 115 died. Today, according to Ahluwalia (1997) the number of deaths per annum has crossed the 150 mark. Santosh Yadav, the Indian Woman mountaineer, who enjoys the distinction of having climbed Everest twice, reminisces about a particular difficult night at South Col in 1993, "I spent the night resting my head against a rock which was jutting into the tent. Imagine my horror when I woke up in the morning to find it was not a rock but a dead body." Nepal Mountaineering Association has attempted to clean the Himalaya.

National Parks and Sanctuaries

Though 9.2 per cent of country's land falls in the category of protected area which includes 85 National Parks with 1.08%, 446 Sanctuaries with 3.43%, and 531 protected areas with 4.5% of the area; visitors and local population pressure, unsavoury conflicts among NGOs over human and animal rights, spread of industrial interests into protected areas and a major spurt in poaching activities with rhino horn and tiger bones fetching thousands of dollars in the international markets are some of outstanding issues that threaten our national parks and genetic wealth they hold. In Rajasthan efforts are going on to extend the dolomite mining work even it falls in protected areas like the Sariska Tiger Reserve.

A third of the Melaghat National Park is being denotified in the guise of reducing human and wildlife conflict. The Indian Institute of Public Opinion study showed that in 1989, 56 per cent of the national parks and 72 per cent of the sanctuaries surveyed had population within their boundaries. Bansda in Gujarat had a density of 56 persons per hectare. The growing human population is putting tremendous pressure on protected areas by increasing the demands for fuelwood, fodder and other forest produce.

Additional Inspector General (Wildlife) S.C. Day has estimated that more than 250 million tonnes a year is extracted as fuelwood from our forests. "If population grows at the current pace there will be no forests in 50 years, forget about biodiversity" he says. Whereas a large number of national parks and sanctuaries without any funds or means for proper protection and conservation cannot be supported. Care has to be taken to obtain a balance, and conservation of core areas and endangered species of both flora and fauna have to be ensured. The Nilgiri bioreserve which spreads over the borders of Karnataka, Kerala and Tamil Nadu constitutes 15 per cent of India's total protected area also repeats the same story. The reserve shelters around 100 mammalian species, 550 species of birds and 30 reptilian ones-thus acquiring an unparalleled biological status that has led to its blatant plunder by the international wildlife trade cartel.

In Kerala, construction of roads have disturbed the wildlife of Periyar National Park. The Kerala Forest Department's proposal to construct a network of roads within the famous Periyar Tiger Reserve, located at Thekkady in the Idukki district, may cause negative impacts on wildlife habitat. The department proposes to strengthen its patrolling and provided more protection to wildlife by constructing seven motorable roads of 138 kms. to canned various parts of the sanctuary with the existing approach roads. The five-year project, to be completed in phases, would link places like Mavady, Mullakudy, Mullathode and Thannikudy-all situated within the thick evergreen forests. The blasting of granite for the first phase of the project linking Mavady and Thannikurdy had already begun.

Again, the road construction activity seemingly violates the forest management guidelines prescribed by the Union Ministry of Environment and Forests. The proposed roads would cut through areas with a high density of tigers and with the rising human pressure and cutting of trees during the construction, wildlife there could be greatly dislocated. The Gir lion reserve also does not feel safe. Noise and air pollution are making the survival of the lion increasingly difficult in the 1,412 sq. kms. protected territory of the Gir sanctuary. Disturbed by the increasing presence of man and affected by the pollution caused by vehicles passing through the five state highways crisscrossing the Gir, many lions are exiling themselves to the periphery of the jungle, often becoming easy targets for poachers and poisoning by villagers. Some visitors come to the Gir under the pretext of a pilgrimage, and leave behind a large number littered on the road, which are harmful to the animals. Cattle grazing along the boundary and inside the forest has increased in number, which explains that the lions have moved to the outskirts of the jungle. Bandhavgarh, once known hunting ground of Maharaja of Rewa estate, is now a national park. Although a small park compared to parks like Kanha and Corbett, it boasts of an incredible variety of species of mammals, birds and reptiles. But today, Bandhavgarh has begun to realise discord between human beings and nature, resulting in the destruction of the latter. It is only because of the lack of knowledge and understanding on the part of the human beings. A check in the number of visitors to the park on any given day is required to be observed. It is necessary to determine the carrying capacity of the park. In recent years, many camps and lodges have come up around the national parks, and contrary to popular belief, the interest of those who run the camps goes beyond just financial gains.

The forest department will do well to take these organisations into confidence. The operators are ever ready to assist in enforcing a strict code of conduct within the park, for the very existence of these camps and lodges depends on a healthy and natural environment. The Jim Corbett National Park, the first national park and tiger reserve of the country receives tremendous threat to its tigers from poachers. Under "Project Tiger" scheme launched in 1973, apart from 520.18 sq. kms. of the Corbett National Park the 301.18 sq. kms. of the Sonanadi Wildlife sanctuary and 496.54 sq. kms. of the reserve forest also became-part of the protected area. The Corbett Tiger Reserve is among the 23 such reserves in the country. The local people here say that most of the poaching cases go unreported unless an animal carcass is found or some persons arrested with animal parts. According to sources here, most of the poaching is done in the peripheral divisions where the forest staff is engaged in routine work and not properly equipped. The forest officers have no magisterial powers and they do not have arms either. In the foothills of the central Himalaya near Hardwar, the Rajaji National Park has been facing the increased and continued biotic pressure on the forest area in and around the park. The *Gujjars,* a Muslim pastoral tribe, and their cattle have expanded to three times or more of their original number. With their buffaloes, cows, ponies and sheep, the *Gujjars* are causing depletion of the precious Sal forests. The effects ate visible all over the park where the undergrowth is disappearing and trees are dying due to excessive lopping. In the eastern past of the country, the Kaziranga National Park, famous for one horn rhino, also faces the problem of poaching and hunting. The Rhino Foundation, set up in 1994 with funding from some 90 tea garden companies, has played an important role in building awareness against poaching. A lot of rhinos are shot during the monsoons when they leave the security of the park to cross over to the high grounds of the tea gardens. The US Fish and Wildlife Department is providing funds for follow up of the poaching cases. As direct incentives to the field staff, the Foundation has been distributing water filters to the forest camps and hunting boots, raincoats and warm sweaters to guards. However, the forest guards need training in use of rifles and the initiative has to come from the Government. They also need country boats, speed boats and elephants for patrolling inside the national park. Plans to expand the protected area of the rhino terriroty by 490 sq. kms. and ensure a corridor for their migration to the hills in the monsoons is providing difficult as local people are not allowing the government to acquire their lands. But if the rhino is to be saved and protected, there is urgent need to acquire some 430 sq. kms. at Burapahar where migrating rhinos run straight into the bullets of poachers. The 470 sq. kms. Manas National Park of Assam, a world heritage site, has become the home of armed Bodo militants and poacher gangs who have been felling trees and killing wildlife as well as foresters. The World Wide Fund (WWF), as a part of its framework for regional cooperation in south Asia to generate a more realistic and focussed approach towards overall conservation programmes, has chalked out a Comprehensive Tiger Conservation Action Plan to strengthen ongoing efforts for protection of tigers through new and innovative initiatives.

The strategy includes mobilisation of support for tiger conservation at political and policy making levels, generating grassroots support through local communities and a support mechanism by way of information collection and dissemination, education and awareness.

The strategy also emphasises the need to facilitate inter-governmental consultations to discuss transborder issues between India and Nepal and field level discussions on tiger conservation work in the region, in collaboration with Nepal and Bhutan. Further, effective campaign on illegal trade-"Don't buy trouble"-has been undertaken as an initiative under "WWF 2000 Living Planet Campaign," to address both supplier and consumer countries of animal parts. During implementation, this strategy will be subjected to continuous monitoring and periodic review and focus will be on the 12 Indian states which account for about 93 per cent of the country's tiger population.

In the field of coastal tourism, India has achieved significant position. Some of the states even have started to receive direct charters from overseas markets. The latest coastal management plan of the Union Environment Ministry, imposing severe restrictions on coastal constructions, is likely to affect various developmental projects mainly in the tourism sector in Kerala, which has a 600 km. long coastline. A series of ambitious beach and backwaters tourism projects on the cards, like the Bekal Fort project, and the Varkala Beach and the Chennai Beach projects could end up as a non-starter once the plan is implemented strictly. The tourism industry, which is going to be the worst affected, has represented to the Government to get the Environment Ministry revamp the plan taking into consideration the special circumstances of the State. Barring deserts and snow, Orissa offers every other conceivable tourist attractions. Yet tourism in the state is languishing for want of thoughtful planning. The State Government ostensibly gives it high priority but does relatively little to build up an infrastructure necessary for a larger tourist inflow. The famous Sun Temple of Konark, one of the 16 monuments in the country and the only one in the eastern India listed as a world heritage monument built by Narasingha Dev I, needs comprehensive conservation plan for restoration. The original spire *(Vimana)* which was once believed to have been more than 200 feet high, has been reduced to 120 feet. Further, the continuing process of erosion has also harmed the temple. Records show that iconoclasts once attempted to destroy the temple and took away the cooper *kalash* and the crowning' *Padmadhwaja,* while the Surya image and the pillar called, *Aruna stambha,* were removed to the Jagannath temple at Puri. It is a temple already ruined. The British, for obvious reasons, were not keen on reviving its glory. The only thing they did was to fill the interior with sands. Now the Archaeological Survey of India (ASI) have taken up the problem. The Udhagamandalam (Ooty) Lake, one of the major tourist attractions of the Nilgiris, has become an eye sore of late due to pollution and excessive siltation. The 172-year old lake was artificially created by John Sullivan to meet the irrigation needs of the hills. It was then a vast reservoir of water extending up to Charing Cross, some three to four km. from the present boundary but gradually the area has shrunk. Though it has shrunk in size, it continues to attract visitors and is a great money spinner as it generates an annual revenue of Rs. 10 million for the Government. A boat ride on the lake used to be a pleasant experience cherished by the young and old alike. But of late the sewage from the town which is released into the lake has caused the pollution. The Kodappamund Channel, originating from the Sholas, passes through many villages before joining the lake. The channel is being used as a conduit to carry the sullage from the wayside villages. As the sewage constantly mixes with the waters of the lake, it leads to heavy sedimentation of the bed. It is estimated that at least 90,000 sq. meters of the lake are now silted.

6

Ecotourism Management

The primary advantage of ecotourism is that it provides an impetus to expand both conservation and tourism development. On the conservation side, ecotourism is the conservation benefit which is most easily sold and thus incorporated into decisions about land use. In concrete terms, entrance and other fees associated with ecotourism can supplement existing governmental conservation budgets and can provide incentives for private sector conservation. On the economic development side, ecotourism can bring employment opportunities to remote regions.

Many observers voice the concern that ecotourism has not reached its potential as a tool of conservation or economic development, in part because many worthwhile projects cannot find financing, in part because host countries have yet to receive the full revenue potential inherent in ecotourism, and in part because relatively little of the revenue which has been generated has directly supported conservation and economic development.

In an effort to expand ecotourism's contribution, this chapter outlines strategies for: setting tourism fees, using these fees to finance ecotourism development and traditional conservation management; and increasing ecotourism's contribution to the economic development of communities near ecotourism destinations.

Collecting and utilising basic information must be part of that process. Ecotourism will provide the greatest benefits, and thus best meet objectives, when management is informed. Unfortunately, there has been little rigorous data collection and analysis. Information needs are discussed In this Chapter, and effective management will require collection and utilisation of this data.

Tourism Fees

Lower fees for domestic residents can be justified on the grounds of both economic efficiency and equity (Lindberg 1991), but such decisions often also include social and political considerations beyond the scope of this chapter. Readers interested in the experience of the United States and Canada regarding pricing for domestic visitation should refer to Aukerman (1990), Walsh (1986) and Rosenthal (1994). Child and Health (1990) also question the appropriateness of developing countries subsidising the foreign visitors through low fees. Several countries, including Peru, Ecuador, and Kenya have raised fees for foreigners while maintaining lower fees for residents (Olindo,1991). Such differential pricing is common within the traditional tourism industry. For example, airlines often charge more for tickets purchased close to the departure date, based on the premise that such travellers have greater willingness to pay and less flexibility. Likewise, hotels often reduce rates during the off season in response to variations in seasonal demand. In effect, parks and similar facilities will need to act like business when providing tourism opportunities to foreigners, such behavior often requires bureaucratic, and occasionally legal, changes. At the same time, parks need to continue traditional activities, such as conservation and, where appropriate, provision of subsidised recreation to residents. Fee levels will depend in large part oil national and local objectives. Two possible objectives are to charge fees which equal the cost of providing the service (cost recovery) or to charge fees that will generate as much profit as possible. There may be additional objectives, which may modify or replace these two. For example, fees may be kept low to encourage increased visitation and thereby increased economic opportunities for tourism-related businesses in the region. Alternatively, fees may be raised to encourage the private sector to develop ecotourism facilities that would not. be profitable as long as fees for "public" destinations were kept artificially low. Regardless of which objective is chosen, knowledge of demand for the ecotourism attraction will be necessary to set fees. That is, how many tourists will visit the attraction and how much are they willing to pay? Methods for estimating this demand will be described after the following discussion of management objectives. Case Study examples of pricing for different objectives follow the methods section.

Profit Maximisation

The focus of this objective is to set fees such that they generate as much profit as possible. Fees should more than offset the cost of providing the tourism opportunity. The profits (revenues minus costs) can then be used to help finance traditional conservation activities, subsidised recreation opportunities to residents, or other program activities. In practice, there is often insufficient information to accurately determine the financial,, not to mention tile ecologic or social, costs of ecotourism. Since both of the above objectives require knowledge of these costs when setting fees, a high priority should be placed on obtaining accurate cost information. Managers trying to maximise profits should keep in mind that this goal is not the same as maximising revenues. Revenue maximisation generally results in trying to attract as many tourists as possible, but profit maximisation may occur at lower visitation levels Since the financial, ecologic and social costs of ecotourism can increase more quickly than revenues at high visitation levels.

Cost Recovery

The focus of this objective is to set tourism fees such that they generate enough revenue to pay for providing the ecotourism opportunity. Fees should, at the minimum, offset capital costs (such as construction of a visitor center) and operating costs (such as maintenance of facilities, salaries for guides, and so on). Ideally, they should also offset such "indirect", costs as the cost of ecologic damage and the cost of negative impact on local communities, though such costs are difficult to quantify.

Other Objectives

Purely from the financial view point of the attraction owners, ecotourism opportunities for foreigners should only be provided if fees at least cover costs. However, additional objectives may lead owners, particularly governmental owners, to provide opportunities even when costs are not covered. For example, fees may be kept low to maintain high levels of visitation, thereby providing economic Opportunities to tourism businesses (however resulting loss of fees revenues should be explicitly recognised and justified). Or fees for foreigners may not be sufficient to cover all costs, but they may generate sufficient revenue to help subsidise domestic visitation.

On the other hand high fees can be used not only to raise revenues but also to limit and disperse visitors when particular sites have become crowded. Kenya, for example, has considered charging higher fee for crowded attractions in an effort to disperse visitors to less visited attractions, of course this strategy requires that similar attractions to be available for visits. A similar strategy has been recommended for Nepal. In addition experience in the United States suggests that high fees will reduce litter and vandalism at natural areas. These strategies implicitly depend on a trade off between price and visitation levels: as the price is increased, the number of visitors will decrease and vice versa. This is a basic economic principle that should not be Ignored, but current fees are so low for most attractions that even substantial Increases will likely to have little impacts on demand in terms of choosing a destination. Tourists surveys, as well actual tourist behavior, suggests that price is relatively an unimportant factor when choosing an ecotour, and that even when price is a concern tourists are willing to pay higher fees if they know that these fees are being used to enhance their experience or to conserve the special area they have come to see. Several parks have raised their fees without noticeably affecting visitor level and many more are able to do so. In fact, if these revenues are then used to improve the attraction, demand will probably increase. Achieving any of these management objective require that there be sufficient tourists willing to pay fees higher enough to meet objectives. Managers should remember that demand for ecotourism can be very unpredictable and dependent on factors beyond control.

Market Evaluation

The basic concept behind this method is that a given attraction can expect levels of visitation and a willingness to pay fees equivalent to existing attractions which are similar in consumer appeal, cost of travel, and other demand factors. This method is a common basis for determining whether Investments in the private sector will be worthwhile. However, care must be taken to evaluate how new facilities expand the supply of destinations, there by putting, downward pressure on prices for both existing and new facilities. Unfortunately, lodges and other ecotourism businesses typically do not share information on visitation levels and prices, so comparison is difficult. In addition, few national parks arid other "public" facilities have historically charged such fees; when fees have been charged, they, have rarely been based on business considerations such as the cost of providing the service and the willingness of consumers to pay for the service. Even private reserves, which generally charge more than public parks, often set low fees since costs are partially underwritten by other programs, such as scientific research arid foundation grants (Alderman, 1990). Even when data is obtained from similar facilities, they must be adjusted to take into account' differences in demand factors, such as quality, of attraction and travel cost. Ideally, it will be possible to identify an attraction which ranks roughly the same on all factors.

Survey A Tourist Demand

The fundamental concept behind this method is that tourists estimate their own demand for the attraction in response to specific survey questions. A survey of this type in Costa Rica revealed that both Costa Ricans and the foreigners agreed that entrance fees to the three most popular national parks should be raised. Furthermore, both Costa Ricans and foreigners agreed that foreigners should pay more than residents, even though that was not government policy. The weakness, of this method is that the results likely underestimate actual demand and thus the potential fee level. In part this is due to tile general difficulties in obtaining accurate responses to surveys (tourists often underestimate what they would actually be willing to pay). In addition, the surveyors note that responses might have been higher if the survey had been administered during the summer months rather than winter months. Furthermore, the responses might have differed if questions had been phrased differently.

Demand Curve Analysis

Probably the most accurate, strategy is to set fees using demand curve analysis. A demand curve measures how much tourists are willing to pay to see the attraction, as well as the trade off between price and number of visitors. Demand curves thereby enable managers to Identify the revenue maximising fees. Demand curves have been estimated for developing country parks using the hedonic pricing method and the travel cost method. Researchers can extend the analysis by statistical analysis to estimate the revenue-maximising fee. In the Costa Rica case, the maximising fee was estimated at $1.20.

Market-Based Reactive Management and Auctions

The fundamental concept of this method is to react to the tourism market as flexibly as possible by changing, fees as demand changes. Because of the inherent 'Imprecision in estimating demand as well as the fickleness of the industry, this method Is an important supplement to the three already discussed. That is, fees might be set at $10 based on tourists surveys or evaluation of equivalent attractions. However if the number of visitors continues to increase rapidly, managers should consider rising fees. Like-wise, If the number of visitors decreases rapidly managers should consider lowering fees.

In addition managers cannot use one of the first three methods to estimate demand, they can use reactive management to gradually increase fees until their goals are met. Auctioning permits or other tourism fees will typically align fees with demand since tour operators will bid as much as they are willing to pay for the permit. However, auctions are generally appropriate only when there is a limited number of permits or allowable entries and when the price of such permits is relatively high. This will usually be the case with hunting and such high value tourism opportunities as viewing mountains gorillas in Rwanda. The difficulty with reactive management within the context of government run ecotourism attractions is that agencies rarely have the necessary flexibility to quickly react to changes in the market place. However, the benefits of such flexibility can be powerful force for decentralisation of authority to set fees.

Tourism Fees

Estimated revenues need to be compared with costs to determine whether management objectives will be met. This comparison will often take the form of a financial analysis or benefits-cost analysis, especially if loan is sought to cover such costs.

Funding Sources

Feasible projects may be sent out to funding agencies for review. There are a wide variety of funding sources, some of which require relatively little financial or cost benefit analysis to justify funding.

Ecotourism projects that are financially viable may attract funding from local banks or investors. When these sources are not available, funding may often be obtained from governmental development programs, international development banks, or bilateral aid agencies. These sources often provide capital to promising private sector enterprises.

Projects that are not financially viable, but are economically viable because of the broader benefits to society, may be able to attract grants or concessionary loans from government agencies, bilateral aid agencies, or conservation organisations and foundations in industrialised countries. It is also common for national governments to provide incentives (subsidies) which may make the project financially attractive. For example, a government might provide reduced tax rates or exemption of 'income from taxation for a given period of time distribution of government lands for tourism-related purposes, provided the majority remained in a natural and managed state;, tax credits for donations of land to ecotourism/conservation projects, exemptions from import tariffs and commodity taxes; and low interest loans. Governments seeking funding for ecotourism and conservation projects can explore similar resources such as conservation foundations, as well as sources available only to government.

Management Issues in Tourism Fee

The evaluation necessary for setting fees can also inform planning for the future. An Important consideration for both conservation and the tourism industry is the stability of demand for ecotourism in general, and an individual attraction in particular. An examination of demand factors suggests that expected increase in population and income in source countries will lead to increased general demand for ecotourism attractions in future. However demand is based partly on taste, which for ecotourism is thought to be heavily dependent on public awareness and the concern about the natural environment. Future ecotourism demand will depend in part on the level of concern in source countries for environmental preservation. Individual sites need to worry about the destination country's political and economic stability.

There is inevitably uncertainty in forecasting future demand so caution must be used when estimating future ecotourism revenues. Knowledge of demand factors can also help planners choose appropriate ecotourism development sites and determine priorities for increasing the ecotourism product. For example, qualification of demand factors for tourism in Greece demonstrated that an increase in promotion within source countries would be cost effective way to increase demand by improving destination image. In the case of ecotourism, other areas for cost effective investment might include improving the quality of the experience through guide training or development of facilities.

Once overall fee policies have been determined, managers must decide for what goods and services specific fees should he charged and how they should be collected. Although there is some overlap in terminology, the following are some of the categories for fees.

- *Use fee.* A fee for use of a specific object or opportunity.
- *Entrance fee.* A fee charged to enter a park or similar attraction.
- Licence or permit. Similar to a use fee, this category includes fees such fishing or hunting permits.
- *Admissions lee.* A fee for admission to a specific tacility, such as a visitor center.

- *Sales and concessions.* Souvenirs, lodging, and other goods and services can be sold directly by the park (with profits being considered tourism fees) or through a concessionaire agreement.

Direct on-site collection. In this case, fees are collected directly from tourists, usually at an entrance gate or as the good or service is purchased. There are at least two benefits of this method: one it directly correlates payment of fees with the service provided and two, it provides direct contact between tourists and park personnel, and thus an opportunity to inform, regulate, and count visitors. Indirect collection through tour operators. In such a system, fees are paid by the tour operator, with the cost passed on to the tourist as part of the tour package price. This strategy is similar to direct collection, and in fact is often used as a complementary system. Although there is less contact between park personnel and visitors, this system can contribute to cooperation between the park and the local tourism industry.

In addition, it will often reduce administrative costs while still allowing visitation levels to be monitored. Another benefit is that the fees are hidden in the cost of the tour package, thus possibly reducing the effect of higher fees on visitation levels.

On the other hand, indirect collection through other sectors of the tourism industry. This method, with fees usually charged through hotel or transportation taxes, provides benefits similar to tour operator fee systems. However, it is often critical for industry acceptance that fees be levied only when there is a strong correlation between the fees and park use. Additional sources of revenue should also be utilised when appropriate. For example, an opportunity should be provided for tourists, and others interested in the area, to donate funds for management of the destination. This mechanism can generate substantial revenue and may be most efficient when set up through a non governmental organisation.

The best fee system for any particular area will he based on the type of visitation (individuals versus groups), the level of cooperation with the industry, bureaucratic efficiency, and other relevant factors. Charging a low entrance fee and a relatively high guide fee may generate substantial revenue from wealthy tourists interested in hiring guides while at the same time maintaining visits by less wealthy tourists who may be more likely to frequent local tourism businesses, which thereby support the local economy. However, the number of different fees should be kept to a minimum to avoid tourist confusion and frustration.

One of the main rationales for developing eeotourism is that it can provide much needed funding for conservation budgets, If existing budgets are reduced as tourism revenues increase, there is little benefit from eeotourism. Indeed, the infrastructural and management costs brought on by the introduction or expansion of visitation may actually reduce funding available for traditional management activities. The instability of tourism revenues may also be worse than the instability of the existing government funding. Whenever possible, establish trust funds to ensure continued funding during low points in tourism cycle.

National policies, such as choosing between cost recovery and profit maximisation objectives, should be developed for fees charged at government attractions, however, managers of individual parks should have flexibility in setting fees based on specific local resource conditions as well as changes in demand for the attraction. If the decisions remain with the central government, the authority to change fee should at least remain as flexible as possible. For example, the executive branch, such as a parks agency, can generate respond more quickly than can the legislative branch, such as a parliament or congress. Recognise that fee collection will not be worthwhile at all attractions, Fee collection may simply not be cost-effective at sites with low levels of demand or high administrative costs. Develop and maintain accurate accounting and financial management systems for both revenues and expenditures. Informed decisions oh fee levels require knowledge of both the cost of providing the tourism opportunity and the revenue generated through fees. Efficient decisions can only be made when such information systematically collected and incorporated into the decision making process.

Ecotourism has been embraced by many as an opportunity to generate income and employment in areas relatively untouched by traditional development efforts. Such goals have often been achieved in part, but there is a realisation that little of the money spent by tourists remains at or near the destination itself. There are at least three reasons for increasing local benefits from, and participation in, ecotourism development. First, it is equitable insofar as conservation of the area for ecotourism reduces or eliminates traditional resource utilisation. Second, when residents receive benefits they usually support ecotourism, even to the point of protecting the site against poaching or other encroachment. Conversely, if residents bear the costs without receiving benefits they often turn against ecotourism and might intentionally or unintentionally damage the attraction. Third, the ecotourists, as consumers, often support the importance of tourism benefiting local residents. The amount of money which actually reaches the destination region, less the amount leaked out to pay for outside goods and services, has not been adequately quantified. However, a common estimate is that less than 10 percent of tourists spending remains in communities near ecotourism destinations.

To some extent this is simply due to the nature of the tourism industry, substantial funds are spent on marketing and transport before tourists even reach the destination. However there are opportunities for expanding ecotourism's local economic benefits. Many of these are currently being pursued by privately or publicly funded programs. As these programmes progress, we should he able, to determine which is most effective in achieving economic development goals. Some of the mechanism for increasing local benefits form ecotourism include: local ownership and management of the ecotourism resource; leasing, partial ownership or profit sharing arrangements between the tourism industry and local residents, direct payments to communities from tourism revenues and local employment in the tourism industry.

Probably, the most obvious opportunity for providing local benefits is employing local residents in the tourism industry and the industries which support it. The money spent by tourists is circulated through the economy as the tourism sector and its employees buy goods from other businesses. Thus, tourism might support not only a local lodge manager but also a local former who grows the food sold in the lodge. On the other hand, if the local lodge imports its food, the money "leaks" away and produces fewer local benefits. To increase local development, tourism should be "linked" to other sectors so that money helps develop the local economy rather than being leaked away.

The following points illustrate opportunities for reducing the leakage of tourism revenue:

— Improve linkages to the local transportation industry. Ecotourists often need to and want to, use existing local modes of transportation, ranging from the traditional, to the modern. Whenever possible, local boats, canoes, mules, taxis and porters should be utilised. In some cases, cooperatives can be formed to purchase more expensive transportation equipment. For example, the boats that carry tourists from Puno to Taquile on lake Lake Tilicaea in Peru are owned by a local cooperative.

— Improve linkages within the tourism industry. Perhaps the most obvious opportunity for local residents to benefit from ecotourism is through employment and income in the industry itself. In the short term, this employment may center on unskilled labour. However, training programs should be developed so that residents are able to fill skilled positions, such as guides and managers. In addition, financing should be made available for local entrepreneurs to establish their own tourism operations.

— Improve linkages with agriculture and fishing. Substantial tourism expenditures go toward purchasing food, much of which is currently imported from regions distant from actual tourism attractions. Ecotourists tend to be interested in local cuisine, provided that quality standards are met and maintained. Lodges and restaurants often need to be more willing to spend the extra time developing sources of food. Meanwhile, local farmer and distributors often need to recognise the importance of quality and reliability.

— Develop local handicrafts and other souvenirs. Souvenier sales are often the easiest way for local residents to benefit from tourism spending, but many destinations sell souvenirs from other regions or even other countries. Instead, a commitment should be made to developing local handicrafts while considering what is appealing to tourists.

— Improve linkages with construction, equipment, and maintenance sectors. Because ecotourism infrastructure is typically small-scale, and located in remote locations, local labour and materials are often employed in its construction. This linkage should be maintained and expanded.

These linkages will develop spontaneously to meet immediate needs. However, active involvement by community leaders, industry, government officials, nongovernmental organisations will often be necessary. For example, the industry can work with local communities to identify opportunities for employment in the industry or for providing goods such as food and handicrafts. The government can often play a vital role in providing credit to the entrepreneurs or training through extension programmes. Nongovernmental organisations can play important role in training and other activities. These varied groups will need to cooperate in order to: identify opportunities for local development, identify training credit and other programs necessary for realistically achieving these opportunities, implement these programs, and evaluate programs successes and failures, trying new strategies where appropriate.

Employment and Training Approaches

Although this program was not intended to substitute for a full degree in interpretation, the results have been positive. The guides formed a local cooperative (Nawcoop) and were successful in finding employment on both a part time and full-time basis.

Training programs have also been implemented to develop reliable and high quality food sources improve sanitation standards and more. In Bali, Indonesia, an experimental farm was established to improve the quality and variety of fruits, vegetables and poultry products for sale to tourist hotels and restaurants, An important component of this program focused on marketing, including organising a reliable supply of products. Meanwhile, Kenya reduced its food imports from 77 percent of tourist food consumption in 1984 to 14 percent in 1988, Nepal's Annapurlu Conservation Area Project (ACAI) not only chanelled entrance fees back into the local region but also included training to upgrade service quality, standardise menus and prices, and improve sanitation and waste disposal standards.

The converse of reducing leakage is increasing tourists spendings. Studies in Latin America and Thialand suggests that additional revenues can be earned by developing infrastructure and services at or near ecotourism attractions. These might include lodging, restaurants or snack bars, souvenirs shops, visitors centre, cultural performances and so on. Careful planning is particularly important when developing these additional facilities. It may be best to locate infrastructure outside the park, thus reducing negative ecological impacts while increasing opportunities for local residents to participate in the tourism economy. However, locating facilities in villages may increase negative social cultural impacts, while at the same time foregoing the park's ability to regulate ecological impacts. Care should be taken to avoid indirect damage to the local environment, culture or economy. Handicrafts should not be based on consumption of flora or fauna when this consumption will endanger the species or local customs. Coral and bird feather souvenirs are often cited as examples of how handicrafts production can cause severe damage to natural resources. Throughout the planning process, consideration should be given both to local cultures and economic traditions and to tourists' tastes and desires.

Tourism also puts new demands on local economies, particular those in remote areas. Consumption of local products can be important benefit of ecotourism, but this demand should be managed carefully so it does not shock local economies or the local environment.

7

Sustainable Tourism in Protected Areas

There has been considerable debate over the concept and meaning of 'sustainable development' since the term was popularised in the 'Brundtland Report' (otherwise *Our Common Future*, World Commission on Environment and Development, 1987). That report defined it as development that: seeks to meet the needs and aspirations of the present without compromising the ability to meet those of the future.

In Australia a number of working groups were set up in 1990, to report to the Prime Minister on the implications of the pursuit of ecologically sustainable development for several sectors of the economy. One of these looked at tourism. Its report (Commonwealth of Australia, 1991) did not attempt a definition of sustainable" tourism development, but did enunciate a number of arising principles and characteristics, which included:

— *Improvement in material and non-material well-being:* An ecologically sustainable tourism industry will be one which considers carefully the quality of experiences offered, as well as simply numerical outcomes.

— *Intergenerational and intragenerational equity:* An ecologically sustainable tourism industry would not diminish the range of educational, recreational and environmental activities available to present or future generations ... Species diversity and ecosystem integrity cannot be replaced or substituted ... tourism ventures should deal cautiously with risk...

- *The protection of biological diversity and the maintenance of ecological processes and systems:* Tourism development should occur in such a way which maintains biodiversity and supports the maintenance of ecological processes.

Several authors have provided definitions of sustainable tourism, or discussed actions required to approach sustainable tourism, which address the full range of environmental, social, cultural and economic aspects of this complex subject (for example Pigram, 1990; Butler, 1991; Hunter, 1995). We propose a definition of sustainable tourism that draws on ecological economics, a relatively new interdisciplinary branch of study that addresses 'the relationships between ecosystems and economic systems in the broadest sense' (Costanza, 1989:1). The purpose of this is to focus on the proper measures of benefits and costs of tourism, and on the critical relationship between investment in management of tourism and sustainable use of natural environments.

Our concern here is only with tourism in protected areas, i.e. areas such as National Parks or WHAs where legislation controls private sector commercial, and individual recreational, activity in the interests of conservation. In such areas, we propose that sustainable tourism can be defined relatively simply in terms of two criteria:

1. Tourism must provide a non-declining stream of net economic benefits
2. Tourism must be compatible with the conservation of the existing natural environment

Considering only protected areas simplifies one area of dispute in the debate over the meaning and implications of sustainable development, and leads directly to the first of these criteria. The dispute concerns the possibilities for substitution between natural and man-made capital. Most economists take it that such substitution is possible so that sustainable development requires that the size of the total, man-made and natural, capital stock is constant or increasing. However, some argue that the substitution possibilities are quite limited, so that sustainability requires that stocks of natural capital are maintained intact (see Pearce *et al.*, 1989 for example). The matter is actually quite complicated as it involves not only, as is often implied, substitution in production, but also substitution in consumption. It is conceivable that an area of the natural environment could be converted to a range of 'Disneyland' type developments which could provide a stream of economic benefits equal in size to, or greater than, that based on the original natural environment. However, in the case of protected areas the dispute is effectively resolved. For protected area natural environments, a clear social decision has been made that such substitutions are not acceptable.

Sustainable tourism in protected areas, by definition, requires the maintenance of constant levels of natural capital. The two criteria together mean that the pursuit of economic benefits from tourism is constrained by the need to avoid environmental damage.

It is important that it is net economic benefits that are considered. The distinction between gross and net benefits involves two dimensions. First, economic benefit measurement should take into account investment in management to maintain natural capital; that is, to avoid and repair environmental damage to the protected area. The relevant benefit stream is that arising after such costs have been met. Second, there is a distinction between financial flows associated with tourism and the economic benefits to be properly attributed to it. The economic benefits of tourism are often, incorrectly, discussed in terms of total tourist expenditure. This includes the costs of the inputs to the tourism industry, which are not available for alternative uses by virtue of use in the tourism industry, and so overstates tourism benefits. Total tourist expenditure, on the other hand, understates economic benefits in so far as it is an incomplete measure of the satisfaction that tourists derive from their experiences. However, as discussed in Driml & Common (1995) the data for the proper measurement of the net economic benefits from tourism are rarely available.

According to standard economic criteria, the objective for managing some part of the natural environment is the maximisation of the present value of the sum of the net benefits arising from *all* uses of the area. In figuring the implications of pursuing such an objective, the relative values of uses are to reflect consumer sovereignty criteria. The fact that private recreation and conservation benefits are not, generally, fully registered in markets does *not* mean that they are treated as irrelevant in standard economics. In the last two decades economists have done a lot of research into methods for measuring non-marketed environmental benefits, with the objective of having them included in this sort of planning. The costs to be measured include the actual costs incurred in making the benefits available, plus any losses to one class of benefit arising as the consequence of delivering some other class of benefit.

To the extent, for example, that commercial tourism reduces the benefits of private recreation, that reduction is properly treated as a cost attributable to commercial tourism. The management plan emerging from such a standard economic approach could involve ongoing environmental deterioration. In relation to use of the area for tourism, it would not, therefore, satisfy the definition of sustainable tourism given above.

Meeting that definition would require that the maximisation objective be constrained by the condition that natural capital stocks be maintained intact. Insistence on such constraints arises from the ecological economics approach. In protected areas there are, by definition, constraints in place which are intended to serve the conservation criterion.

Whether the constraints in place in any area are sufficient to realise the conservation objective is an empirical question. The context for tourism in protected areas is as an activity in competition with other potential uses. To the extent that tourism is considered more environmentally benign than other potential uses, it becomes a favoured use. This is evidenced in the many protected areas where extractive uses are banned or limited and tourism is allowed to continue.

In such situations, investment in management to avoid or repair damage is the only way to provide for sustainable use where the tourism activity potentially causes impacts. Critical to the whole issue is whether impacts are able to *be* ameliorated by adequate management or are irreversible.

Tourism to the Case Study Great Barrier Reef WHA and the Wet Tropics WHA

The Great Barrier Reef Marine Park was established in 1975 and the area was inscribed onto the World Heritage List in 1981. The Great Barrier Reef WHA covers an area of 344,000 square kilometres adjacent to the north-east coast of Australia. The rainforests of mainland north-east Australia are represented in the Wet Tropics WHA. This WHA came into effect in 1988. It is 9000 square kilometres in size. Amongst the features which cause this area to be of World Heritage status are the occurrence of representatives of 13 of the world's 19 families of primitive flowering plants. At some places on the coast, where the rainforest meets the fringing reefs, the two WHAs lie side-by-side. Both areas satisfied all four of the criteria of outstanding universal value for inclusion in the World Heritage List.

In both WHAs protection of the natural environment is the primary management objective. The Great Barrier Reef WHA is managed as a multiple use area, with the major uses being commercial tourism, private recreation and commercial fishing. The Great Barrier Reef Marine Park Authority is a Commonwealth Government agency with responsibility for managing the area, in association with the State of Queensland's Department of Environment and Heritage. With the creation of the Wet Tropics WHA, logging of the rainforest was banned. The current major activities in the area are commercial tourism and private recreation. A number of transport, water storage and municipal functions continue. The Wet Tropics Management Authority is a government agency of the State of Queensland and operates in association with the State's Department of Environment and Heritage and the Department of Primary Industries' Forest Service. The congruence of the attractive and interesting natural environments of reef and rainforest, in a tropical setting, has made the region of coastal north-east Australia a very popular tourist destination. When interviewed, tourists to the area nominate the climate, the Great Barrier Reef, and increasingly, the rainforest as the major attractions of the area. Domestic tourism from other parts of Australia is the backbone of the tourist industry. The most popular months to visit are in the Australian winter, as the majority of Australians live south of this tropical area. Visitors from overseas are making up an increasing percentage of visitors.

Most visitors to the Great Barrier Reef WHA visit by boat on day trips departing from coastal towns in North Queensland. Boat sizes range from those carrying less than ten passengers, providing SCUBA diving, sailing or game fishing trips; to vessels which carry 300 to 400 passengers on day trips to permanently moored pontoons at reef sites. These trips offer the activities of snorkelling, SCUBA diving and reef viewing from glass-sided semi-submersible vessels. In addition, there are tourist resorts on a number of the islands within the Great Barrier Reef WHA. Recreational fishing and boating is popular with local residents, using a fleet of over 24,000 small privately-owned boats.

People who visit the Wet Tropics WHA also mainly visit on day trips. They may drive themselves (in their own cars or hire cars) or take a commercial tour. Transport on commercial tours is provided by 4WD vehicles, minibuses, coaches, river boats and a scenic train.

Tourism to both WHAs has increased dramatically in the last decade. The number of visitor days spent on the Great Barrier Reef and the number of vessels supplying commercial trips have doubled in ten years. Around two million visits were made on commercial tours in 1994 (Driml, 1994). It is estimated there were 4.7 million visits to individual sites in the Wet Tropics WHA in 1993 (Manidis Roberts, 1994). The city of Cairns is the most used departure point for reef trips and is the largest source of accommodation for visitors to the Wet Tropics WHA. Predictions for tourism to the Cairns region are for a doubling over the years from 1993 to the year 2001 (Office of the Co-ordinator General, 1993).

It is estimated that tourists and local residents visiting for recreation spend approximately $A776 million per annum in the local economies so that they can visit the Great Barrier Reef WHA. An additional $A377 million per annum is spent by visitors to the Wet Tropics WHA. These estimates are based on expenditure on commercial trips and private recreation trips into the WHAs plus accommodation in adjacent areas: they do not include the cost of travel to North Queensland. Together, the WHAs provide a resource base for an industry worth over $A1.1 billion in gross expenditure terms (Driml, 1994). The financial value of tourism is much greater than other competing active uses in these two WHAs. Some other active uses have been prohibited in both areas; mining and oil drilling in the Great Barrier Reef WHA and logging in the Wet Tropics WHA. The catalyst for the establishment of the Great Barrier Reef Marine Park was a concern that prospective exploratory drilling for oil would damage the reef. As a result, the potential oil reserves have not been investigated, so that the opportunity cost of prohibiting oil exploration and possible production is not known. The continuation of logging of rainforest in the Wet Tropics WHA was not seen as compatible with conservation and so logging was banned in the area in 1987. The gross value of sales of sawn timber from the region was in the order of $A25 million per annum at the time (Driml, 1991). Logging quotas were anyway due to decline as a result of scientific advice that yields from virgin rainforests were declining, so there was little prospect for timber industry growth. The growth in rainforest tourism in the last decade has resulted in the situation where today the annual gross expenditure on tourism is ten times the gross value of timber production in 1987, in real terms.

Management of the WHAs

The creation of the Great Barrier Reef Marine Park in 1975 and its listing as a World Heritage Area in 1981 predated the popularisation of the notion of sustainable development by Brundtland (World Commission on Environment and Development, 1987). Management of the Great Barrier Reef as a protected area has worked towards similar aims to those promoted via this newer terminology (Kelleher & Driml, 1988). The Wet Tropics WHA is a more recent creation but prior to listing, much of the area was managed as National Park or State Forest and the management of tourism in these areas also had similar aims...

Prohibited Uses

Underpinning management of these two WHAs is legislation that promotes multiple-use within a sustainability constraint. However, as already noted, some uses of the areas are banned by legislation — mining or oil drilling in the Great Barrier Reef WHA and logging in the Wet Tropics WHA. Some activities in which reef tourists may wish to indulge are banned by legislation; these are spear fishing on SCUBA and taking fish over a certain length. The relevant legislation requires all other uses to be controlled so as to be consistent with conservation of the natural environment.

Zoning Plans

For both WHAs, zoning is used as a primary management tool. Zoning plans are developed in consultation with users and other interested members of the community. The entire Great Barrier Reef Marine Park has been divided into four sections and zoned, with reviews of zoning occurring every five to ten years. The draft of the first zoning plan for the Wet Tropics WHA was released for public comment in October 1995. The following discussion is therefore largely based on experience with the Great Barrier Reef Marine Park.

Zoning controls tourism by delineating where it is excluded and where it is an allowed activity, subject to commercial tour operators obtaining a permit. Some areas of the Great Barrier Reef Marine Park are set aside as Preservation and Scientific Research Zones and are not to be entered for general tourism and recreation. Some areas are closed on a seasonal basis to protect nesting birds and turtles. Some areas are zoned for no commercial or recreational fishing and therefore are the equivalent of terrestrial National Parks in Australia. These areas are open to tourism and recreation of the 'look but don't take' type. Other areas allow fishing with controls and are thus available for fishing by tourists and local people. In some areas tourist infrastructure, mainly consisting of permanently moored pontoons, is allowed. Other areas are zoned for 'no structures' and are therefore open only to vessels anchoring on a daily basis.

Management Plans

Management plans provide a further level of control between broad zoning and individual operator permits. The need for management plans to guide decisions on use has arisen mainly due to increased demand for tourism to specific sites, in both WHAs. Management plans can specify sites available for particular uses, and limits on numbers of people and activities. Management plans have been developed for some individual reefs and islands, or groups of such, for the

Great Barrier Reef, and more are scheduled. Draft plans are being developed for areas within the Wet Tropics WHA. Public participation is a feature of plan development in both WHAs. In both cases, the management plan is the place where issues have to be façed about reducing current levels of tourism or at least restricting future growth. Delays have been experienced in finalising management plans in both WHAs due in part to the need to take hard decisions, often in the absence of conclusive information on ecological or amenity limits.

Permits

All tourist operations in both WHAs require permits. Permits are the means by which precise control is exercised over actual sites of operation, numbers of people allowed at sites, and conditions of operation. In the Great Barrier Reef WHA, permit requirements have evolved over time and reflect scientific knowledge about actions that can be taken to minimise environmental impact The conditions on any individual permit reflect the complexity of the operation and potential impacts. Examples of permit conditions include requirements that permanent moorings be installed at sites to prevent the damage done when vessels use anchors on a daily basis. Another condition is a requirements for larger vessels to have holding tanks for sewage so that there is no discharge at reef sites. Such conditions are being applied where relevant.

Proposals for larger tourism operations that involve permanently anchored structures require formal environmental impact assessment before any approval is given. Operators may be required to post performance bonds that cover the cost of removal and rehabilitation should the structure be damaged or abandoned. Operators may also be required to fund scientifically designed monitoring programmes. In the Great Barrier Reef WHA, permits for tourist operations have a life of six years and are transferable, subject to the operation remaining substantially the same.

Entry Fees

Entry fees charged on commercial tourist operations are used to collect funds for management. They are not intended to ration use, and at 1 to 2% of average trip price, are not high enough to have this effect. In the Great Barrier Reef Marine Park, the charge is $1 per head. In the Wet Tropics WHA, the charge is $1.15 per visitor who spends up to three hours in the protected area and $2.30 for visits of more than three hours. Fees collected in the Great Barrier Reef Marine Park are allocated in a transparent manner between park management and research. Tourist industry representatives form the majority on the board that allocates the research funds.

Industry Participation

Tourist industry participation in management takes a number of forms. Individual operators and industry associations have input into the development of Zoning and Management Plans, industry is represented on Consultative Committees, and the Wet Tropics WHA has an informal tourism liaison group" that meets regularly with managers. Within industry, moves are being made towards developing self-regulation and accreditation schemes. The tourist industry as a whole supports the principles of conservation and minimising environmental impacts. There is, however, a general expectation that the industry will expand.

Facility Provision

A major management tool in the Wet Tropics WHA is the provision of infrastructure which allows access to sites of interest but which contains impacts to 'hardened' sites. Over the last five years, a sum of $A10 million has been invested in capital works to bring facilities up to standard for current visitor numbers, whilst minimising environmental damage. The infrastructure provided includes new or improved boardwalks, tracks, day use areas, camping grounds, roads and visitor information centres. On the Great Barrier Reef, a programme of installing public boat moorings at sensitive sites has commenced. Much of the infrastructure for tourists at reef sites is provided by commercial tour operators.

Conservation of the Existing Natural Environment

For both WHAs, the physical area actually used for tourist activities is a small proportion of the total protected areas. For example, the Great Barrier Reef WHA contains 2900 individual reefs and 950 islands. There are resorts on 22 islands. The number of vessels with permits to conduct tourist operations is around 540. The operations of these vessels are concentrated on reefs which are at a return day trip distance from major ports. The Draft Wet Tropics Plan identifies current tourism infrastructure nodes at less than 1% of the area and areas surrounding roads at less than 2% of the area (WTMA, 1995).

A recent review of the impacts of tourism in the Great Barrier Reef WHA brought together published information and the observations of users and scientists (Carey, 1993). The information available is the result of a number of projects conducted over the last decade.

The facilities and activities associated with tourism may potentially cause a variety of types of impact. A list of those identified by Carey for the Great Barrier Reef WHA include:

- site impacts from structures, moorings and anchoring
- coral damage from diving and reef walking
- removal of coral and shells
- garbage disposal and littering
- sediment disturbance and dredging
- water pollution — nutrients
- heavy metal pollution

— oil pollution
— sewage discharge from vessels
— sewage discharge from island resorts
— impacts on bird and turtle nesting
— fishing impacts
— fish feeding impacts
— impacts of research and monitoring

In the Wet Tropics WHA, tourism is concentrated in a few areas with road access and within a return day trip distance from Caims. This includes some of the last coastal rainforest remaining (after clearing for agriculture and residential use) and there is concern that this area may be vulnerable to impacts exacerbated by tourism, including road kills of the fauna and minor clearing inadvertently reducing the populations of rare flora. There is only one reported study on impacts of tourism — on impacts of walking tracks (Graham, 1994) — and minimal ongoing scientific monitoring of sites. No comprehensive assessment has yet been conducted of the impacts of tourism in the Wet Tropics WHA.

A Non-declining Stream of Net Economic Benefits

In order to historically evaluate tourism against this criteria, one would need time series data on net economic benefits for the two WHAs. Such data are not available. A full data set would identify: economic benefits to tourists and commercial operators, costs of running commercial operations, expenditure on management, and estimates of the economic value of any environmental damage that is not ameliorated. Only with this information can the full social benefits and costs of tourism, and trends in these, be assessed.

In respect of future tourism, several actions would need to be taken in order to at least establish the conditions for non-declining net benefits. Due to the presence of external effects of tourism on the environment, and on other tourism, the market cannot be relied on to deliver net economic benefits and so management action is warranted. Two actions are suggested.

The first is to ensure adequate investment in management of the type described in the section on 'Management of the WHAs' so that all the constraints to minimise environmental impact are maintained. Adequate investment in management to maintain the quality of the protected area both for natural environment values and as a resource for tourism, is critical to sustainability. The criteria of non-declining net economic benefits requires that attention be paid to costs of management (whether funded by the private or public sector). Better documentation of who pays for management, and who benefits, will allow more informed assessment of the most equitable and efficient ways of funding management. Currently, Government provides over 95% of the funding for management of the WHAs (Driml, 1994). This funding may not be adequate to maintain environmental quality. The Great Barrier Reef Marine Park Authority is concerned that funding is not keeping up with the management demands resulting from increases in levels of use (GBRMPA, 1993). Opportunities exist for a greater contribution from tourists and the tourist industry to management costs. However, it should be recognised that the imposition of regulation to avoid environmental damage has the effect of operators to take out performance bonds is an economic instrument requires them to bear a greater proportion of the true risk of operating in a protected area. The entry fees currently charged are nominal and neither regulate use nor raise a significant proportion of management funds. There may be scope for raising entrance fees without reducing visitor numbers. Research into demand functions would provide managers with information on the likely effects of different levels of fees on visitor numbers. The managers of the WHAs have not yet made any move to capture resource rent by other means, for example, by auctioning permits.

All operators have been awarded permits on application

or have purchased permits along with businesses (allowing the original operators to capture any rent). In an environment where there are increasing limits being placed on use and increasing demand for use, the potential for generation of resource rent exists. The option of capturing resource rent and using this for management should be investigated.

The suggested second action is to pay attention to the nature of demand for tourism in the WHAs with a view to managing for quality of experience. In the case of the two WHAs, it can be expected that the interest in nature-based tourism that is evident internationally and in Australia (Commonwealth Department of Tourism, 1994) will continue to support tourism demand for these areas. Demand for particular destinations can change, however, if affected by perceptions of the destination as crowded, excessively developed or suffering environmental damage (Butler, 1980).

The issue of maintaining the attractiveness of sites is important to maintaining non-declining net benefits. The negative effects of crowding and excessive infrastructure development are generally externalities to individual tour operators and so market processes cannot be depended upon to optimise tourism development. In addition to, or instead of, controls for environmental conservation *per se,* management agencies together with tourist operators might need to set limits on use and development in order to retain attractiveness. It is likely that there is a range of demands from tourists for different 'settings', from wilderness to more intensive use. The Draft Wet Tropics Plan incorporates a recreational opportunity spectrum (Clarke & Stankey, 1979) which describes appropriate settings and activities in areas designated to different opportunity classes.

The management agencies of both WHAs have recognised the need to maintain attractiveness to visitors. Several research projects currently underway are aimed at better understanding the demands and perceptions of visitors and how they might react to different levels of visitor numbers or infrastructure. It is important to note that it is not only the number of visitors to an area that is relevant to net economic benefits. The price visitors are prepared to pay is also relevant. Some visitors will be prepared to pay a premium to visit 'wilderness' or secluded sites, so limiting numbers does not necessarily limit revenue earned.

Summing Up

It is imperative that any tourism allowed in these areas be sustainable in terms of the natural environment and very desirable that it be sustainable in terms of net economic benefits. As Australia is a developed country, with a commitment to ecologically sustainable development and considerable scientific expertise available, it should have an advantage in getting management of tourism in protected areas 'right' in terms of sustainability. When management of tourism in the Great Barrier Reef and Wet Tropics WHAs is judged against the criteria for sustainability put forward in this paper, no conclusive findings can be made. The intention is clearly there to manage tourism to minimise impacts while allowing visitors to enjoy access. However, evaluation of outcomes is limited.

If the first criteria for sustainability put forward in this paper is to be applied, it is critical that management agencies have the information to manage so as not to deplete natural capital. Monitoring and research on environmental impacts of tourism has to date been *ad hoc,* though better progressed in the Great Barrier Reef WHA. There is evidence that the situation will improve through the research efforts of the new Cooperative Research Centres. At a broad level, it seems that tourism in the Great Barrier Reef WHA is sustainable in terms of natural capital. There is very little objective evidence in respect of the Wet Tropics WHA. However, the facts of the small area actually visited and the recent large investment in infrastructure to minimise biophysical impacts, could be taken as suggesting that the area's natural capital is not currently threatened.

Information is not being collected to allow an assessment of whether the benefits of allowing tourism outweigh the costs, or what the trends are in this respect. A critical feature for meeting both criteria is adequate investment in management, including research and monitoring, to support tourism. If the costs of necessary management begin to outweigh the benefits of tourism, the desirability of tourism should be questioned. Similarly, if net benefits decline due to reductions in amenity, management agencies should take action to find a better balance. Currently the agencies are not collecting the information to assess the net economic outcomes of their investments and policies.

REFERENCES

Butler, R.W. (1980) The concept of a tourist area cycle of evolution: Implications for management of resources. *Canadian Geographer* 24 (1), 5-12.

Carey, J. (1993) *Review of Management of Impacts of Commercial Tourism and Private Recreation in the Great Barrier Reef Marine Park.* Report to the Great Barrier Reef Marine Park Authority, Townsville.

Clarke, R. and Stankey, G. (1979) *The Recreation Opportunity Spectrum: A framework for Planning, Management and Research.* US Department of Agriculture and Forest Service Pacific Northwest Forest and Range Experiment Station, General Technical Report PNW-98.

Common, M. (1995) *Sustainability and Policy: Limits to Economics.* Sydney-Cambridge University Press.

Commonwealth of Australia (1991) *Ecologically Sustainable Development Working Group Final Report: Tourism.* Canberra: Australian Government Publishing Service.

Costanza, R. (1989) What is ecological economics? *Ecological Economics* 1 (1) 1-7

Dixon, J.A. and Sherman, P.B. (1990) *Economics of Protected Areas: A New Look at Benefits and Costs.* London: Earthscan.

Driml, S.M. (1991) Research needs for rainforest economics. In N. Goudberg, M. Bonell with D. Benzaken (eds) *Tropical Rainforest Research in Australia.* Townsville: Institute of Tropical Rainforest Studies.

Great Barrier Reef Marine Park Authority (1993) *Annual Report* 1992-1993. Townsville. Great Barrier Reef Marine Park Authority.

Hunter, C.J. (1995) On the need to re-conceptualise sustainable tourism development. *Journal of Sustainable Tourism 3* (3), 155-65.

Kelleher, G.G. and Driml, S.M. (1988) Environmental limits to tourism in the Great Barrier Reef Marine Park. In B. Faulkner and M. Fagence (eds) *Frontiers of Australian Tourism*. Bureau of Tourism Research, Canberra.

Manidis Roberts Consultants (1994) *Data Summary 1993 Visitor Use Survey Wet Topics World Heritage Area*. Report to the Wet Tropics Management Authority, Cairns. Office of the Co-ordinator General (1993) *Cairns Region Tourism Strategy*. Brisbane: Office of the Co-ordinator General.

Pearce, D., Markandya, A. and Barbier, E. (1989) *Blueprint for a Green Economy*. London: Earthscan Publications.

Pigram, J. (1990) Sustainable tourism: Policy considerations. *Journal of Tourism Studies* 1

Wet Tropics Management Authority (1995) *Draft Wet Tropics Plan* WTMA, Cairns.

World Commission on Environment and Development (1987) *Our Common Future* Oxford: Oxford University Press.

8

Wildlife Tourism: A Case of Central Himalaya

Wildlife

Wilderness is a necessity said, John Muir, the sage of Sierra. Thoreau thought the health of civilisation needed the tonic of the wild. Since time immemorial man got inspiration from nature in improving his ways of living and maintaining coordination with surroundings. Frank Smythe found that the hills had a capacity for welding into a harmonious whole the physical, mental and spiritual qualities of man. Such are the qualities of wilderness that man forgets his sorrows, pains and miseries with its closeness. As one passes through hills, dales and mountains, the journey becomes a discovery of new things and self-realisation.

The ancient Hindu sages believed in the healing touch of nature and regarded communion with nature as spiritually elevating. Technical advancement and modernisation are forcing man to think and respect nature as a cure to all kinds of ills that afflict man today. Hence the varied flora and fauna of the region are becoming one of the main attractions for the tourists.

Flora

Hill Area Development Board (1987-88) report has stated the total area of Chamoli and Uttarkashi districts were 906 and 801 thousand hectares respectively. Out of this the area under forest cover was 527 and 710 thousand hectares." The remaining area was under cultivation. The great chunk of uncultivated area can be utilised for wildlife tourism and recreation without disturbing the eco-system.

Thus, the forest of the region can be divided into four zones on the basis of characteristics:

1. The central zone;
2. The northern zone;
3. The northern bush land; and
4. Alpine meadows

1. Central Zone: The central zone of the region is densely populated and cultivated; hence it is more or less devoid of forests and other wildlife. Wherever there is forest it is dominated by chir pine. Other species, which frequently occur with chir, are amla, sandan, timla and kath-mahwa. But in upper reaches of this zone, blue pine often associated with banj, oak and maple is found in abundance. This vegetation is commonly found in both the districts. Moru or tilong is found between 1800 and 2750 m. The kharsu is found between 2200 and 3000 m, Burans the queen of hills is widely distributed in all oak forests mixed with blue pine. The red flowers of burans change the forest scenery from February to April. Ringal an undergrowth companion of banj and kharsu, makes the forest dense. Rich epiphytic moss, lichen and ferns decor the forest most. Panger (Himalayan horse chestnut), silver fir, spruce, locally known as raga and rausala are also found in this altitude abundantly.

2. Northern Zone: The Northern zone is also full of varied flora. In fact it has the richest vegetation of Garhwal. Himalayan oak still dominates the scene; others are burans (*Rhododendron arboreurn*), silver fir (*Abies pindrow*), spruce (*Picea smithiana*), cypress (*Cypressus Jarulosa*) and blue pine etc. When oak starts disappearing Pangar (*Aesculus indica*), kabasi (*Corylusja cquemontii*), kanjula (*Acer caesium*) and ringal (*A. jaunsarensis*) take its place. Ferns, lichen and creepers are abundantly found here. Forest of Har-ki-doon, Tuni, Dodital, Belakkhal, Dingad valley, Yamunotri, Gangotri, Kedar Ganga valley. Wan, Nandprayag, Kedarnath valley,' Tungnath, Rudranath, Ukhimath, Deoriatal, Valley of Flowers and outer Nanda Devi sanctuary etc are the finest examples of this forest. Fir and spruce are densely found from Rudraprayag to Pipalkoti and Ramm to Dibrugheta. Botanical Survey of India and other reports revealed that more than 200 species of Gymnosperms; 180 species of Angiosperms grow in the Nanda Devi National Park." Mr. Batten was surprised to see the oaks of Niti and deodars of Malari valley. Rhododendron dwarfs of Ruinsaratal, Dodital (Uttarkashi district), Kuari pass, Tungnath and Rudranath (Chamoli district) with crimson and mauve flowers change the scenery entirely. Marco Polo praised the vegetation of Dhagirathi valley.

3. *Northern Bush Land:* This is the zone where the tree line ends up with bushes and difficult inhospitable terrain starts along with cold climate (annual precipitation less than 25 cm). But nature's bounty of rich flora attracts people to make a visit. The flora is a xerophytes shrub and bushes scattered thinly all over the earth surface. Safed Purcha (*Artemisia maritima*), Kala Purcha (*A. scarorum*) and Jhaura (*Caragana pygmaea*) occur in between 2750 and 3700 in above sea level. There are-three species of Juniper (*Juniper pseudosabina. Juniper communis* and *Juniper macropoda*). Juniper is the most affected flora by human and animal interference at this altitude. It is easy to ignite even when it is green. Dimar (*Caragana pygmaea*) is common found flora of this zone. Rhododendron bush also appears in this zone. Being aromatic it is used for making joss sticks.

The most suitable time to visit this zone is from mid June to the first week of September every year.

4. *Alpine Meadows:* Meadows of Garhwal are situated in between the bush line and the permanent snow line. Here

the land is most rugged, but abounds of Himalayan grasses, herbs and floral plants. Scanty juniper and rhododendron bushes are found here too. Though altitudinally the Alpine pasture land varies from place to place due to physiographical conditions, but they are generally found in between 3500 and 4900 m above the sea level in Garhwal. It snows there in the month of November and it temains a frozen hostile wasteland for six months. Later from mid April snow starts melting. With brief rain showers the wasteland gets transformed into a miraculous valley of flowers.

Primarily, Garhwal is famous for its Alpine meadows. Most popular are Har-ki-doon, Ruinsara tal, Dayara, Belakkhal, Kush-Kalyani, Tapovan, Nandanvan in Uttarkashi district and Auli, Gorson Auli, Vedni, Bistola, Kuari pass, Madamaheshwar, Rudranath, Tungnath, Valley of Flowers, Hemkund-Lokpal, Nanda Devi outer sanctuary and Manpai in Chamoli district. These beautiful calm and quite places provide a unique and fine retreat, an Eden of flowers to the visitors of scorched plains. Highly nutritious marrila grass locally known as buggi, grows in these high pasturelands. Hence these Pastures are locally known as Bugyals. These grasses bear highly aromatic flowers. Most common among them are Potentialla and blue Primula deliculata. Smythe identified nine spices of Primula in Garhwal, Sexifraga, Forget-me-not, Iris, Marsh-Merry gold. Yellow Buttercups, Pink Geranium, Blue Gentian, Prime rose, Poppy, Rosace, Deep red Thymes, Yellow stripped Slipper Orchid, Blue Delphinium, Aster, Daise, Red Straw Berry, Sedum, Anemone, Brahma Kamal, Globe flower, Himalayan yellow Poppy, Polygonum Affine, Himalayan Lily, Himalayan Rose, Cobra Lily, Jacob's Ladder, Fritilaries and dark purple Monks hood etc. These flowers are densely distributed in the meadows of Garhwal. Mr. Holds worth does some candid speaking when he says, "Let me confess at the outset that as the botanist of the Kamet expedition of 1931, l am an imposter. My qualifications for the post are wholly inadequate, and my opportunities for doing the job thoroughly were naturally rather meager. These flowers are generally found in most of the pastures in Garhwal Himalaya. These flowers in glacial valleys, moraines, under rocks, ledges and crannies present the views of most beautiful rock gardens of earth. August-September is the most suitable time to visit these Alpine pasturelands. End of September is the seeding time, the frost and snow later burn all the flora of this heavenly region and ends the floral life. These pastures are the real Himalayan holiday resorts imparting lots of things to explore, enjoy and recreation.

Fauna

Northern areas of Garhwal are rich in varied fauna. Here the fauna adapts itself to enjoy the ecological factors like cold, aridity, snow cover and humidity with the increase in altitude. The fine adaptability is clearly visible in their body cover (hair/feather and colour) that provides resistance to insolation and radiation. The forest of pine, oak, blue pine, rhododendron, cypress, fir, spruce, birch, juniper, ringal and the Alpine meadows provide an ideal habitat for wild animals and singing birds.

Animals: The most commonly found animals are langur, red monkey, brown bear, black bear, common fox, leopard, snow leopard, barking dear, sambar, musk dear, serow, porcupine, tahretc. Butterflies of different colours and sizes and beetles are also found in this area.

Birds: The higher region of Garhwal is full of colourful singing avifauna. Most commonly found are-Himalayan whistling thrush, Himalayan golden crest, western variegated laughing thrush, monal and koklas pheasant, partridge, Himalayan golden eagle, Himalayan bearded vulture and snow partridge etc.

Fish: Besides the rich mammals and avifauna, higher Himalayan water bodies of Garhwal are rich in aquatic life also. The river and streams abound in fishes. Most common are mahaseer (Indian salmon), Indian trout and goonch (fresh water shark), kalabans, pharkata and chilwa. Alaknanda, Mandakini, Pinder, Bhagirathi and Yamuna are the ideal habitat for fresh water fish but rivers and lakes of upper Garhwal abound in the Himalayan trout.

In facts, the rulers of Garhwal made fish hatcheries in 1910, one in Kalyani (Uttarkashi district) and the other at Tilwari (Chamoli district) by procuring a consignment of eyed ova of brown trout (*Salmo frutta fario*) from Kashmir. In 1951 these hatcheries were transferred to Animal Husbandry Department of U.P., but the condition of these hatcheries started deteriorating and the stock of fish went down. Now there is a separate Directorate of Fisheries and both the hatcheries come under the Assistant Director of Fisheries, Uttarkashi. In Talwari the original stock of trout perished which was replaced by the seed of rainbow trout (Salmotrutta gairdner). For flora and fauna some areas of these two districts of Garhwal are very famous.

NATIONAL PARKS

At present Parks are becoming very popular, when life has become very much mechanical and lethargic in the cities. Park resources—flora and fauna are very much in demand list of the tourists. Parks are part of large tourism recreation conservation system. Tourism development also is part of a large tourism recreation conservation system. It depends as much on the identification and protection of natural and cultural resources as it does upon the building facilities. According to Indian Board of Wildlife, "A National Park is an area dedicated by state for all time to conserve natural and historical objects of national significance and wildlife and where provision is made for enjoyment of the same by the public.

Two national parks are there in Chamoli district. Valley of Flowers and Nanda Devi are world famous for their beauty."

(a) Govind National Park

In 1955 Upper Tons valley was declared as Govind Pashu Vihar (sanctuary), after the name of Pandit Govind Ballabh Pant. Later in 1990, it was notified as national park, comprising the·whole of Supin range in the Tons forest division. The area of 953 sq kms is a thick forest of pine, blue pine, oak, rhododendron, fir, spruce, deodar, cypress, rhododendron dwarf, birch and Alpine herbs and shrubs. The inhabiting animals are-common fox, langur, wildcat, red monkey, Himalayan black bear, brown bear, barking deer, sambar, musk deer, Indian marten, leopard, serow, thar, marmot and snow leopard. Snow leopard is declared as an endangered species, and a plan to protect the snow leopard is reportedly proposed.

Game Birds: Among the game birds monal pheasant, westerner horned pheasant, cheer pheasant, peura partridge, khalij pheasant, chukor and black partridge are the main attractions. At higher altitudes red billed and yellow billed chough, snow pigeon, Himalayan nut-cracker (specially in blue pine forest) are the main attractions for bird watchers. But at moderate heights red-billed babbler, blue magpie, whistling thrush, red-billed scarlet, minivet, verditer forest, perhaps the finest of all the Himalayan song birds) are commonly found Flycatchers and gray-winged black bird commonly found.

Har-ki-doon valley has a perfect backdrop of snowy mountain peaks and dense forest of pine, deodar and other coniferous that meet the vast stretches of meadows. It is said that Bhog Daft, a great warrior of Mahabharata who fought against the pandavas, resided here. It is therefore, that Duryodhana, the eldest of the Kaurava is worshipped in Tons valley. The best time to visit is from June to September. The altitude variation in the park is from 1400 to 6100 m. From May to August one can see the wild flora of the park in full bloom. Marshall described the wilderness as, "Timeless dimensionless, all encompassing dynamic uncluttered by the artist's conception and a form of beauty that gratifies all the senses." But with the arrival of winter (cold, frost and wind) most of the flora bums and all the pastures get tanned. A cloudless sky gives an opportunity to enjoy the wide scenery of white wealth of the nature.

(b) Valley of Flowers National Park

Mr. Frank Smythe, the famous mountaineer, first discovered Bhyunder valley widely known as the *Valley of Flowers* in eastern Garhwal in Chamoli district. He was so much fascinated with this expedition, in valley that he later returned and collected many species of flowers. He has recorded his thrill in his book entitled, *'The Valley of Flowers'*. This 8 kms long and 2 kms wide valley is full of colourful flowers of different sizes, shapes and aroma. The surroundings are unique. On the north of this valley stand cliffs 2000 m high and on the northeast is the beautiful mountain Rataban, that catches the attention of the visitors and gives perfection to the scenery. Smythe rightly says, "...No photographer can do justice to the grandeur and ethereal beauty of such scene." The wide stretches of northern slopes are decorated with silver birch punctuated with Alpine meadows; the southern slopes are carpeted with lush green grass and colourful flowers. In fact the valley lies in between Bhyunder Kantha pass (5090 m) and Khuntakhal pass (4425 m), from Baminidhar (3560 m) to the base of Rataban peak (6166 m). The entire valley falls into the Bhyunder-Ganga catchment area and covers Hemkund-Lokpal, Pushpavati valley and its tributaries. The scenery and flora changes from Ghangaria (a halting place enroute to Valley of Flowers). It is 5 kms from Bhyunder village. From here the real ascent starts with terrific natural beauty. It is a very beautiful valley with magnificent forest and tumbling streams. In 1981 the valley was declared as one of the Hiamalayan national parks; The 3.5 kms trek from Ghangaria to the Valley of Flowers is most enchanting. The forest of silver birch merges into the green stretches, decorated with colourful flowers, mud, boulders, rivulets, rocky cliffs and white mountains. Some of the flowers of the valley are Potentilla (*P. afgyrophylla*) in red, yellow and orange colours. Primula minutissima. Primula nivalis. Primula stuartii. Anemone (*A. obtusiloba*). Gentian (*Gentian stipitata*), Androsace (*A. rotundifolia*), monk's hood (*Aconitum heterophyllum*), purple ipomea (*Ipomea purpurea*), globe-flower (*Trolluis acaulis*), musk thistle (*Carduus nutans*), cream yellow Himalayan lily (*Lilium oxypetalum*). Himalayan rose (*Rosa macrophylla*), snowy Lindelofia (*Lindelofiaspectabilis*), cobra lily (*Arisaema costatum*), Jacob's ladder (*Polemonium caeruleum*), Himalayan yellow poppy (*Meconopsis paniculata*), Wallich's blue poppy (*Meconopsis wallichii*), Saxifraga (*S. flagellaris*) and Ids (*L kumaonensis*).

The nature's Eden changes its hue and, colour weekly, fortnightly and some times daily. The life-span of flowers varies from few days to months. In the month of May snow tends to melt and seed sprouting begins, June watches the small plants with buds and few flowers, July witnesses the blossom but August is lucky enough to see the valley in prime youth and colours. So are the lucky visitors of August as they watch the youthful valley. From September onwards the colours and youth of the coloured valley starts fading and the arrival of dry autumn heralds the decay and decomposition. October comes with frost and cold and tans the valley and again it becomes an isolated, desolate pocket of earth. The most suitable time to visit the valley is mid August.

(c) Kedarnath Musk Deer Park

The forest of Kedarnath valley this valley is a paradise on such a high altitude. Musk deer is the most sought-after animal of the valley. With a view to protect this endangered animal this valley was declared as musk deer sanctuary in 1972. The area of the sanctuary is 967.2 sq kms and the entire sanctuary lies in Kedarnath forest division. Therefore it is named as Kedamath musk deer sanctuary. Kedarnath shrine and other old temples-Trijuginarayan, Madmaheshwar,

Tungnath, Rudranath and Ansuya Devi are also situated within the bounds of this sanctuary, the Chamoli-Ukhimath motor road skirts this sanctuary from the south and serves as an excellent approach road for the sanctuary.

Flora: The beautiful thick forests along with road and the valley are the main attraction. Here pine grows up to 2000 m but moist hillsides are clad with oak. Above this, the forest mainly comprises deodar, fir, spruce, thuner, cypress and blue pine. Among broad-leaved trees rhododendron, walnut, oak and horse chest-nut are the main species. But birch occurs after coniferous forest. Above this lies rhododendron dwarfs, juniper and other thorny bushes. In between the bush line and permanent snow line lies the pastureland which abounds in a number of medicinal, aromatic and other plants.

Birds: Among avifauna khalij, koklas and monal pheasants, snow partridge are fairly common. Hunting and poaching have created a critical condition for the birds. Monal pheasant and musk deer are declared as endangered species. A drive from Ukhimath to Mandal is most fascinating. A man who has ever been to that area can never forget that dense mixed forest of oak, blue pine, cypress, fir, rhododendron and birch. One shivers even in the month of June due to cold. The beautiful earth slopes of Chopta can be used for snow ski in winter.

Fauna: Due to varying climate and vegetation a large number of wild animals are found all over the sanctuary. Up to 3000 m above the sea level, barking deer, sambar, wildcat, panther, black bear, ghoral and wild boar are found. Above 3000 m Himalayan thar, bharal, snow leopard, musk dear, serow, ghoral and Himalayan brown bear are found.

(d) Nanda Devi National Park

Nanda Devi National Park is situated at 30° 16'-30° 32' N and 79° 49-80° 21 E with an area of 800 sq kms. This park is drained by the Rishi Ganga and is clustered between the glaciers of Gangotri and Milam. Nanda Devi is the second highest peak of India. Altitude variation of the sanctuary is from 2100 to 7817 m. The whole area is known as Nanda Devi sanctuary, a name first bestowed on it by Mr. Ruttledge of Everest fame. Eric Shipton and Bill Tillman took years to get into the sanctuary through Rishi Ganga. Finally in 1934 they got success in penetrating the sanctuary and reached at the height of 6227 m. Later in 1936 H. Tillman and N.E. Odell of Anglo-American expedition got success in reaching the summit.

It was the cherished dream of world mountaineers. In 1939 at the Instance of Shipton and Tillman the 182.63 sq kms of Nanda Devi basin was declared as Nanda Devi Wildlife sanctuary. A huge amphitheatre of mountain range, offering ice walls, demarcates the cup-shaped sanctuary; corniced ridges and almost seventy named and unnamed peaks. The sanctuary has got two horseshoe shapes, one outer sanctuary and the other inner sanctuary. The outer sanctuary is a dense mixed forest, which has Alpine pasture lands adorned, by beautiful seasonal colourful flowers. The inner sanctuary includes a number of high peaks and major glacier system. It consists of Ramini, Changabang and north Rishi glacier in the north and south Nanda Devi glacier, south Rishi, Trisul, Bethartoli, Round and Nanda Ghunti glacier in the south. Each glacier system gives rise to streams and all the streams end in Rishi stream. Ultimately this enters the awe-some lower gorge guarded by overhanging cliffs, and skirts Lata Peak to merge with the Dhauli Ganga near Reni village. Some of the well-known peaks from west to east are Dunagiri (7066 m), Changabang (6864 m), Kalanka (6931 m), Nanda Devi East (7434 m) and Nanda Devi (7817 m). From cast to west Nanda Kot (6631 m), Devasthan (6678 m), Maiktoli (6805 m), Mrigthuni (6855 m), Trisul (7120 m) and Bethartoli (6352 m). The area is segmented by a series of parallel ridges and the most important is Devasthan-Rishikot ridge, which divides the Rishi gorge at the base of Nanda Devi and separates the inner sanctuary from the outer sanctuary. The northern wall from Lata to Rishi pahar is the divide between the Nanda Devi basin and the Dbauli Ganga.

Due to its beautiful surroundings and rich wildlife, the sanctuary was declared as national park along with the Valley of Flowers under the Wildlife (Protection) Act, 1972 in September 1983. Monsoon begins here from third week of June. Thundering clouds are a very common sight in the valley. Inside the park the snow line is well above 4500 in. Though the park receives little precipitation, it supports a lush green vegetation cover than the other valleys.

Flora: The forest forms a very small percentage of the flora of the sanctuary and is restricted to the Rishi gorge. The coniferous trees grow in Dudh Ganga valley and Dibrugheta glade. Fir (*Abies pindrow*) is most dominant, deodar (*Cedrus deodara*) is found at Lata, but rhododendron and white and pink rose (*Rosa brunonii and R. macrophylla*) are found in admixture with fir and deodars. Birch (*Betuld utilis*) is found all the way from Dibrugheta to Ramni. Lichen and moss covers the tree trunk. The Botanical Survey of India and expedition reports reveal that more than 200 species of plants (*8 species of pteridophytes, 5 species of gymnosperms, 188 of angiosperms*) grow in the park. About 15 species e.g. *Aconitum spp., Circeaster agrestis, Epipogum lislerasp, Meconopsis aculeata, Nardostachys grandoora, Orchis latifolia, Podophyllum hexandrum, Saussurea obvallata* are considered rare and endangered." Between the timber line and the permanent snow line there are the extensive meadows with scant but evergreen shrubs (*e.g. Rhododendron anthopogon. Juniper and Salix species*), herbs (*e.g. Aconitum, Cyananthus and Polygonum species*) and grass (*e.g. Lantonia, Festuca and Poa species*).

From Lata Kharak to Sarsupatal the trek is full of Alpine vegetation with beautiful aromatic flowers. These are generally found in Lata Kharak, Dhransi, Didrugheta, Deodi, Ramni and Sarsupatal. The local people believe that the first Brahm-karnal should be plucked for the Goddess Nanda, otherwise she will be offended and make journey hazardous. Most of the flowers found in Valley of Flowers are found here too.

Birds: Very rich and varied avifauna live in this park. Lamba during his study in 1981-84 found 80 birds of 27 families. Outstanding among them are Himalayan golden eagle (*Aquila chrysaetos hodgsoni*), black eagle (*Ictiraetus malayaensis*), Himalayan bearded vulture or larnmergeier (*Gypaetus barbatus*), snow partridge (*lerwa leswa*), Himalayan snow cock (*Tetraogallus Himalayensis*), chukor partridge (Alecioris chukorj, Himalayan monal (*Lophophorousimpejanus*), koklas pheasant (Ceriornis macrolophus), west Himalayan snow pigeon (*Columba leucondta),* Indian spotted dove (*Sirtptopelia chinensis suratenses*), Himalayan great barbat (*Megataima virens marshallorum*), western variegated laughing thrush (*Trochalopteron variegatum similie*), Himalayan whistling thrush (*Myiophoneus caeruleus temminckii*) and western red headed tit (*Aegithaliscus concinnus redalei*).

Fauna: Nanda Devi National Park is rich and varied in its faunal wealth. Among the mammals found are langur, Himalayan black bear, yellow-bellied weasel, leopard, snow leopard, serow, Himalayan tahr, bharal or blue sheep, goral, musk deer, mouse hare and Indian field mouse.

9

Ecotourism in Eastern Europe

Tourism Patterns in Earlier Period

Tourism resources of Eastern Europe may conveniently be divided into five categories:

1. Heritage—the long and complicated history of the region is selectively represented in museums, exhibitions, statues, architecture, domestic artefacts, artisan crafts, music, song, dance and costume. Yet throughout the region, architectural splendour of notable historic centres such as Cracow in southern Poland, recognised by UNESCO as being of global importance, have long been threatened by atmospheric pollution from heavy industry and increasing levels of vehicle emissions.
2. Sand, surf and sun—From Poland's short-season Baltic coast (Dawson, 1991) to Albania's still largely unspoilt Ionian littoral (Hall, 1991b). Marine pollution problems, arising both from the pressure of tourism itself and from other sources, are increasingly posing environmental.
3. Winter sports—these now attract large numbers of Western tourists and major land use conflicts have arisen, such as at Bansko in the Bulgarian Pirin Mountains, where a winter sports resort was opened in 1981 within National Park.

4. Wildlife—though all countries of the Eastern Europe possess the equivalent National Parks and have designated areas devoted to the protection of fauna and flora, considerable land use conflicts exist. Hunting and fishing have been important and highly profitable tourist pursuits. The association of this activity with the now discredited eastwhile communist leaderships, however, together with increasing environmental awareness, has ensued substantial debate on the merits or otherwise of its continuation.
5. Spas—mineral springs and curative treatments have served a wealthy, often foreign clientele, since classical times and in recent years the Middle East has been a notably lucrative source of clients. Although care has been required to protect the quality of the waters of such locations, they have not been immune from atmospheric pollution.

Tourism under State Socialism

No doubt, tourism was becoming increasingly popular in Eastern Europe the inter-war period, particularly in upland areas, the post-war imposition of the Soviet model of political, economic and social development introduce new roles and patterns for recreational activity. Economic barriers, constraints on mobility, ideological hostility and the low priority given to service industries, coupled with general Cold War perceptions, rendered Europe behind the Iron Curtain an unattractive propositions for most Western vacationers. Priority was given to domestic recreational activities in the region, with administration, transport and accommodation being subsidised by state enterprises and trades unions for the benefit of working families. Cross-border movement normally; entailed exchanges of 'friendship groups' between like-minded countries. De spite the human rights clauses of the 1975 Helsinki agreement, until the end of the 1980s the region's nationals, other than Yugoslavs, wen rarely permitted to travel westwards. Currency inconvertibility, restricted access to hard currency, relatively low living standards and stringent exit vis; policies proscribed most forms of extra-bloc tourism except for the privilege *nomenklatura,* who also had access to hard currency shops and the other benefits of the 'more equal'.

When, the West European package holiday business was takin off in the 1960s, Eastern Europe was ill-equipped to respond to expanding market demands and was largely ignored by Western tour operators. The one exception was Yugoslavia, which adopted a pragmatic attitude to labour and tourism mobility. There followed a rapid growth of tourist arrivals in Yugoslavia from the West, a development unmatched elsewhere in the region. Although absolute numbers of international tourists to Yugoslavia were not significantly greater than those to several other countries in the region, the dominance of the Western market did secure a higher level of tourist income, which, by the end of the 1980s, was greater than the total for the rest of the region and, moreover, was mostly in hard currency.

When state socialism was near eclipse, considerable growth in tourist (as opposed to all types of visitor) arrivals was experienced in the region. Growth was particularly notable for the land-locked states of Central Europe: Czechoslovakia (41.4% increase 1985-8, 16.7 per cent rise 1988-9) and Hungary (8.6 and 37.2%). Poland fared less well (-9.2% 1985-8), but recovered in 1989 (32.0% up). The beach holiday destinations—Yugoslavia, Bulgaria and Romania—showed modest growth up to 1988, but both Yugoslavia and Romania saw downturns in 1989, a trend to be continued subsequently in the former, as the federation began to enter its death throes. By contrast, arrivals in Romania in 1990 showed a 34.6 per cent increase, albeit in large part because of a cross-border influx of low spending Soviet citizens from Moldova, emphasising the continuing need to treat all statistics in the region with great caution. Romania aside, the most spectacular growth in tourist arrival numbers in the early transition period came about in

Hungary, with increases of 37.2 per cent for 1989 and 41.5 per cent for 1990. Otherwise, somewhat surprisingly, the region witnessed a considerable reduction in the growth of tourist arrivals for 1990.

With the exception of Yugoslavia under state socialism, the economic impact of international tourism remained relatively small, certainly by comparison with Western Europe. In 1988, the last full year of state socialism in the region, for example, Bulgaria's tourist income was just 2.2 per cent of that of Spain and Romania's was the equivalent of just 7.3 per cent of that earned by Greece (WTO, 1990). That Turkey could raise its level of tourism receipts by more than 600 per cent between 1980 and 1988 was a salutary example for the region. By contrast, receipts declined substantially in Romania, largely as the result of the deteriorating image of the country's domestic conditions, and they fell dramatically in Poland in the early 1980s, only to later recover. In Bulgaria and Czechoslovakia, however, receipts increased at rates comparable with the major Western tourist economies, in Hungary even more rapidly, and in Yugoslavia the fastest.

At the time of early stages of transition, as intraregional mobility of low spending visitors increased in response to the easing of cross-border movements, levels of receipts rose less than proportionately, such that in 1989, all countries of the region except Romania saw a decrease in receipts per arrival, and in 1990 only Bulgaria and Yugoslavia recorded per capita increases, in the latter case reflecting declining rather than increasing tourist arrival.

Central Europe, and particularly the land-locked states of the Czech Republic and Hungary, have experienced growth in international tourism development which the troubled Balkan societies have been poorly placed to pursue. Relative stability, more advanced economies, a concentration of international funding and initial advantage have contributed to this division. A sample of more recent figures for Hungary can exemplify that country's position as the region's leading tourist destination in terms of numbers, and, since the Yugoslav upheavals, also in terms of tourist receipts. Hungary derived a tourism income surplus of $170 million for the first seven months of 1991, a 30 per cent increase on the previous year's figure. The industry became the country's largest balance of payments contributor. For the first six months of 1992, despite a six per cent decrease in tourism income. Hungarians travelling abroad spent 21 per cent less, rendering a surplus of $202.1 million, an increase of $30 million. The Balkan countries, despite possessing the most favourable climatic and coastal conditions for mass tourism, have experienced stagnation or even decline in tourist numbers, reflecting an initial lack of clarity of political change, continuing instability and a generally lower degree of road transport accessibility from major West European markets.

Further, tourists from the northern part of the region, no longer restricted to Soviet bloc vacation destinations, started to abandon their post-war Black Sea coast holiday playgrounds for more enticing Western venues. However, in Bulgaria at least, preliminary figures for the first half of 1992 were showing an increase of 23-25 per cent in foreign visitors compared with the previous year, perhaps the result of deflection from the former Yugoslavia, where the tourism industry has been dismantled, although both Slovenia and Croatia are now vigorously promoting themselves. In response to mass market demands, and not least the growth of 'business tourism', accommodation, transport, utilities and telecommunications are gradually being overhauled with assistance from the major international funding institutions and commercial transnational companies. For tourism to be more environmentally sensitive and sustainable. however, a greater emphasis on more modest to medium grade accommodation is required, coupled with an encouragement of small-scale rural developments which can supplement farm incomes and reduce farmers' desire to pursue ecologically harmful intensive agriculture.

Practically environmentally sensitive tourism must involve the local population in decision-making as well as participation in accommodation provision, conservation and education (Murphy, 1985; Wells *et al.*, 1992). Not surprisingly, however, tourism training in Eastern Europe has tended to focus on hotel management, catering, travel agenting and such areas as computing, telecommunications and languages, to cater for the new growth markets. The region is vulnerable to tourism fashion changes, which are themselves sensitive to the instability and the short-term problems with which the region is currently beset. The impact of socio-economic change is witnessing rapidly rising crime and accident rates. Although such developments can exert a repulsion effect on tourism activity, the extent of tourism's contribution to their growth may not be insignificant. Again, one way of ameliorating such problems is to more closely involve local communities in the tourism development process. At the same time, the uncertainty of transition and the instability of which it is a part tend to create an organisational vacuum within which the medium-term priorities for developing a tourism industry cannot be clearly established. Legislative and regulatory frameworks for privatisation and joint venture development, including provisions for insurance and guarantees, may be slow to arrive. Hidden power structures and agendas arising from such situations may not be readily apparent to outsiders. The authors are aware, for example, of one particular former active party member who is now one of the most forceful tourism entrepreneurs in his country. The danger for the region of falling into a dependency relationship with the West, becoming dominated by Western multinational accommodation, transport, agencing and financial organisations is ever present.

To become a cheap tourist playground, a number of localities could rapidly reach saturation level, with increased overcrowding, infrastructural strains, environmental deterioration and host antagonism.

Change and Conservation

Water management, in Eastern Europe particularly for flood control and agricultural development extends back to at least the eighteenth century. With increasing population pressures and the growth of organised timber exploitation in the later nineteenth century, soil erosion became recognised as a serious problem and forestry protection legislation began to be introduced (Turnock, 1988). This acted as the basis for nature reserve and National Park designation, which developed from recommendations predating the First World War. The first reserves were set up in southern Bohemia as early as 1838 (Carter and Turnock, 1993: 205), although National Park legislation, inspired by North American and West European concepts of wilderness, was not elaborated until the inter-war period. Bodies set up to oversee and administer such areas included Poland's Council for Nature Protection (1919) and Romania's Commission for Natural Monuments (1933). Although much genuine environmental concern was shown in the post-war period, in the face of policies emphasising rapid and heavy industrialisation based on outmoded technologies and inefficient fuels, environmental considerations were given a low priority. Two forcibly promoted dogmas exacerbated this situation: (a) that socialism harnessed to science could overcome all natural obstacles; and (b) environmental problems only resulted from capitalist exploitation and thus, by definition, did not exist in socialist Eastern Europe. The extent of resources required to ameliorate environmental damage thereby inflicted on the region has been a matter of some subsequent debate.

Change and Cooperation: The European Trust for Natural and Cultural Wealth was established in Prague in 1991 with the backing, of the Czech Government and a grant from the World Bank's Global Environment Facility. Inspired by the World Wide Fund for Nature (WWF) and links with environmentalists in Eastern Europe, the trust aimed to preserve the region's natural heritage by establishing an 'ecological backbone' across Europe. The first targets were the natural habitats along largely uninhabited and previously militarised border areas— 'ecological bricks'—where it was hoped to foster cooperation between neighbours.

A few large sites are attracting most attention and funding, many other conservation projects have involved cooperation between Eastern and Western Europe. Bilateral and multilateral funding have been made available for an increasing number of projects appearing within assistance packages since 1989. Funding takes two forms: specific support, usually for the establishment of protected sites and their management plans, and more general funding to improve the recipient countries' administrative framework and public awareness. At government level, the EC, particularly through the PHARE programme (European Community Environmental Assistance to Eastern European Countries, initially Poland/Hungary Assistance for Restructuring), the World Bank and the European Bank for Reconstruction and Development (EBRD) support projects and project implementation units in several countries. The Polish, US and Dutch governments are involved in the Green Lungs project, a subregional nature conservation strategy in north-eastern Poland which might be extended to neighbouring countries. At a more modest level the IUCN-East European Programme (IUCN-EEP) has, through bilateral funding, established specific nature conservation project coordination units in the Czech Republic. Poland and Romania. The WWF is involved in wetland projects in Hungary and Poland. The Ramsar Bureau has also placed a high priority on projects in Eastern Europe, having applied to the GEF for $2 million to fund small-scale wetland conservation projects.

On the other hand, cross-border environmental cooperation in the region extends back to the 1920s when Czechoslovakia and Poland agreed on joint protection measures for an area which eventually became the Pieninsky/Pieniny National Park. In the post-war period the two countries again jointly developed cross-border National Parks in the Tatra (K) and

Karkonosze (Q) mountains. Generally, however, little bilateral action was taken within the framework of the Council for Mutual Economic Assistance (CMEA or COMECON) and no effective supranational environmental agency was created within the region. Indeed, for over 40 years the borderlands between the countries of the region, and particularly between those countries and the West along the line of the 'Iron Curtain', were largely uninhabited and inaccessible. Although regularly patrolled and fortified, with large tracts forbidden to human activity and movement, these no-man's lands became unconsciously protected natural areas.

One of the most valuable natural areas is the Sumava Biosphere Reserve (D), 700 square kilometres of forests and wetlands on the Czech-German border. It was faced with the development of intensive agriculture and forestry, the growth of uncontrolled tourism and long-range air pollution. The Czech Government agreed to set aside 70 000 hectares as a National Park, with the remaining 92000 hectares designated a protected landscape area, including a 3000 hectares 'strict' nature reserve. A management plan to promote sustainable resource management was sponsored by the Czech Government, the Czech Green Circle and the WWF. Completed in 1991, it envisages a core area of about 20 000 hectares, a recuperation zone of 5000 hectares, a traditional use zone of 40 000 hectares and a public use zone which it is hoped will attract ecotourism. Within the traditional use zone, forest intervention will be permitted for a 40 year period, the time required to convert artificial spruce monocultures into dynamic systems.

The National Park is to be used as the *Leitmotif* for the Bohemian/Bavarian forests region. Situated on the 'green roof of Europe', it is hoped that the park designation will promote, rather than hinder, the process of helping forests which are. historically, part of a single economic and cultural region, to grow back together again and to overcome political division. It is one of the Cold War's ironies that the lower

Odra/Oder valley between Poland and Germany shelters the Baltic's last community of salmon, which annually swim up the river to lay their eggs in small streams on the Polish side. There are 500 types of plant 226 species of bird, 19 species of amphibians and reptiles, 56 types of mollusc, 50 species of fish and 50 types of mammals here. Up to 100000 migrating geese, ducks and swans rest here in spring and autumn. Osprey and sea eagles are relatively common sights, and beavers and otters live in the marshlands.

A National Park has been established which covers 32884 hectares (22384 in Germany, 10500 in Poland) encompassing three zones: (1) reserve areas, with no human use (7390 hectares): (2) environmentally protected areas with some human use (9110 hectares): and (3) surrounding areas compatible with the park but with some human use (16384 hectares). Financed by the Government of Brandenburg, one of the new east German provinces, with support from the German Foundation for the Promotion of Culture, the park extends 60 kilometres south from Szczecin to the villages of Cedynia/Hohensaaten on either bank of the river. Aside from two outstanding land use problems—a power station and the network of border patrol roads—revived land ownership claims, attempts to exploit gravel deposits and new potential tourism pressures require strong conservation reinforcement measures (Springate, 1991). The development of ecotourism as a means of satisfying at least some of the economic pressures on the area could see the development of 'gateways' and 'honeypots' on both sides of the border, filtering tourism pressures into selected sites away from the reserve areas.

Current Problems of Ecotourism Development

Now recognition is being extended to the need for 'sustainable', 'green' and 'eco' tourism, as, for example, stated in the Romanian and Albanian national tourism programmes Spaho, 1992; 1993) and in the objectives of a number of environmental NGOs attempting to influence policy both in the region's governments and in the major Western funding agencies.

There often appears to have been little conceptual discussion and analysis of the appropriateness of adopting at national policy level what may be little more than fashionable buzz-words and 'marketing babble' (Wickers, 1992). This can result in contradictory and conflicting policy statements, particularly where a government's tourism and environment departments have not been coordinated. Such crucial questions as defining and recognising tourism carrying capacities and 'saturation levels' have barely begun to be addressed and may be neglected because of skill shortages, inadequate resources and political in-fighting (Hall, 1991a). Further, a newly unleashed entrepreneurial sector may have neither the resources nor the inclination to take a longer term view of tourism's environmental impacts. Nor will local populations be sympathetic to environmental conservation policies if these interfere with such traditional local activities as hunting, fishing and smuggling.

This emphasises the need to involve the local community in decision-making and participation in conservation and tourism provision to persuade them that environmentally sensitive tourism can be in their own economic interests. At a general level, as 'ecotourism' implicitly requires management, control and proscription, there will be an inevitable reaction within the region, particularly from the newly privatised sectors, against any policies echoing aspects of the old communist regimes' practices.

It is great irony that just at the time when the shackles of communist control have been thrown off and Western consultants have been flooding the region extolling the virtues of the 'free' market, so others have come along arguing that some aspects of people's newly won freedoms should be limited and that restrictions on access to certain areas should be reimposed and even extended. Superficially, for example, the old Albanian 'prescriptive' approach to tourism, whereby foreigners were herded around in a group along a few prescribed routes in prebooked state transport and full-board accommodation and were 'policed' by guides, drivers and sundry onlookers, had a great deal to commend it in minimising cultural and environmental contagion.

Local Participation: The active participation by the local population in the conservation and education dimensions of the tourism development process is an essential element of ecotourism. In Eastern Europe, however, attempts to involve local communities have been inhibited both by the lack of experience of bottom-up development from which citizens can draw, and the often dismissive or at best patronising attitude taken by some officials towards local populations, particularly in rural and more remote areas. Local citizen participation is often seen as a threat to the power structure of both local and central bureaucracies and to the very valuable perks which accompany the membership of such structures. Attempts to break such ingrained structural relationships will not be easy, although local NGOs are receiving financial, organisational and moral support from their Western counterparts. Local populations in their turn may be suspicious of any 'official' approaches. For example, when researchers from the Danube Delta Institute surveyed relatively isolated local residents on their attitudes towards accommodating tourists in farm tourism and on other ways of being drawn into 'ecotourism' processes in the Delta (DDITRG, 1991), they were met with large degree of apprehension and suspicion.

Support Requirements: Inventories of natural and human resources, entailing data collection and collation, processing, analysis and representation are still required in much of the region. Particularly in the Balkans, shortages of often basic equipment and access to literature arc commonplace and constrain implementation: computers, word processors, photocopiers, fax machines and accurate measuring instruments are all urgently needed, together with access to spare parts and case of servicing. The ability to learn from experience elsewhere is constrained by the lack of availability of appropriate literature.

Documentation centres need to be established to house both comprehensive databases from which information can be easily retrieved and libraries of relevant scientific books and papers from around the world. Linking mechanisms to ensure essential cooperation and rationalisation of effort, resources, skills and experience are often lacking. It has been the authors' experience that tensions can arise from a number of sources, such as between: (a) public and private sector representatives; (b) environment and tourism administrators; (c) ecological and economic objectives; (d) central and local government; (e) those with and those without appropriate skills and training.

Training programme requirements for staff reveal critical needs in such areas as ecology, social survey techniques, marketing, computing, languages, cartography, photogrammetry, geographical-information systems, guiding and information centre staffing. Selective knowledge and experience, rather than holistic perspectives, have been the norm. This partly results from the activities of professionals, who. whilst specialists in their own fields, have usually received training within relatively narrow disciplinary confines and have hitherto been unable to take a broader ecological view of any particular geographical area.

Suitable legal and administrative frameworks may still need to be established in some countries to clarify land and property rights, control transport and accommodation and establish insurance guarantees and tax regimes. These should also include codes of tourist conduct in protected areas updated to meet new conditions.

In the case of Hungary as post-communist agricultural intensification began to threaten species and their habitats, nature conservation laws were passed in 1991 and 1992 to establish a Nature Conservation Authority (NCA). This body administers the prevention of areas of international importance from falling victim to indiscriminate privatisation and of foreigners buying protected areas. Unlike the region's traditional approach which focused mainly on species protection, the new regulations will stress habitat protection. Special attention will be paid to environmentally sensitive areas and to establishing a comprehensive network of ecological or 'green' corridors connecting major protected areas. The NCA is able to exchange land of comparable value and to lease and license land on terms favourable to farmers with the aim of compensating any losses resulting from conflicts of interest with nature conservation. A Nature Conservation Trust has been established for coordination.

Consequently the new political and legislative framework, the WWF has been able to complete an inventory of Hungary's steppe grasslands and has prepared a legal protection and management proposal. The WWF is also promoting traditional extensive farming systems, entailing such practices as grassland management, rotation of crops and the appropriate use of marginal land such as planting native tree species rather than non-native pines. Small-scale farm tourism should be built into this process as a means of broadening the rural population's economic base and as a form of compensation and disincentive to pursue intensive agriculture.

Information Requirements: Clear statements of the nature and aims of ecotourism need to be incorporated into literature and publicity material to educate and encourage active participation by interested parties (tourism organisations, local populations, local and national state bodies and individuals), as well as for potential tourists themselves. Fundamental education and information programmes on environmental protection amongst the local population must be effective, especially through the medium of schools, and put into practice, recruiting locals as wardens and deploying them on financially beneficial training courses to strengthen tourist control mechanisms. The interest, support and participation of the local community is vital, especially where ecotourism strategies are perceived as threatening its economic interests. Bottom-up information flows may not be easy to stimulate in the short term given the nature of past decision-making practices in the region.

Strategy Formulation: Apparently, six types of action study are required for an ecotourism strategy plan: (1) a strategy for assessing tourism demand and targeting specialist markets/niche groups; (2) the establishment of a working formula for assessing tourism carrying capacities; (3) an interim plan for matching different tourism activities/types of tourists, their likely environmental impacts and economic benefits; (4) an interim-plan for a system of prescribed routeways and transport forms appropriate for different ecological conditions within and adjacent to the designated area (Hall, 1993b; 1993c); (5) a longer term plan for the nature and location of information/education centres, coordinated with local educational programmes, for 'gateways' into, and at, 'honeypots' on the periphery of protected areas; and (6) an interim plan for prescribed infrastructure and services, accommodation and activity areas, their access and seasonally. These would also act as 'tax' collection points, permit issue centres and questionnaire survey points. Production of a final composite plan/strategy should ensure its complementarity and integration with local, regional and national environmental, tourism and other planning strategies and methods.

Summing Up

Sustainable forms of tourism are a relatively new concept for Eastern Europe, although past practices did see the restriction of tourists' mobility, albeit not necessarily for environmental reasons. Eastern Europe is vulnerable to tourism fashion changes, which are themselves sensitive to the instability and myriad problems besetting the region.

Despite this, the region's cultural and environmental diversity provides the potential for substantial market segmentation. Targeting niche markets—ideally high spending groups with minimal adverse impacts and season-extending activities—should emphasise the significance of 'green' forms of tourism. The region's substantial heritage potential and natural protected areas can be used to considerable educational as well as economic advantage to the area.

There are very real dangers of ecotourism being cynically taken up as a development objective simply because of: (a) the propaganda value for governments and agencies of being seen to be 'greening' development and particularly tourism development; and (c) its role as a means of gaining access to development Aid funds from the West; (b) the fashionability of the concept. Apparently, too many projects are being developed based on Western European (or American) experience, despite the cultural and environmental circumstances and the nature of consequent pressures being very particular to the region itself. Indeed, there may be better lessons to be learned from the experience of the developing world than from the developed. In short, there is more than a slight danger of eco-ethnocentrism being superimposed on the application of ecotourism in Eastern Europe. Some projects currently being pursued have not been mentioned in this chapter precisely because they have fallen into this trap, led by people and institutions of whom we would have expected better. For tourism development to be successful and acceptable, sensitivity of implementation and sustainability and local participation must be more than just cliches in national or corporate plans. Most importantly, local populations must be involved and shown that conservation and tourism can complement each other to the economic advantage of the local community.

REFERENCES

Albrecht. C., (1987), Environmental policies and politics in contemporary Czechoslovakia, *Studies in Comparative Communism*, 2(3-4), 291-302.

Allcock, J.B. and Przeclawski, K., (1990), Introduction. *Annals of Tourism Research*, 17, 1-6.

Boo, E., (1992a), *The Concept of Visitor Currying Capacity as it Applies to Developing Countries*, World Wildlife Fund, Washington.

Buckley, P.J. and Witt, S.F., (1990), Tourism in the centrally-planned economies of Europe. *Annals of Tourism Research*, 17, 7-18.

Carter, F.W., (1985). Pollution problems in post-war Czechoslovakia, *Transactions of the Institute of British Geographers (New Series)*, 10, 174.

Carter. F.W., (1991a), Bulgaria, in Hall, D.R. (ed.) *Tourism and Economic Development in Eastern Europe and the Soviet Union*, Belhaven Press, London and Halstead. New York. 220-235.

Cater, E., (1991), Sustainable tourism in the Third World: problems and prospects, *University of Reading Department of Geography Discussion Paper 3*.

Cerovsky, J., (1990), IUCN and Eastern Europe, *IUCN Bulletin*, 21(4), 1-4. Cerovksy. J. and Podhaiska. Z., 1990, Czechoslovakia, in IUCN, *Environmental Status Reports 1988-1989*, Vol. 1. IUCN-EEP, Cambridge, 3-53.

Cohen, E., (1989), Alternative tourism—a critique, in Singh, B. *et al.*. *Towards Appropriate Tourism*. Lang, Frankfurt. 127-142.

Dakov, M., (1976), *Environmental Management in the People's Republic of Bulgaria*, Sofia Press, Sofia.

Dawson, A.H., (1991), Poland, in Hall, D.R. (ed.) *Tourism and Economic Development in Eastern Europe and the Soviet Union*, Belhaven Press, London and Halstead. New York. 190-202.

Elkins. T., (1990) Developments in the German Democratic Republic, *Geography*, 75, 246-249.

Forster, D.P. and Jozan, P., (1990), Health in Eastern Europe, *The Lancet*, 335,453-460.

Golembski, G., (1990), Tourism in the economy of shortage. *Annals of Tourism Research*. 17, 55-68.

Hall, D.R., (1984), Foreign tourism under socialism: the Albanian 'Stalinist' model. *Annals of Tourism Research*, 11, 539-555.

Hall, D.R., (1990a), Eastern Europe opens its doors. *Geographical Magazine*. 62, 10-15.

Hall, D.R., (1990b), Stalinism and tourism: a study of Albania and North Korea. *Annals of Tourism Research*, 17, 36-54.

Hall, D.R., (1990c), The changing face of tourism in Eastern Europe. *Town and Country Planning*. 59,348-351.

Hamilton, G., (1991), Amex sets initiative for Ecotourism development. *Business Eastern Europe,* 20, 412.

Hinrichsen, D. and Enyedi, G. (eds), (1990), *State of the Hungarian Environment,* Statistical Publishing House, Budapest.

Hughes, G., (1991), Are the costs of cleaning up Eastern Europe exaggerated? Economic reform and the environment, *Oxford Review of Economic Policy,* 7(4), 12-24.

International Union for the Conservation of Nature (IUCN), (1992), *Conservation Status of the Danube Delta, IUCN-EEP Environmental Status Reports* Vol. 4, IUCN-EEP Cambridge.

Jenner, P. and Smith, C., (1992), *The Tourism Industry and the Environment,* E.I.U. Publications. London.

Michalak, W. and Gibb, R., (1993), Development of the transport system: prospects for East/West integration, in Hall, D.R. (ed.). *Transport and Communication Development in the New Central and Eastern Europe.* Belhaven Press. London.

Ostrowski, S., (1991), Ethnic tourism—focus on Poland, *Tourism Management,* 12, 125-131.

Ramsar, (1992), New opportunities for cooperation in Europe, *Ramsar Newsletter,* 13. 2-7.

Russell, J., (1990), *Environmental Issues in Eastern Europe: Setting an Agenda,* RIIA and IUCN. London.

Shaw, D.J.B., (1991), The Soviet Union, in Hall, D.R. (ed.) *Tourism and economic development in Eastern Europe and the Soviet Union,* Belhaven Press, London and Halstead, New York, 119-141.

Spaho, E., (1992), Tourism: promising contracts, *Albanian Economic Tribune,* 6(10). 17-19.

Springate, C., (1991) Where eagles dare. *Green Magazine,* 3(3), 26-29.

Standring, K., (1991), Eastern bloc-buster, *Birds Illustrated,* 1(1), 76-81.

Thompson, J., (1991), East Europe's dark dawn. *National Geographic,* 179(5), 37-69.

Turnock, D., (1979), Water management resources in Romania, *GeoJournal,* 3,609-622.

Waller, M., (1989), The ecology issue in Eastern Europe: protest and movements. *Journal of Communist Studies, S.* 303-328.

Wells, M., Brandon, K. and Hannah, L., (1992), *People and parks: Linking Protected Area Management with Local Communities,* The World Bank/World Wildlife Fund/ US Agency for International Development, Washington.

10

Case Studies on Ecotourism Development

I

A COMMUNITY-BASED CONSERVATION EFFORT IN BAR, VALLEY, GILGIT, PAKISTAN

Pakistan, with its geography ranging from sea level to the second highest mountain in the world, hosts a rich variety of flora and fauna. In order to reverse the process of deforestation and improve the status of wildlife, the Government of Pakistan has created a number of environmentally related departments at both the federal and provincial levels. In addition several NGOs have initiated efforts to enhance the process of reforestation. However local participation, the essential requirement for the success, has largely been ignored. Local communities were largely involved in the protection of natural resources on government land. Likewise technical and financial support needed to improve communities' skill and ability to manage their resources on private lands was virtually nonexistent.

The World Wide Fund for Nature/Pakistan (WWF/Pakistan) has been actively trying to improve the environmental situation by including local communities in natural resource management. This paper details WIVF/ Paki stan's efforts in Bar Valley in the Northwestern Frontier Provinces of Pakistan.

The project, begun in 1990, capitalised on the popularity of hunting in the area and the possibilities of linking ecotourism based on sustainable hunting), conservation and community development.

Bar Valley

Bar Valley is situated about 35 kilometers from the town of Gilgit in the Nagar subdivision of the North Western Frontier Provinces of Pakistan. Bar valley was once known for its large number of Siberian ibex *(Copra ibexsibirica).* However, their numbers has declined due to uncontrolled hunting by the local people for food and outsiders for trophies. Although wildlife department staff was present they were largely ineffective controlling and managing hunting inside the valley.

There are three main villages in Bar Valley with a total of 2.10 households. These communities depend mainly on livestock for their livelihood. Having already over grazed the areas close to the villages, the people began grasing their Livestock in the alpine pastures that were once the exclusive domain of wild animals including the ibex.

Winters are hard in Bar Valley. The minimum temperature in January often dips well below freezing and the valley remains covered with snow. During these harsh winters, the villagers bum large a-mounts of fuel wood to keep warm. The main source of fuel is the 'juniper tree, which is one of the only forest trees found in the local mountain ecosystem. It is slow, growing and endangered throughout the country. In addition, the people collect huge quantities of alpine grasses for stall feeding their livestock in the winter. The combined effect of deforestation and removal of grasses has resulted in erosion, and the deterioration of the habitat needed for the ibex and other wildlife.

The continuous loss of habitat and uncontrolled hunting of ibex created a dire situation in Bar Valley-in 1990, WWT/

Pakistan initiated activities to alleviate the process of degradation and improve the status of the ibex by establishing linkages among local communities, local administration and other NGOs, as well as adapting integrated management approaches.

The core of the plan was to motivate villagers to take responsibility for protecting the ibex until the population could grow to a level when commercial exploration would be feasible. The objectives of the project were to:

— protect wildlife species of the area against illegal, uncontrolled and unauthorised hunting;

— generate income opportunities for the local communities and improve their lifestyle through the sustainable use of the environment (both natural resources and wildlife);

— preserve and improve the local biodiversity;

— create awareness with regards to the value of environmental conservation;

— provide training and research opportunities to students and graduates of universities, both local and foreign; and

— provide practical examples of resource conservation (biodiversity in general and wildlife in particular) and-development through local participation for replication in other parts of the country.

Project Implementation

Protection of Wildlife

After holding several meetings with the local communities, a protection procedure was suggested and adopted. Three villages of Bar Valley elected 10 members to form a management committee for one year. The committee was comprised of five hunters and five non-hunters. This committee was given Rs. 4,500 (USS 150) 1) per month to carry out protection duties and other conservation-related activities. The project was to stop giving this money when new sources of income were generated as a result of the project's activities. However, activities would continue to be sponsored by the community with the new sources of income. The local wildlife and forest departments %ere also persuaded to appoint two observers to ensure the wildlife protection and forest rules were not violated.

Trophy Hunting Programme

As mentioned earlier, the core concept behind the project was for sustainable hunting of the ibex. The project was heavily dependent on the cooperation of the 41 local hunters. The complete ban on hunting not only affected the hunters directly but also other community members. While not all members of the community hunted, many benefited indirectly from the hunting activities by receiving meat from their relatives and friends who did. Efforts were thus needed to appease the hunters as well as the other villagers to avoid the possibility of poaching. Even if a few non-hunting families had remained unattended by the project, total control over hunting, which was the utmost priority of the project, would have become difficult.

The feasibility study had already proposed that a sum of Rs.240,000 (US$ 8.000) be given for distribution amongst the 240 families of Bar Valley. This would not only compensate the community immediately for the loss of the wild meat, but also involve every household in the programme. Additionally, it was assumed the communities would either change their food habits or replace wild meat with meat from other sources. This money was a loan and was to be returned to WWF/Pakistan upon the commencement of the trophy hunting programme.

Regular censuses were conducted, and the ibex were counted bvl-age and sex. It was recommended that 10% of the mature males (over 8 years of age) could be used for trophy hunting, when there was a minimum population of 30 mature and over mature animals in the entire valley (273 km^2) and the total population of ibex was approximately 500. Except for two minor violations, there were no reported poaching problems. As a result, the animal population grew and in April 1994, more than 500 animals were counted.

Based on the population census of ibex for April 1994, the government of the Northwestern Frontier Provinces recommended that five ibex be allowed for trophy hunting. This was endorsed by the local administration and a formal request was sent to the Federal Government to lift the ban and issue the permits for hunting to take place. Because the villages' protection activities were successful, the Government of Pakistan allowed five trophy hunting permits and endorsed the Idea that the local communities would earn a profit as proposed In the project. The Government of Pakistan allowed five licenses for the hunting of ibex in the valley; 75% of the revenue was to be given to the local communities and 25% to the government as a management fee.

A fixed license fee and quota was agreed upon in consultation with the wildlife department and other partners of the project. The fee for international hunters was USS3,000 while Pakistani hunters were charged Rs.25,000(USS830).

The local village council and WWF, Pakistan decided upon the use of revenue from trophy hunting and other tourist related activities to fund further development and conservation projects. Government departments were encouraged to use their share of the income for conservation purposes, preferably in the project or surrounding areas.

From the revenue collected a health care center was constructed. Currently (1996),WIAT/Pakistan is also training selected villagers in organising tours to some of the famous valleys in the area to further diversify the ecotourism activities in the area.

Developing Bar Valley as an Ecotourism Destination

In order to prepare and promote Bar Valley as a tourist destination, WWF/ Pakistan worked with the local communities to improve tourist facilities as well as develop promotional material on the valley. Moreover, when the project first began it was uncertain whether the government would allow trophy hunting in the area, and more importantly whether the villagers would be permitted to keep the profits generated from the hunting if allowed. In response to this possibility, the community identified various aspects of their natural and cultural environment that were of potential interest to tourists. Campgrounds were designated, and 20 tents and other camping equipment were given to the local communities to accommodate tourists visiting scenic spots in the valley. Other ecotourism activities were designed to diversify the range of activities for the tourists.

These activities included:

- — The availability of riding facilities (on horses and yaks);
- — Cultural shows for tourists in Dainter Village on weekends;
- — Training of guides and porters for trekking and hikes
- — Training of local people in the preparation of hygienic local and foreign food; and
- — The availability of transport facilities to and from the nearest town where transport services for other destinations are available.

Many of the activities have begun and several families are now earning a substantial amount of money. Rates and charges were fixed through mutual consultations with partners, and the quality of services in the valley has been regularly monitored.

Bari Darukush, an area which represents a mosaic of

mountain habitats, grasslands and wetlands was closed for all uses except trophy hunting and limited grazing. This area will be maintained for limited camping, tourism activities and research studies.

Other Development Activities

The Project also linked conservation with local development activities. Since the area does not support a vast array of resources it was important to assist the local communities in land use practices and improved agriculture techniques. Activities included assisting local landowners in establishing, fruit orchards and improving the existing agricultural practices. The project also assisted in the rehabilitation of about 15 acres of land (jointly managed) by constructing an irrigation channel near Bar Valley. Moreover the possibility of soft loans for the purchase of transport, better breeds of livestock and seed are being explored.

Local communities were also persuaded to establish nurseries for fuel wood and forage species. The project and local communities established a demonstration nursery to increase the area under plant cover. Similarly areas have been designated as limited-use zones, where grass cutting and fuel wood collection is banned. In collaboration with other development projects in the area, fuel-efficient technologies were introduced and subsidised for adoption in each household of Bar Valley.

In order to improve potential income generating opportunities, activities such as training in carpet making, the establishment-of a basket and wood cutlery industry, and improved marketing techniques for local handicrafts are also being explored.

Creation of Environmental and Conservation Awareness

The project also felt that it was important to create an environmental awareness campaign to educate the local people in the importance of resource conservation. Local NGOs were encouraged and assisted to prepare and provide material on environmental education for distribution in the area. Likewise, the education unit of the project, in collaboration with the education staff of WWT/Pakistan, conducted special workshops for schools in the area and prepared special education material for school children, teachers and other interested groups. Environmental slogans on important environmental issues were also displayed in prominent locations throughout the valley.

Another important aspect of this education campaign was to provide training and research opportunities to students and graduates of both local and foreign universities.

Selected graduate students were encouraged to undertake field oriented research studies. They were also encouraged to analyze project activities to further improve the project. Six university graduates were given training opportunities on various project activities which eventually helped them find employment in organisations relevant to their subjects.

Replication of Project in Similar Areas

WWF/Pakistan felt that the Bar Valley Project could be replicated in similar areas. Two additional project areas were selected based on the following criteria:

- The area should have a minimum of 100 ibex, 50 markhor or 10 musk deer within the project boundaries:
- The local people should be willing to protect wildlife and their habitats; and
- The local people would sign a written conservation-cum-development agreement with WWF/Pakistan, where by they would be bound to abide by the rules and regulations of such agreement for a specified period of time.

Activities and strategies were to:

- — Ensure complete protection of wildlife species against poaching
- — Ensure the sustainable utilisation of natural resources
- — Help people to reduce, and ultimately eliminate, their dependence on critical and endangered natural resources, especially the forests and wildlife species of the area
- — Make the project sustainable within 10-15 years; and
- — Persuade and convince local people, NGOs, and government agencies to replicate these ideas in other parts of the North Western Frontier Provinces.

Problems Encountered During Implementation

While implementing the project, a number of problems emerged, some were anticipated while others were not. Although frustrating and time consuming, the project had to design and implement various activities to manage such problems. These problems were of two broad categories: community related and government related.

Community Related Problems

As mentioned previously the project had to rely on the cooperation of local hunters. The project plan was that revenue from licenses and visitation would be distributed equally amongst the households of the community, without regard to whether or not an individual was previously a hunter. The hunters were not eager to cease their activities for the questionable promise of future revenue. Another problem was if the hunters were given an incentive, villagers who did not hunt might attempt to receive this incentive.

Not every hunter in the community was eager to adopt the new rules of the project. The project had already identified several hunters who might violate the rules and continue to hunt. A comprehensive monitoring system was needed in each important ibex habitat to deter such hunters. Since there was no source of immediate income, and the local people were not accustomed to investing in such projects, the project had to either rely on volunteers or had to pay a group people to act as guards to protect the area.

The people, although generally ready to stop hunting, were reluctant to spend days in the remote parts of the valley to guard against poaching for no financial gain, it was thus decided that those who were willing to perform such duties would be paid by the project. Although the guards' salary was not high, every ad it in the valley wanted to participate. However, the project could only afford to pay 10 guards for a limited period. The project anticipated that once the community began to collect revenue from trophy hunting, these guards would then be paid by the community.

Government Related Problems

In order to be sustainable, the Bar Valley project relied heavily on the trophy hunting programme, though in fact, the federal government had banned all hunting. A long procedure was involved to relax the ban. Without government approval for the trophy hunting permits, the people of Bar Valley would most likely begin uncontrolled hunting again, and any chance for future conservation efforts would be unlikely. Another problem was that the relationship between the forest department and the local communities was bad. On several occasions, the local communities of Bar valley had negotiated with senior civil administration officials for a sustainable wildlife use project, but these discussions were hampered by serious conflicts with the forest and wildlife department. It was feared these past problems, would hinder the goals of the project. However, because of effective liaison by the project between the local people and the forest department, the relationship improved and now the forest department is cooperating with the trophy hunting project.

Sharing Revenue with People

Before the initiation of this project, there had been no precedent in Pakistan where revenue from wildlife resources had been shared with the local communities. However, the Bar Valley project had two major strengths:

1. Communities were involved in the protection of wildlife
2. WWF/Pakistan was helping communities in its management

The original proposal suggested that 70% of the revenue generated from trophy hunting should go to the local communities (and 30% to the local government). However, the Prime Minister changed the ratio to 75% / 25%. and thus a new rule emerged in the country which allowed local communities to be eligible to share in revenue from natural resource conservation, provided they participate in its protection.

Sustainability of the Bar Valley Project

Although it is hard to fix specific rules for the sustainability of natural resources, certain lessons can be learned from the project in Bar Valley.

Community Organisation and their Improved Management Skills

Over the last five years, the local communities have learned the importance of wildlife conservation. The community is well organised and has developed the necessary management skills to sustain their activities.

One example of improved the management capacity is the), stem of protection that was established. The system for protecting the ibex habitat has been done on a locally initiated basis which has satisfied all the members of the community. Protection activities are now being carried out on a regular basis with few conflicts. Likewise, the management committee is taking on other rural development issues.

Popularity of the Programme and its Replication in Other Areas

WWF/Pakistan is receiving a number of requests from communities in other valleys to assist in setting up similar projects in their areas. Popularity of the programme outside the project area is another indicators of is Success.

Cooperation of Government Agencies

Although essentially a community-based initiative, supported technically and financially by an NGO, government agencies are extending full cooperation to the programme.

This interest and confidence on part of the government was developed through several internal and external consultations as well as collaborative research such as the wildlife census programme in the valley.

Availability of Non-ambiguous Target Point

Any project which deals with the sustainable utilisation of natural resources, must have a terminating point-a point where the project will be taken over by local partners. If such a point is well identified, and local capacity developed, such a project or activity should be sustainable. The Bar Valley Project has a fixed ending target. It aims to improve ibex populations to a level when the surplus can be harvested through trophy hunting in such a way that a viable ibex population is maintained, while a new and sustainable source of income is generated or the local community.

Summing Up

The Bar Valley Project has become an example in Pakistan of participatory natural resource management. The project's community involvement and income generating potential showed tremendous promise for its sustainability. As of 1996, the available number of ibex in the Bar valley was about 900 with 50-60 animals ready for cultivation.

This could bring much needed income into the valley and generate further development initiatives that demonstrate to the local people that conservation of biodiversity and wildlife promise much in return.

II

MAHENDRA TRUST FOR NATURE CONSERVATION WITH ECOTOURISM

Ecotourism means different things to different people. ACAP began work before the word ecotourism had been coined. While ACAP has been implementing ecotourism style projects, this was not the goal of ACAP. Even the academic literature on ecotourism or sustainable tourism, ACAP is often used as an exemplary model.

The King Mahendra Trust for Nature Conservation (KMTNC)

KMTNC is an autonomous, NGO established in 1982 by the KMTNC Act, to meet the challenge of conservation for development. The Trust initiated its programme in Nepal's nature and wildlife conservation areas and later extended it to include sustainable community and tourism development, with the unique approach of directly benefiting the local people. The trust has emerged as a people-orientated institution relying essentially on local people for their support in conservation efforts. Its goal is not to seek a solution on its own, but to help the local people find answers. This approach to solving, problems aims to bring about attitudinal changes for conservation and development among the people rather than to impose predetermined ideas.

Since 1982, KMTNC has undertaken over 60 projects across Nepal, in the fields of nature conservation, biodiversity protection and sustainable tourism and community development. It established the, Nepal Conservation and Research Training Center (NCRTC) on the outskirts of the Royal Chitwan National Park in southern Nepal and extended wildlife research, monitoring and community-oriented programmes for residents in the buffer zones around the Royal Chitwan and Royal Bardia National Parks. The trust's recent undertakings are the Kathmandu Central Zoo and Manaslu Ecotourism Project in North Gorkha. The Trust currently employs over 400 staff.

Mission Statement of KMTNC

The mission of KMTNC is to conserve, manage and promote nature in all its diversity, balancing human needs with the environment on a sustainable basis for prosperity ensuring maximum community participation with due cognizance of the linkage between economics, environment and-ethics through a process in which people are both the principal actors and beneficiaries.

ACAP: An Innovative Approach to Nature Conservation and Community Development

In 1985, His Majesty King Birendra Sir Bikrarn Shah Dev of Nepal visited the Annapurna region and soon insisted it be given protected status. Thus, in 1986 the KMTNC committed itself to an undertaking known as ACAP, with a goal of conservation for development.

Despite careful planning, the pilot project launched in the western village of Ghandruk in 1986, was met with skepticism by the community. The concern stemmed form the bitter experiences of the visiting trekking guides from the Khumbu or Mount Everest region who are familiar with the National Park Programme. The Ghandruk residents feared that they as the people from the Khumbu region.

This skepticism retarded the project's progress for almost two years. However, it made the project implements realise the importance of gaining the trust and confidence of the local people in order to achieve the long-term goal of making them the custodians of their resource base. This realisation became instrumental in placing the Conservation Education and Extension Programme (CEEP) at the center of ACAP. The CEEP target groups include all direct and indirect resource users-from students and local residents to trekkers.

Protected Area Context

The Annapurna Conservation Area Project is Nepal's first and largest (7629 sq. km) conservation area in the country and is home to more than 125,000 people. The objective of the ACAP is to integrate tourism management, nature conservation, cultural resource conservation and community development for the benefit of local people and thousands of international visitors and their support staff, it is the first protected area to allow local residents to live within its boundaries and maintain their traditional rights to access and use of its natural resources. It is also the first protected area managed by local experts that does not use assistance of the army to protect the dwindling resource base on which the region depends. Instead, it invests the financial resources that are available for community development and local capacity building in the region. KMTNC receives no regular government funding for ACAP, but has been granted the right to collect the entry fees from trekkers. The fees collected (NRs 1,000 or US $20 per person), have been used to create an endowment fund with the aim of making it financially self sustaining. This has become an exemplary achievement, as it has proven that an NGO can return a significant portion of tourism revenue back into conservation and development activities.

Tourism Context

The Annapurna Conservation Area is Nepal's most popular trekking destination and receives close to 50,000 trekkers per year and an equal number of support staff such as guides and porters. In the 1970s, there were few lodges in the Annapurna region. The influx of "hippies" followed by budget trekkers, changed the nature of tourism in Nepal, leading to the proliferation of lodges along the main trekking routes, where public land encroachment became a trademark. Today, the Annapurna region has over 1,000 lodges and tea shops catering mainly to independent trekkers. Some of these lodges have been built in areas never before salted in, such as Ghorepani, the Annapurna Base Camp and Tolka. Even though such settlements are illegal, activities have continued. In the Annaprna region, as in other parts of Nepal, the response to tourism has been spontaneous where demand eventually led to development. The tourism industry was developed mainly through private initiatives without much public intervention or forethought.

Forty years of booming trekking tourism has led to the proliferation of lodges and related trades, but at a cost. Forests were cleared to build lodges and tea shops, some in areas never settled in before. Barren fields were used as camp sites. Fuel wood was indiscriminately used. There was no mechanism of local control over usage of natural resources or for that matter, over tourism. Solid human waste was discarded indiscriminately. Rapid deforestation, landslides, loss of top soil, land and water pollution and loss of wildlife habitats became evident-threatening the environmental quality of the region and the livelihood of local people.

Philosophy and Strategy

Environmental and socio-economical concerns in the Annapurna region are multifaceted. In this regard, instead of prescribing one single mitigating measure, the problems have been addressed holistically with a multi-land use concept. An integrated and grassroots approach, with flexibility in its programme implementation, has been devised to incorporate the relevant issues in which local communities are the key players and beneficiaries of the process.

Working Principles

People's Participation

The project involves local people in the decision making process, in identifying needs, completion of programmes, and maintenance of completed activities. For instance, the Conservation and Development Committees (CDCs) make decisions on how, when, where and how much the local people are allowed to use the forest. Furthermore, local people also contribute financially, both in cash and kind, and provide up to of the total programme cost to complete ACAP assisted initiatives. The chairman of Sikles CDC pointed out: "Motivation is the most important factor for the project's success. People's participation cannot be achieved unless the people realise that the projects will make an immediate benefit to them. Projects that are not desired by the local people should not be encouraged, as that will only cause greater loss of resources".

Catalyst or Lami

ACAP's role as a catalyst is directly linked to the amount of participation by the people. In a sense, this helps refine the division labor between the project and the local people. As most of the population is deprived of basic facilities such as drinking water, health care and education, ACAP plays the part of facilitator, by bringing in outside resources to help fulfill the needs of local residents.

Sustainability

There are no guarantees of automatic success, but the use of such working principles could help create an environment conducive for success. Development schemes often face skepticism during programme implementation (as in Ghandruk). Conversely, despite all the education and emphasis on people's actions, villagers still perceive KNITNC as a savior. Hence, preventing over expectation is essential if local efforts are to be sustained.

Ecotourism Development and Circuit Trekking in the Ghalekharka-Sikles Area

In 1992, building on the previous experiences of KMTNC/ ACAP and with financial assistance from the Asian development bank (ADB) and His Majesty's Government of Nepal, KMTNC Pioneered an ecotourism development project in Ghalekharka-Sikles area. The Project aims to:

— minimise undesirable environmental and socio-cultural impacts of tourism;
— generate and retain tourism income in the local economy;
— strengthen links between tourism and local development; and
— diversify tourism products.

To achieve these objectives, the trust has launched an integrated scheme comprised of a micro-hydro electricity, kerosene depots, local capacity building, visitor information centers, camping grounds, waste disposal, community lodges, publicity and promotion, eco-friendly toilets, conservation education and extension, research and monitoring, and other community development and nature conservation activities.

The seven day Ghalekharka-Sikles trekking route in the southern region of ACAP has advantages over the rest of the Annapurna region. The number of trekkers is less then 1,000 annually and the problems of crowding and congestion are less prevalent in this area thus, exerting less pressure on the natural and social environments. The Gurung are the dominant ethnic group in the area. Their rich culture is much the same now as it has been for many centuries. The environment is varied, ranging from temperate jungle to sparsely vegetated hill tops. It possesses some of the few remaining virgin rhododendron forests in Nepal and is comparatively free from pollution. The project area covers ten Village Development

Committees (VDC's), with a total population of over 20,000. Tourist development in this area has been carefully conceived, planned and implemented to diversify the tourism product within ACAP as well as to diversify Nepal's spectrum of tourism opportunities

Mechanism and Strategies

Tourism in the Ghale-Kharka Sikles area is still relatively new, thus the local people have little experience in this industry. The small number of tourists passing through the area (1,000 in 1993) does not exert much pressure on natural resources or require larger infrastructure development. Its impact on socio-economic and environmental conditions is also minimal. This presents several advantages. With careful planning, coordination of efforts, and implementation of. programmes, it is possible to avoid some of the problems experienced in other tourist destinations of the country, such as unreasonably high expectations of the local people, haphazard growth of tourism services, and lack of managerial intervention to mitigate problems. With an integrated and holistic approach, tourists are not regarded merely as a source of cash or income but as a partner in the development and conservation process.

The Ghalekharka-Sikles ecotourism project is a pioneering project in many ways:

Quality Experience

Around the Annapurna circuit, there are over 1,000 tea shops and lodges, it is not possible to walk, for more than half an hour without coming across one of them. In addition, problems of excessive litter pollution, rapid deforestation and encroachment into forests and public land exist. The Ghalekharka-Sikles route provides the trekker both the opportunity of walking through unpolluted, temperate jungle and virgin rhododendron forest for several hours without coming across a tea shop/ lodge.

Proactive Approach

In other parts of ACAP and Nepal, the approach has been reactive, responding to the existing tourism related problems, rather than emphasising the planning and development process. The approach in the Ghalekhacka-Sikles area has been proactive, designed to meet the needs of trekkers, while maintaining the environmental and socio-economic integrity of the area.

Demand Creation

Instead of responding to spontaneous tourism development, the ecotourism project has focused on creation of new and distinct products to achieve a symbiotic relationship between tourism and the environment. Local people have been made aware of the negative impacts of tourism, and social and Physical infrastructures are being developed to minimise them.

Decentralised Framework

Instead of relying on laissez fair development, the objectives and policies of the project are set forth and designed to strengthen the capacities of locally formed institutions. For instance, the lodge management committee is responsible for proper waste management, provision of alternative fuel technologies, setting standardised prices, and participating in lodge management training.

Community Ownership

Community ownership of tourism related products and facilities are encouraged and handed over to local communities to provide equitable distribution of tourist income. In the long run, community owned facilities, such as campsites, lodges and micro-hydro schemes, will become assets for generating income and employment, provided they are managed well. In other parts of Nepal, a tension exists between those who receive tourism income and those who do not. The community ownership will help maintain a collective and cohesive outlook in the community, rather than degenerating into competition amongst individuals.

Information Dissemination

Information dissemination, through brochures, signposts, and information centers has been emphasised, thereby creating self-responsibility rather than predetermined responsibility among visitors and locals. Visitors are informed as to their impact on the local culture, economy, and natural environment, and that they are regarded as partners in developing and sustaining the tourism initiatives.

Initiatives and Achievements

To sustain project initiatives, various local institutions have been formed and the capacity of their members built to strengthen the decentralised approach to tourism management. Under the CDC, forest management, camp site management, micro-hydroelectricity service, lodge management, kerosene and gas depot management committees are now effectively operating in the project area. The Camp site management responsibilities have been handed over to various village groups based on their ability to manage the fund and infrastructure being developed. For example, the Parche Mothers Group collected over NRs 100,000 (USS 2000) in 1996. The money was used for maintaining camping facilities and trails and for community development activities.

The provision of reliable alternatives to fuel wood is the only realistic way of protecting the forests. Alternative energy sources such as kerosene, micro-hydro electricity and back-boilers all contribute to reduce wood usage. For instance, the use of electricity not only reduced dependency on kerosene, but also brought over a 40% reduction in fuel wood consumption of the 200 households in the Sikles and Parche villages over the past two years. An energy expert indicated that 80% of energy is lost for heating, while only 20% is used for cooking. In response to this, a low wattage cooker known as *Bijuli Dekchi* (an electric pot used to boil water at night and cook during the day) and the back boiler have been introduced in the project area.

The use of electricity has had a positive impact on the local villagers' health, children's education, and night work. It has been proven in the Sikles area that with electricity, children study longer at night, and other family members tend to work after dark to produce both household and income generating materials. In addition, according to health experts, the incidence of chest and eye infections caused by smoke is also reduced by the use of electricity. The project his also introduced income generation activities such as traditional carpet weaving, poultry farming, and vegetable, kitchen gardening to add this diversification. Likewise small scale community development, such as the improvement or building of schools, safe drinking water systems, and trail bridge repair and maintenance has begun. As usual, the villagers are required to make a contribution of between 30-70% of the total programme cost, either through the provision of labor or the partial financing of each project.

Opportunities and Constraints

There is a Question of how far NGOs like ACAP can go towards fulfilling the objectives of an eco tourism programme. The very nature of NGOs is that they rely on money from various sources. The consistency of this money is not guaranteed. The above question is also a warning. There are increasing numbers of academics who see NUC)s as anew tool or the third path in development. Such optimism can be dangerous as it raises false expectations. After all, NGOs operate in the global economy as do all companies and organisations. At present, the world economy is in overall contraction, which simply means that there is less money to be spent on development. Another question is how far should NGOs go in implementing development programmes? The fact is that where democracy exists, the elected government should be held accountable for implementing development programmes.

The future of ecotourism in Nepal relies heavily on who is responsible for marketing, setting the trekking quotas, increasing the entry fees once, the infrastructure is in place and the carrying capacity of a tourist destination themselves. It is not sustainable if KMTNC remains the overseer of the area. At the same time, it is KMTNC that has the most experience in running such types of projects-so it remains to be seen whether this knowledge and experience can be transferred to the local people.

There is also an issue of ownership. Can the local interest groups or communities stop the emergence of private lodges and camping sites and compete with the private sector?. Again this raises the question of how far local people can be empowered in the control of their newly created resources, and whether or not they can transfer the skills and leadership they have developed to future generations. It is likely that the number of trekkers will increase rapidly once the infrastructure is in place. This may lead to the area being overrun and overused, and end in a classic case of the "boom and bust" scenario. All of these questions must be addressed seriously if ecotourism to a given area is to succeed.

As already mentioned, KNITNUACAP often faces the problem of over expectations from the villagers. KMTNC/ ACEP also faces over expectations from donor agencies. Successes such as the development of Ghandruk village are quite naturally emphasised, while Iess glamorous projects receive little attention. This can create the impression that KMTNC, ACAP is constantly successful. This, of course, can cause some negative results, such as:

— Donor agencies may expect their money to be used for projects that attract a lot of publicity. The reality is that the majority of KMTNC/ACAP's work goes unseen by the general public and so receives little attention from the media and other Information sources.

— Donor agencies, may question why KMTNC/ACAP needs large amounts of money, when the projects (or the projects that are seen) seem to be so easy to implement with almost guaranteed success.

— The very concept of the grassroots approach has caused KMTNC/ ACAP to have high overhead costs. Methods for measuring costs are usually based on the quantity and quality of the infrastructure implemented. This ignores the key issues of social development and difficult working conditions. The impacts of motivation and education are difficult to quantify. Similarly, nature conservation is also difficult to measure in economic terms.

The philosophy behind the actions of KMTNC/ACAP is to create an ecotourism project that is holistic. In other words, the natural environment, local people, tourists and the activities of ACAP have been coordinated-as far as possible to fit together in a mutually beneficial manner. Many opportunities exist in Nepal for greater improvements in the quality and benefits brought about by tourism. ACAP has attempted, with recognizable success, to start a process of sustainable ecotourism development. ACAP will keep working on various projects, but it cannot succeed-alone. The challenge Des with other groups, NGOs, tour operators, hotel owners and the government to create conditions favorable to sustainable ecotourism development.

III

A CASE STUDY FROM SIKKIM, INDIA

The Sikkim Biodiversity and Ecotourism Project (SREP) is a collaborative initiative designed to conserve the biological diversity of key destinations. At the heart of the project are participatory approaches that link enterprise operation with conservation action, while merging traditional cultural practices. Working with communities, the private sector and government. The project builds upon people's skills, interests and knowledge to:

— increase awareness of resource conservation in the communities and private sector

— increase economic returns from ecotourism services and enterprises,

— contribute to policies that meet ecotourism and conservation goals.

The project is a joint effort of the Mountain Institute and the G.B. Pant Institute of Himalayan Environment and Development. Project collaborators include the Travel Agents Association of Sikkim (TAAS).

Green Circle (a Sikkimese NGO), the Khangchendzonga Conservation Committee la community NGO) and local communities at key tourism sites.

Project Area

Khangchendzonga National Park and communities in surrounding areas in western Sikkim are the focus of the project. Within the park is Sikkim's major trekking route, the Yuksam-Dzongri Goecha La Trail. The trail offers an exhilarating climb through dense forests and impressive mountain views. The forests and alpine meadows are some of the most biologically diverse in India and contain over 30 species of rhododendrons, 400 species of orchids and many other flowering plants. The park and surrounding areas also contain a large mammal population (over 80) and more than 300 species of birds and butterflies.

The spiritual and physical focus of the area is Khangchendzonga the World's third highest mountain peak (8548 m) and revered as the protective deity of Sikkim. At the trail head is Yuksam, Sikkim's first capital. From Yuksam, visitors can take short walk to several archeological ruins and to Dubdi Monastery, Sikkim's oldest monastry. A variety of ethnic groups, including Lepchas (the indigenous people of Sikkim), Bhutias (long-time Tibetan residents) and Nepalis, as well as Tibetan refugees, live in this culturally and historically rich area. The majority of the population pursues traditional agricultural livelihoods, while in recent years some have ventured into tourism activities. Other project sites include Khecheopalri lake, one of Sikkim's most sacred and popular lakes, and Pelling, a settlement near Pemayangtse Monastery.

Project Components

The SBEP focuses its work in three key areas that link conservation with ecotourism enterprises.

Increasing Community and Private Sector Biodiversity Conservation Initiatives Activities Include

— community ecotourism plans covering site-enhancement and trail and site maintenance

— natural resource management and monitoring, and conservation education

— supporting fuel wood reduction by trekking operators and local lodges

— supporting local NGOs working in ecotourism and conservation.

Increasing Economic Returns From Community-Based and TAAS Ecotourism. Activities Include

— training in ecotourism services (e.g. for guides, lodge-owners, cooks, porters);

— supporting new community ecotourism enterprises (e.g. vegetable growing indigenous foods, fuel wood-saving equipment and short, guided treks);

— developing marketing strategies for community-based ecotourism and TAAS ecotourism activities; and

— conducting market research and developing new

ecotourism products such as off-season activities and eco-lodge designs.

Improving and Contributing To Policy-Making On Conservation and Ecotourism. Activities Include

— scientific and participatory monitoring of project activities and impacts-

— applied research on conservation and ecotourism • sharing of research and monitoring findings among policy-makers, communities and the private sector; and

— promoting public-private sector dialogue through workshops, exchanges and policy review.

Innovation figures strongly in the project. Participants are invoked in ecotourism planning, training courses and conservation management and utilise participatory learning tools that build upon best practices and the positive attributes of Sikkim's natural and cultural heritage. A combination of appreciative inquiry' and modified participatory learning and action (PLA) tools provide the basis for planning, implementing and evaluating community ecotourism activities. Using the same approach, the project is exchanging experience and expertise with mountain peoples and affiliated projects in Nepal and other parts of India.

Community Ecotourism Planning

A critical element of planning and subsequent actions in ecotourism is the focus on appreciative inquiry, a process which finds and builds upon positive attributes and values in local environments and groups of stakeholders. Unlike traditional rural development efforts that incorporate PLA techniques and focus on problem identification and solving, appreciative inquiry asks questions such as:

— What do you value in your community and environment?

— What excites you most about where you live?
— What is the most positive vision you have of your environment and community in the future?
— What do we need to do to realise a vision of the future?

The focus is on finding the causes of success and motivation rather than failure as the basis for community planning. PLA tools have been modified to help investigate these questions. This includes: trend lines of issues such as waste disposal, wildlife, and forest cover which are projected over 10-20 year horizons; schematic maps are created to fore see future community and natural resources status; mapping of current and potential ecotourism resources; and ranking of ecotourism attributes such as sites and services. A similar approach is adopted during the evaluation of community conservation and ecotourism activities, when the focus is on "What worked well and What needs to be improved"?

This lesson outlines the experiences from community ecotourism planning at Yuksam. Yuksam has served as the basis for further planning in other project sites in western Sikkim, and many of the lessons learned have been incorporated into other project activities such as training in ecotourism professions. The case study of Yuksam is interspersed with field notes from the various sessions.

In May 1996, participatory community ecotourism planning was conducted in Yuksam. The team of five project staff and six local residents worked with local community members to gather information and generate site-specific ideas for linking tourism related activities to conservation efforts. One major problem identified was that tourists were spending a relatively short period of time in the area. Local community members felt that the opportunity for increased income generation lay in extending the stay of visitors to the area. On an initial experimental basis, team members used a framework of appreciative inquiry and modified participatory learning techniques to suit the purposes of ecotourism planning

All participants were asked to "discover" the elements in their environment and community that represent the best of what they have to offer. Positive attributes identified by villagers Were:

— Lots of greenery
— Community unity seen in actions to help others
— Meeting tourists from many different countries;
— Fresh air;
— Dense forests
— Historical Importance of Yuksam, the first capital of Sikkim

Participants were then asked to dream and to think of what the best vision of Yuksam might be in ten years time. Participants were asked, what would you like to see in Yuskam ten years from now. Their responses include:

— More forest cover
— More tourists in Yuksam
— No litter in Yuksam and along the trails
— Local conservation groups or NGOs
— More income from tourism
— Yuksam perceived as a little Switzerland

The next phase was to use PLA tools to collect some of the information needed to design a plan for achieving the common dream, one that was inclusive of participants' aspirations, and focused on the issue of increasing income from existing tourists. A preliminary report was prepared by participants and included:

— A listing of environmental and community attributes

— Ecotourism resource maps
— Local stories about sites and history
— Maps and analysis of the availability and use of forest resources
— Socio-economic analysis of tourism benefits

The final step was to identify actions to be taken in the next three to six months that would begin to deliver their vision. Thus, in addition to the report, specific outputs from the planning exercise-were agreed to be implemented in the following four to six months. These included:

— beautification activities (e.g. planting of native tree species and cleanup campaigns
— training courses for lodge-operators, naturalist guides
— collection of material to be used for a promotional brochure about Yuksam and its attractions.

In addition to the activities identified, in October 1996, 28 village members organised their own cleanup campaign of the major trekking route, generating a small initial amount of funds for further activities through the recycling of bottles and tins.

In December 1996, a participation-valuation of activities since the previous May was conducted and a plan developed for 1997. In addition to the use of PLA tools (such as pair-wise ranking and standard ranking to assess activities) narrated stories of community action in conservation were also documented. Yuksam residents have readily accepted the principle of local contributions to project activities and enthusiastically attended the training courses as well as showed a keen interest in enterprises such as low-cost vegetable production, community-wide cleanups and afforestation campaigns. Another activity was a lodge-operators' training, where participants developed standard tariffs and menus. Operators now maintain visitor registers and issue receipts to customers.

The evaluation was very insightful highlighting areas that the Project and the Community needed to work on (e.g. dissemination of results, the nature and benefits of participation, and the role of community groups and institutions in ensuring widespread and enthusiastic participation). Local communities were concerned that the benefits of participation In project activities were seen to be fair, and that the community itself should visibly participate in the decision-making Process. For example, the villagers decided who should attend study tours and how the rest of community might share in the benefits of visiting other sites.

Based on the evaluation, local community members and project staff prepared an action plan for 1997. Tools and outputs, such as mapping trekking routes and future maps of the village, were used as the framework for designing and deciding activities. The final plan used more traditional planning tools such as logistical framework, re-sponsibilities, time frames and indicators of success.

A critical element developed by village participants during the use of the methodology was the commitment to an action plan, demonstrating as the villagers say," that we should go beyond talk and do something" In the first exercise it was a cleanup of the village by teachers, schoolchildren and other villagers, in the second session, villagers proposed to raise funds for garbage management and visitor education. By March 1996, three signboards and six garbage bins were in place throughout Yuksam. Community identified activities for 1997 included:

- — garbage management in the village and along the trail
- — trail repair by local residents
- — plantation work and management
- — training for porters, lodge-operators, guides, pack animal operators, trek cooks;
- — conservation education of visitors and residents

— completion of the Yuksam promotional brochure.

Other results of community ecotourism planning in Yuksam included:

- A series of projects and other events to form the Khangchendzonga Conservation Committee (KCC). KCC developed a COC for visitors to follow in the area. Signboards with the code were erected in Yuksam, and visitors now receive a copy of the code at the lodges.
- Yuksam community members participating as resource persons for a community ecotourism planning effort at nearby Kecheopalri Lake.

Lessons Learned and Further Opportunities

While the community planning methodology is in its formative stages, it was found that the following appear to be critical elements in the process.

- A framework of appreciative inquiry needs to be developed which focuses on what is done well, what works among and excites the groups of stakeholders, and what helps participants develop a positive vision of the future. The purpose here is to start identifying the factors that lead to success among stakeholders. Maps, drawings, lists and discussion all serve to develop and represent people's ideas and visions.
- A process of participatory learning about the environment, stakeholders and other groups and communities that informs the design of plans. Several advantages to this process are to:
    1. engage a larger section of the population and to develop rapport and trust with local people.
    2. provide a training function among local com-

munities in community-based conservation and ecotourism planning.

3. generate data which serves as planning information and a baseline for monitoring the initial participatory process helps in providing the foundation for subsequent participation.
4. produce documents and information that can be used by the villagers. Local people use them as reference material, guidelines, source of promotional material, and the community assistant regularly refers to it as a work plan and monitoring too. These reports also serve to document the process and its progress.

— Developing a participatory plan of action. Often the first plan is one that emerges out of the participatory learning session, covering one to six months and always initiated by one joint action and commitment during the learning phase. A larger plan is usually developed after the completion of the first set of activities. Elements of the plan include: what activity, who is responsible, what is the schedule, what is the level of co-financing and what are the indicators of success. However, this set of steps is not set in stone and can and should be adapted to the needs and interests of the communities. This plan is presented by the participants to the community for discussion and revision.

— Co-financing by participants is an essential part of project activity implementation. Nearly all activities have a local contribution by communities in the form of cash labor or materials. This helps local people decide which activities are most wanted and usually ensures follow through with project activities.

— Community evaluation of action plans on a periodic basis using participatory indicators and methods, followed by modification and further action plans as required.

Conclusions

Local communities have responded to and participated very positively in the process of planning and action for conservation and tourism. Project staff has always been concerned with ensuring that the process avoids being an expert driven approach. The process used and its elements are as much the efforts of community participants as the efforts of project staff. Local villagers worked with staff to develop the protocol of questions, defining elements and procedures for evaluation.

The approach may have a tendency to lead community members to develop visions that the project simply does not have the mandate to assist with. To avoid unrealistic expectations of the project and its staff, the boundaries of the project are made clearer in the process. This did not hamper the process, nor has it dampened the excitement. On several occasions staffs have helped communities to find other assistance for activities that the project could not support.

In a state such as Sikkim, where the central and state governments have traditionally been the source of development and conservation support, it has been very encouraging to see a ready acceptance of the concept of local contributions to community-identified actions.

IV

THE LOWER, KINABATANQAN: THE IMPORTANCE OF COMMUNITY CONSULATIONS IN ECOTOURISM DEVELOPMENT

Tourism was officially recognised as an industry in Sabah by 1986, albeit on a very small scale. Sabah's reputation as one of the major nature tourism sites in Malaysia is based on its abundant range of forest habitats and wildlife species. Most of these sites are within protected areas where local communities use of forest and land resources is nonexistent or minimal. The need to communicate and consult local communities to develop ecotourism activities within these areas did not arise. The lower Kinabatangan a vast floodplain and with a catchment area of about 16,800 square kilometers, is one of Malaysia's main wetland areas. The upper parts of the Kinabatangan catchment area are rugged, forested hills and mountain ranges. The lower parts are swamps and lowlands, with small sandstone hills and limestone outcrops dotting the landscape. Much of the region remains under forest cover and owned by the government, but usage of land by private owners and conversion to agriculture has been, and is still proceeding at a fast rate. Policy decisions on land use in the 1930s resulted in large areas of the lower Kinabatangan being used for timber harvesting and areas which had not been issued with titles or long-term leases for agriculture were demarcated as forest reserves. Later, it was decided that agriculture deserved precedence over forestry, and during the 1970s most of these areas were made available to investors in agriculture projects. For communities along the banks of the river, these decisions provided the impetus to apply for unclaimed land. Windfall profits were made from selling rights to timber on that land, and later by selling the land for agriculture development. Since then, a relatively small number of companies have been acquiring most of the land in lower Kinabatangan for expansion of oil palm estates. These developments point to a future where eventually all available land will be converted to agriculture, riverine communities may cease to exist traditionally, and livelihoods dependent on natural resources like fisheries, timber and farming can no longer be supported. In 1989 it was proposed that an area of about 30,000 hectares (it has since been, reduced to under 30,000 hectares) in the lower Kinabatangan be reserved as a wildlife sanctuary to protect a range of habitats which

6

Ecotourism Management

The primary advantage of ecotourism is that it provides an impetus to expand both conservation and tourism development. On the conservation side, ecotourism is the conservation benefit which is most easily sold and thus incorporated into decisions about land use. In concrete terms, entrance and other fees associated with ecotourism can supplement existing governmental conservation budgets and can provide incentives for private sector conservation. On the economic development side, ecotourism can bring employment opportunities to remote regions.

Many observers voice the concern that ecotourism has not reached its potential as a tool of conservation or economic development, in part because many worthwhile projects cannot find financing, in part because host countries have yet to receive the full revenue potential inherent in ecotourism, and in part because relatively little of the revenue which has been generated has directly supported conservation and economic development.

In an effort to expand ecotourism's contribution, this chapter outlines strategies for: setting tourism fees, using these fees to finance ecotourism development and traditional conservation management; and increasing ecotourism's contribution to the economic development of communities near ecotourism destinations.

has caused misunderstandings between tour operators and members of the community.

For tourism to support conservation, development and equity welt-thought-out policies and programmes need to be in place involving all the major stakeholders, especially local communities who now face a future of depleting natural resources and the inability to fully capitalise on emerging economic activities.

To gain a better understanding of these villages, and to understand whether tourism can really be an effective tool for conservation, in 1996 a six month survey was conducted in five selected villages as part of the multi-disciplinary Sabah Biodiversity Conservation Project. The survey was carried, out by Sabah Wildlife Department with technical assistance 4 from WWF/M, and funds from the Danish Cooperation for Environment and Development (DANCED). The survey was the initial part of a project to look into the possibility of starting a model community-based tourism project in the area. The primary results of the study and the feasibility of community-based tourism are described in the following sections.

Methods

Methods involved formal and informal discussions with village representatives, tour operators and relevant government agencies, with visits to existing and potential tourism sites.

Consultation with Community Leaders

It was acknowledged before the tourism survey began, that a participatory consultative process with village authorities and members of the community would be key to understanding the social structure and hierarchy of decision makers in the selected villages.

Consulting with the village authorities was, however,

not an easy process. The relatively recent change of government in Sabah had also been accompanied by changes of the village authority. Dialogue sessions with the community leaders were looked upon with a degree of suspicion by certain individuals. Eventually, after Setting the support of the community, leaders in two villages, community meetings % ere arranged to again clarify the objectives of the survey.

During these community meetings, it was found that the presence of the Wildlife Department, and the process of establishing a wildlife sanctuary were referred to, repeatedly, as sources of various problems. For example, some individuals complained of crop damage by elephants, asserting that this problem is due to the existence of a sanctuary and failure on the part of the Wildlife Department, in fact, elephants have always periodically raided village gardens and, if rates of damage have increased recently, it is more likely due to the expansion of plantations..

These community meetings also tended to be dominated by certain individuals, usually men, with little representation from the women or youth. After four decades of timber harvesting being the main economic activity in the region, it was difficult for them to understand the concept of a service-based economic activity such as tourism.

The failure of resident tour and lodge operators to involve the community in the development and management of their operations has also denied the local people an opportunity to understand the tourism industry.

All tour operators interviewed during the survey mentioned that they had, at one time or another tried to involve local residents and encourage local tourism initiatives but with limited success. The high turnover rate of local staff was attributed to, their unreliability and unrealistically high salary expectations. This is not surprising as they were not properly introduced and exposed to this type of Industry.

Consulting the village leaders about the survey and its objectives was an important step in establishing rapport with the village, but for them to believe that community based is economically-Oable and sustainable, there had to be proof of its benefits.

Village Authority and Cohesiveness

As a separate activity of the SBCP, a local boat service was initiated among some boat owners in Sukau, where they agreed to use a rotation system. This system was thought the most suitable as many of the boatmen also had other activities or were away for a few months a year to collect edible bird nests and hence could only be involved part time.

The village Development and Security Committee (VDSC) was responsible for organising the boatmen determining the standards of the service and monitoring its progress, while SBCP provided the necessary technical support. The eagerness and confidence of the boatmen involved was notable. Subsequent meetings in the development of this initiative, however, highlighted the lack of widespread support from the village. The root of this dissatisfaction and lack of cohesiveness was not fully nor easily understood, and this presented a problem in providing an example of a viable community tourism project.

As most government-supported development plans go through the normal official procedure the VDSC will eventually be the implementing agency for these plans or programmes. Various government agencies are keen to develop the human resources in rural area but if the village authority structure is not strong enough to capitalise on these opportunities, they will be left behind in favor of larger towns.

The need for constant assistance and support of the VDSC in developing this initiative made the decision to appoint a local village facilitator more significant.

Villager Facilitator

The idea to appoint a local village facilitator was initially made to overcome main constraints: a lack of communication and a lack of information. Although three out of the like villages are accessible by road, there are no telephone communications with them. The role of the facilitator is to liaise between SBCP and the village. The facilitator is also involved in identifying village priorities and the significance of tourism on the priority list. The problems encountered in developing the boat service highlighted the need for facilitator supported communication and problem solving. It was decided that there should be one facilitator in each village. Generally, this approach has been well received.

Initially, when the time came to select a village representative to be facilitator and be trained to use PRA (Participatory Rural Appraisal) methods, the idea was met with indifference. Only one village readily chose a representative during an organised village meeting. The consultative process within the villages did not materialise. Because the villages were only visited on average once a month for one or two days, the need for continuity in communication and consultation, preferably by an NGO or other neutral party became evident. A project extension has been proposed by WWF/M, and one of the recommendations is to have a site-based facilitator or manager who would be able to provide the neutrality in organising further discussions among the different interest groups.

Although tourism can serve as a catalyst to improve the local economy, infrastructure development, social development and conservation of natural resources, the roles of all stakeholders must be clearly defined to meet these objectives.

So far, only two of the stakeholders in this area, the tour lodge operators and the local communities, have been actively engaged. The other stakeholder groups (i.e. the major land owners in the region who are not local villagers) were conspicuous in their absence during the main workshop at the end of the tourism survey.

Dialogue Sessions among Major Stakeholders

Oil palm companies are the major land users in this area and have cleared tens of thousands of hectares of forest land bordering the proposed wildlife sanctuary for oil palm cultivation. The level of pollution caused by effluent from, the processing mills appears to be quite high, and its effects have not been mitigated adequately. Decisions made in the 1970s and early 1980s; by the government to release forest reserves in lower Kinabatangan for timber production, along with the decisions made to locate two or Sabah's six Integrated Timber Complexes at Sandakan and to ban log exports, contributed substantially to the conversion of forest to agriculture in the area region.

For community-based tourism to develop in the lower Kinabatangan, there must bean integrated approach to land-use planning and natural resources management among the major stakeholders the Government, oil palm industry, timber industry and local communities. At present, the situation from a local resident's point of view is that the burden of maintaining the integrity of the wildlife sanctuary is on their shoulders, and local communities have to adhere to a certain set of conservation "do's" and "don'ts". At the same time, an oil palm or timber company can clear forested lands larger than the sanctuary and make enormous profits. Obviously this competition in land use and benefit sharing has to be resolved. The Sabah government is fully aware of these issues, and development of a regional tourism plan has been proposed.

Even though the idea to develop this management plan is excellent, the time frame required to achieve and implement it might be too long as land conversion is being carried out at a rapid pace. After analysing the results of the survey, other options are being explored. One of them is forest rehabilitation on privately owned land for timber production where some local individuals have expressed interest. The conservation, and potential tourism value of this venture is, however, severe])-challenged by the ability of residents to make much quicker profits by simply selling the land.

Faced by this competition, the possibility of actually-purchasing tracts of private land before they are sold to be converted to oil palm estates has even been considered. Another option is that contributions from the government (Forestry Department), private sector (timber and oil palm companies and tour operators) and tourists can support a community forestry programme. Whether or not this is feasible will require more thorough investigation on the actual land use and ownership scenario. Linking tourism with other community projects such as this would require a greater awareness of the positive values of tourism and how they can help to increase the quality of life in a community. However, in formational material on conservation and environmental awareness is lacking in many rural areas.

When the local boat service was initiated, it presented a good opportunity to develop hew information materials that could be used as guidelines to encourage good environmental practices. One of the preliminary activities was a mini-workshop in Sukau to highlight the positive and negative aspects of tourism, and how communities ought plan and manage the tourism product together to minimise the negative impacts. The other activity now being pursued is the production of information leaflets on the local tourism services in the village as an economic incentive to maintain an acceptable standard in their services.

Information Dissemination

For a nature-based tourism product to be sustainable, the elements that make up the product itself must be properly managed. In the case of the lower Kinabatangan, it is the natural habitats, diversity of wildlife populations, local history and culture. During dialogue sessions with the communities involved, it was suggested that for a community based tourism product to be viable, it has to compete with existing products. This resulted in a number of ideas based on additional knowledge of the area, which can be developed into a variety of programmes for tourists and the general public to appreciate. Drafts of informational leaflets that were made to introduce the local boat service in Sukau, and a guided jungle walk through a nearby limestone hill, could not be disseminated as hoped because the VDSC could not decide on who should coordinate the potential tourists wishing to use these services.

Returning to the example of the local boat service, the rotation system, although thought fair, raised the question of unequal distribution of tourists per boat and loss of turn if they happened to be busy elsewhere. Although the system was discussed many times, there is still, the misconception that being part of the boat service is similar to holding a permanent job with a guaranteed income. On the other hand, those that have held full-time jobs with the resident tour lodges state that working full-time is not suitable, and the hours are too long. It is these views and varying perceptions amongst villagers that make information dissemination to outsiders an issue requiring much thought. Information, training and exposure are crucial to create a better understanding and awareness of each other's role in the economic development of a community. Screening of information to ensure credibility is also important. For example, SBCP was asked to include the availability of a village guesthouse for overnight tourists in a proposed informational leaflet when in fact the guesthouse was lacking essential amenities.

The concept of information flow among the major users of the natural resources and land in the lower Kinabatangan is an important step, but more importantly, how can this information and understanding of each others' roles be used to overcome pressing is sues in formulating an integrated approach to appropriate land use in this area?

As Malaysia moves into the information technology era, there is an opportunity to tap into all the available resources to address the above issues by improving communication between rural and urban areas, and between policy / decision makers and the affected public.

Conclusion

When this tourism survey first started, the main objective was to look into the potential of community-based tourism projects in the lower Kinabatangan that would help support the wildlife sanctuary without denying the local communities access to the natural resources within the sanctuary. Not only was the process of consultation and dialogue important in achieving this objective, but it also heightened appreciation of the complex social structure of each village. From this process, it is hoped that a long-term relationship, based on the trust that tourism can be an effective tool to promote conservation, social development and equity, can be created.

11

Wildlife Legislation and Administration

Wildlife Legislation

The native rulers in India took certain steps and created hunting or shooting reserves and prevented these areas from the free use and movement of the local population. After independence till 1972, when the Wildlife (Protection) Act, 1972 was enacted, no uniform national legislation was there to control and regulate the wildlife activities. Much was left on the mercy of the people. Though a few voluntary conservation agencies like Bombay Natural History Society were trying to create public awareness among the mass for protecting the wildlife. No major steps were taken, with the result that most of the colourful wild fauna and flora are today threatened and endangered. The Bombay Natural History Society, established in 1883, as a private agency took a first stop in formulating a comprehensive and detailed act for Bombay in 1951, which was known as Bombay Wild Animals and Wild Birds Protection Act 1951. The other special legislation enacted by the different State Governments were, the Elephant Preservation Act, Rhinoceros Preservation Act and the Games Act. These acts made local impacts only and helped to control the wildlife activities of certain areas. None of these were national in scope. There was a need to enact a uniform and national legislation on wildlife activities. Covering all the aspects of wildlife control, administration, management, National Parks and Sanctuaries and trade in the animals it was essential for the protection, conservation and efficient management of the left over wild heritage of our country. Keeping them objectives into consideration, the Wildlife (Protection) Act 1972 was enacted and this act has been extended in all the States except Jammu & Kashmir and Nagaland. Jammu & Kashmir Govt. has since enacted its separate act on the similar pattern. Now, the Wildlife (Protection) Act, 1972, is the Primary legal document to control the wildlife management in all over the country. Before 1976 the forests and wildlife were State subjects but by virtue of 42 Amendments, in 1976, wildlife and forests have been brought under concurrent list of the Indian Constitution, thereby vesting the Central Government with power and authority to exercise more control over these subjects. This step was taken when most of the State Governments were neglecting the cause of forests and wildlife, at the cost of development activities. The sequel of this was the Indian Forest (Conservative) Act 1980, which prevents the denotification or use of any forest area for non-forestry purposes. Recently an amendment has been passed by the Parliament, which deals with the transportation of the wild animals, under Indian Wildlife (Protection), Act 1972.

The Wildlife (Protection) Act, 1972

The act provides for the protection of wild animals and birds and for matters connected therewith or ancillary or incidental thereto. It has seven chapters and sixty-six sections and five schedules of animals. These chapters deal with Administration of Wildlife Organisation, hunting of wild animals, Sanctuary and National Parks. Trade in animals and animal articles, prevention and detection of offences and miscellaneous. Chapter one of this act deals with the preliminaries and definition. Chapter second from section 3 to 8 deals with the appointment of officers such as Director of Wildlife Preservation of the Central Govt., Chief Wildlife Warden and Wildlife Wardens in the States, their duties and powers. It also deals with the appointment and duties of the

Wildlife Advisory Boards in the States. The most important contribution of this act is the controlling of hunting of wild animals. It is dealt in chapter third from section 9 to 17. For the purpose of controlling the hunting, the wild animals, birds, amphibians and reptiles have been grouped into five different schedules. Under schedule 1st are all the endangered and rare species and their hunting is completely prohibited throughout the country. For example tiger, Indian lion, leopard (*Panthera pardus*), Kashmir stag (*Cervus elaphus hanglu*), binturong (*Arctictis* binturong), black buck (*Antelope cervicapra*), crocodiles (*Crocodiles palustris*). Great Indian bustard (*Choriotis nigriceps*), Siberian white crane (*Grus leucogeranus*), lion tailed macaque, whales, leopard cat (*Felis bengalensis*), Indian wild ass (*Equus hem/onus khur*), bharal (*Pseudois nayaur*), four horned antelope (*Tetraceras quadricornis*), brow antlered deer or thamin, python, serow (*Capricornis sumatraensis*), peafowl (*Pavo cristatus*), lesser or red panda (*Alurus fulgens*) musk deer (*Moschus moschiferus*) etc. Schedule second consists of special games. These animals require more attention in protection and the hunting of which is allowed by issuing license under very exceptional circumstances. The schedule includes animals such as Indian elephant (*Elephus maximwn*), Bison or Gaur (*Bos gaurus*), Nilgiri langur (*Presbytis johni*), Himalayan brown bear (*Lusus arctos*), Himalayan black bear (*Selenarctos thibetanus*), Dolphin, Stump tailed macaque (*Macaca speciosa*), Giant squirrels etc. Schedule third includes big games like chinkara, or Indian gazelle (*Gazella gazella bennefti*), Chital (*Axis axis*). Nilgai (*Boselapnus frpgocamelus*), Sambhar (*Cervus unicolour*), Mothbear (*Melursus ursinus*), Hyena (*Hyaena hyaena*), Hog deer (*Axis porcinus*), Barking deer (*Muntiacus mutjak*), Tibetan wolf (*Canis lupus*). Schedule fourth comprises small games such as Hares (Common Indian desert, Himalayan mousehare), Marmots (*Marmota bobak himalayana*), otters (*Lutra lutra*), Falcons, Finches, flamingoes, Hornbills, Ducks, Cranes, Bustards, Pigeons, Pelicans, Swans. The last schedule includes the vermins, such as common crow, mice, rats etc. The schedule pattern has brought uniformity in the control and supervision throughout the country and the animals and birds are protected with equal measure everywhere. On the recommendation of the subcommittee of Indian Board for Wildlife these schedules are revised, depending upon the results and experience gained on the particular animal or bird. Now, through a notification in 1980, separate schedules have been drawn for the flora part of Wildlife, on the same pattern. For example, Dioscorea deltoidea in I-B. Red panda of family Orchidaceae, in I-B, Frerea indica of Asclepiadaccae in II-B, Fern sp. or Cyathed, sp. II-B etc. Chapter four of the act exclusively deals with the creation, management and legal provision for the National Parks, Sanctuaries, Reserves and close areas. Details of specific rules for their creation and control are dealt with separately in the chapter dealing with National Parks and Sanctuaries in the preceding pages of this book. Now, the concept of creation of "Biosphere Reserve" is also to be brought within the purview of the act. Now trade or commerce in wild animals or animal products has also been regulated through Section 39 to 49 of chapter fifth of the act. All the animals and their products have been declared government property and no body can engage himself in the trade or custody of the animals or their product without the prior permission of competent authority i.e. the Chief Wildlife Warden or Wildlife Warden or any other officer empowered in this behalf. Further provision is made for using certificate of ownership by the Chief Wildlife Warden to the persons, who are in lawful custody of any wild animal or animal article, trophy etc. Adequate provisions are made in regulating the transfers of animals and their products from one State to another, from one owner to another. Every trader has to register himself and he should maintain all records and keep the records open for inspection to the authorised officer. Stringent provisions and penal measures have been made for hunting the animals of schedule I and schedule II. Chapter V of the act describes the penalties and preventive measures for violation of the provisions of the act. Chapter VI of the act describes the powers of the officers in preventing commitment of offences, enforcement of penalties, punishments, for violating the provisions of this act. It includes section 50 to 58 of the act. The last chapter deals with the miscellaneous aspects such power to alter entries in schedule, power of Central and State governments to make rules etc.

Administration of the Act

Before the enactment of Wildlife (Protection) Act, 1972, the administration of wildlife was the part of the normal duties of a forest officer and no separate organisation was specially created for it. But the Wildlife (Protection) Act, 1972 made elaborate and comprehensive provision for the administration of wildlife, both at Central as well as State level. Wildlife Wings have been carved out of the forest departments in all the States. At the Central level, the Inspector-General of Forests is the highest exclusive dealing with forests and wife life in the Ministry of Agriculture and he is assisted by one Joint Secretary for Forest and Wildlife, designated as Director of Wildlife Preservation, Government of India, the purpose of carrying out the provisions of Wildlife (Protection) Act. There are Deputy-Inspector General of Forests and Assistant Inspector General of Forests to assist the Inspector General of Forests, in the day-to-day work. There are four Zonal Assistant Directors of Wildlife Preservation stationed at Delhi, Madras, Calcutta and Bombay for the northern, southern, eastern and western zones respectively. The main function of Assistant Director is to, keep strict watch on the export of wildlife and animal products, which are exported through the main four parts of the country. All international trade in wildlife and their products can only take Place from these four parts of country and the species allowed to import or export are mentioned in the central export policy, which is banned from year to year. At the State governments level, Chief Wildlife Warden is the highest authority having statuary power under Wife Life Act, 1972. The rank and status of the Chief Wildlife Warden is different in different States. In some States the Post is equivalent to Chief Conservator of

Forests. While in other he may be an Additional Chief Conservator of Forests or a Conservator of Forests. Chief Wildlife Warden heads the separate wildlife wing within the forest department. The Chief Conservator of Forest is the over ail in charge of both forests as well as wildlife. There are demand from some quarters that wildlife wing should be completely separated from the forest department and be given the status of a separate department, The demand, of course, is debatable and controversial and involve issues of considerable risk. At present forestry and wildlife are the integral parts of the forest administration. The Chief Wildlife Warden enjoys statuary power under Wildlife (Protection) Act 1972. There are Wildlife Wardens and Assistant Wildlife Wardens who exercise their power as per the provision of the act. At present in most of the States the Divisional Forest Officers are also designated as Wildlife Wardens. In some States separate Wildlife Wardens have been appointed so that more pointed attention is paid and the wildlife is managed with more care and efficiency. For enlisting the co-operation of the general public and taking benefit of the knowledge and interest of wildlife enthusiasts, honorary Wildlife Wardens an also appointed. This has helped in the protection and propagation of the message of preservation of wildlife. Thus a line of administrative set up has come up both at Central as well as State level, for guiding and monitoring the wildlife management. In addition, the Zoological and Biological parks are also becoming popular in attracting the common public and the States forest departments under the direction of wildlife wing manage most of these parks. Forest and wildlife are inseparable as the blood and flesh in any animal body. The true status of wildlife depends upon the co-ordination of forestry practices. Forests constitute the habitats of wildlife and its management is directly linked with the wildlife of the area. But recently a decision has been taken to separate the wildlife wing from the forest department and shift it to the newly created Department of Environment. The main argument for this is that more pointed and scientific attention is paid to the management of wildlife. Apart from the Government organisation, Indian Board for Wildlife is the main body which advices the Union Government on all the wildlife policy matters. The members of the board include officials of the government as well as eminent conservationists and naturalists. The board was first constituted in 1952 and was called as "Central Board for Wildlife" with 25 members. The board suggested measures for protecting and safeguarding the wildlife. The board was later on re-designated as "Indian Board for Wildlife" IBWL). The membership of the board at present has gone around 70. The Indian Board for Wildlife has created separate wings within itself for paying specialised attention to a particular group of wildlife such as zoo wing, flora wing and the bird wing and then recommending to the government for taking up appropriate steps. Following are the main functions of *IBWL.*

— To advise the Central and State Governments on the ways and means of conservation and control of wildlife through coordinated legislature and practical measures with particular reference to seasonal and regional closure, and the declaration of certain species of animals as protected animals and the prevention of indiscriminate killing.

— To promote public interest in wildlife and the need for its preservation in harmony with the natural and human environment.

— To sponsor the setting up of National Parks, Sanctuaries and Zoological Gardens.

— To advice the Government on policies regarding export of living animals, trophies, skins, furs, feathers and other products of wildlife.

— To review from time to time the progress in the field of wildlife conservation in the country and suggest such measures for improvement as are considered necessary.

— To perform such other functions, which are relevant to the purpose for which, the Indian Board for Wildlife is constituted.

— To do all such other things either alone or in the conjunction with others or on the direction of the Government of India, which the board may consider necessary, advisable or conducive to the preservation and conservation of wildlife or for other similar purposes for which it is constituted including those mentioned herein.

There are significant achievements of IBWL The main achievement has been the inaction of comprehensive and united legislation for wildlife conservation, in the form of Wildlife (Protection) Act 1972. The board from time to time also recommends amendments in the act and in shifting and adding any species of wildlife in the schedule of the act. These schedules of the act are the guiding principles for hunting and due *to* this step considerable success has been achieved in protecting certain endangered and threatened species. Now, we have a clear picture species-wise with regards to the status the wildlife. The Indian Board for Wildlife through its recommendation and pursuation has been able to create as many as 221 reserves which include 85 National Parks and 448 sanctuaries for ensuring the protection of endangered and rare flora and fauna, specially listed in schedule I and schedule II of the Wildlife (Protection) Act 1972. Before the creation of the board there were only 33 reserves for wildlife. The establishment of a modern Zoological Park at New Delhi in 1955 was the result of the decision taken in its -first meeting. In this park the animals are given a feeling of their natural habitats. Visitors can see the animals in the enclosures. The expert committee set up by the Board has examined the overall condition of the existing wildlife reserves, in, its recommendation in 1970, the committee has suggested creation of more and more wildlife reserves, parks and sanctuaries and improvement measures for the existing reserves. The committee had also recommended that about 4% of the total geographical area of the country should be earmarked for the management of wildlife by creating more and more wildlife reserves. On the recommendation of expert committee Central Government has started extending financial assistance through the Five Year Plans for the creation and development of National Parks and sanctuaries. The fund is gradually increasing in every Five Year Plan. The various wings and expert sub committees of the IBWL are the center point of the knowledge gained through scientific application of the various wildlife management principles. This forms the technical guideline to the Central as well as State Governments for taking adequate steps to preserve the wildlife resources of the country. Not only this IBWL has been instrumental in creating a viable public opinion in favour of wildlife by organising seminars, celebrating wildlife weeks, setting up of Nature Clubs, conducting tours and organising essay and painting competition, film shows etc. Special measures are taken to educate the children and students of the various universities about the values and importance of wildlife conservation. With the help of University Grant Commission, many universities have opened separate faculties for forestry and wildlife. This should be further encouraged specially among the students, who are the future custodians of wildlife reserves. Indian Board for Wildlife has studied the trade in wildlife and animal produce and through its recommendations to the Central Government has been able to control and strictly regulate the trade in wild animals and their produces. The Wildlife (Protection) Act 1972, rigidly regulate the trade and certain species has been completely prohibited. The Zonal Assistant Director of Wildlife Preservation exercises powers and control the export of wildlife products. The export and import of wildlife has further been checked. When India became a party to the Convention on International Trade in Endangered Species of Wild Fauna and Flora in 1976, the member countries, by co-operating with each other have been able to bring the illicit trade to a minimum level.

International control and watch is exercised and it has become easier since the endangered species of India have been included in the appendices of the CITES. The convention regulates trade, by using licenses to the member countries and no member country can import or export any species listed in CITES, unless it has got valid license. To implementing the provision of the convention each nation has to appoint a separate management authority. The Inspector General of Forests and Director of Wildlife Preservation are the management authorities whereas Director, Zoological Survey of India, Director, Botanical Survey of India and the Director, Central Marine Fisheries Research Institute, have been declared as scientific authorities. Indian Board for Wildlife has also been instrumental in formulation of a National Environmental Conservation Policy and played a role in the revision of the national forest policy, keeping the position, of wildlife into consideration. A new forest policy and a new draft of Indian Forest Act is under/the consideration. In the same line, as in the Center, as per the provision of most of the Wildlife (Protection) Act 1972, State Governments have set up State Wildlife Advisory Boards for assisting the State Government in formulating broad principles of wildlife managements. These boards provide expert recommendation after considering the local factors'.

World Wildlife Fund (International)

Another non-official agency, which has played a vital role in the preservation of wildlife all over the world, is the World Wildlife Fund. It acts in close relationship with the International Union for Conservation of Nature and Natural Resources, which was established in 1961. It is a voluntary organisation with its Headquarters at Glands, Switzerland. A Board of International Trustees manages, the Fund. In 1969 it launched its National Appeal in India when the 10th Central Assembly of the International Union for Conservation of Nature and Natural Resources was held in New Delhi. World Wildlife Fund, India, has its headquarters at Bombay.

The success of any effort depends upon the resources available. The problem of conservation of wildlife is a Herculean task and involves raising of adequate fund for meeting the various requirements in connection with purchase of sophisticated equipments and know how to be made available for vigorous protection of wildlife. Most of the fund collected comes in the form of donation, appeals and by selling posters on wildlife, greeting cards, calendars and bearing conservation notes printed on them. Indian wildlife conservation owes a great deal to it. World Wildlife Fund, India has given financial and equipmental assistances to the following projects:

— Project Tiger
— Gir Ecological Research Project
— Project Hangul
— Himalayan Musk Deer

All these projects have been launched with the financial support of World Wildlife Fund (WWLF). The contribution of WWLF had done spectacular improvement in the status of these species viz., tiger, lion, hangul and mask deer. The success of Project Tiger has specially been marvelous. Its main function has been to provide financial support for National Tiger Conservation Programme, mainly for the purchase of equipments "and for the provision of expert scientific know how. Adequate transport facilities have been provided for effective movement. Advance electronic equipments and Radio and Wireless facilities have helped a great extent in capturing the poachers and enforcing strict vigilant watch over the area. It has also helped in frequent communication and co-ordination. Further special viewing devices, which were useful in darkness by emitting, light but not disturbing the animals has assisted in studying their behaviour more closely and accurately. This is particularly true in case of tiger and other nocturnal creatures. The World Wildlife Fund India also renders help by organising "Conservation Education Programme in the various educational institutes. In all the parts of India, viz. Northern, Southern, Eastern and Western, Nature Clubs have been set up, the highest being in the western zone, i.e. 291.

Wildlife Preservation Society of India

Wildlife Preservation Society of India was established in 1958 by some Indian wildlife enthusiasts and naturalists with its headquarter at Dehra Dun. The society is engaged in organising photo exhibition, symposium and lectures on the wildlife topic; it organises tour for students and other interested persons to the sanctuaries and national park. This helps in the propagation of wildlife conservation and also infuses interest among the people for wildlife. The society also publishes a quarterly journal called as "Cheetal", which contains articles, which are based upon the various field works done in connection with preservation of the animals. The main object of this society is to create public awareness for the preservation of wildlife heritage of the country. The society attempts to achieve:

- To promote interest in and impart knowledge regarding the preservation and conservation of all forms of wildlife, vegetation, water and environment, particularly among the youth of the country.
- To promote wildlife tourism.
- To carry out publicity and propaganda for the preservation of wildlife in India by means of monographs, journals, bulletins, films, film strips and other fusible methods.
- To assist the government in enforcing the provisions of Indian Forest Act and Wildlife (Protection) Act and helping in bringing the culprits to book.
- To advise and render help to the government organisation for better management of National Parks and Sanctuaries, preservation of wildlife and rare species and in the introduction of exotic species and finally rehabilitation of the rare species etc.

— To raise funds for meeting it's objectives and the object to create wildlife libraries and reading rooms and museum etc. so that more and more people are educated and imparted knowledge in wild fife.

— To carry out research work in matters of wildlife management, rare and threatened species and related matters

— To promote sportsmanship in Shikar and to recognise well regulated shooting and fishing as a means of preserving wildlife, thus, recreational use of surplus wildlife.

The society has been able to get significant success in its efforts in propagating the idea of wildlife conservation particularly among the youths.

Bombay Natural History Society

Bombay Natural History Society is only one of its kind in the sub continent. Since its foundation in 1883 as a private body at Bombay it has vastly contributed in the field of research, conservation, education and disseminating and extending the knowledge of flora and fauna among all categories of the population. The society is represented in Indian Board for Wildlife and State Advisory Boards of many States. The journal of the society publishes the articles contributed by the professional scientists, research workers, specialists and amateurs on various topics of natural history concerning with observation studies, survey and experiments, thereby making it a journal of very high international standard. The journal is one of the best sources of information and knowledge on the oriental flora and fauna. The society has also contributed towards the better understanding of flora and fauna through publication of superb books such as *Indian Birds* by Salim Ali, book of Indian Animate *by* S.H. Prater, India's *Wildlife* by M Krishnan, Birds of India and Pakistan by Salim Ali and S. Dillen Ripley. These publications are unique contribution made by the society illustrated with beautiful photographs. These publications had helped in propagating the idea of conservation of flora and fauna and better understanding of nature and in disseminating the knowledge of flora and fauna of the sub continent, i.e. India, Pakistan, Ceylon and Burma. The Society has a library consisting of more than 6000 publications in various subjects of natural history such as botany, zoology, ornithology, entomology etc. The Society is also engaged in the Nature Education Scheme by teaching school children in natural history subjects. The Society also guide the postgraduate research scholars in the field of ornithology and for this purpose is affiliated to the University of Bombay. It also assists in the form of grants in aid for carrying out fieldwork in natural history to students, specialists and naturalists from the fund created such as Dorabji Tata Trust Field Work Fund, the Salim Ali—Lake Wan The Ornithological Research Fund etc. Further the Society in collaboration with foreign agencies also carries out the research projects. It carried out the survey of Indian mammals from 1911 to 1923 and it constitutes the greatest achievement. The ornithological survey which started in 1929 in the Western Ghats are still continuing. A large number of specimens were captured from all over India and studied. Studies are going in the ecology of Gir lion and wild ungulates in the Gir forests of Gujarat. This project was taken with the Yale University and Smithsonian institution. The Society has vivid and comprehensive collection of specimen of flora and fauna. The collection includes about 20,000 mammals, about 23,000 birds, 1,500 fishes, 4,000 reptiles, 1,000 amphibians and 80,000 insects etc. The students, research workers and specialists are allowed to make use of the collection for further understanding of natural history. Other than the above-described organisations there are several independent or associate programmes going in India and other parts of the world, whose contribution towards the conservation of wildlife is immense. The Central Crocodile Breeding and Management Training Research Institute has come with the assistance of Food and Agriculture Organisation and UNDP.

APPENDIX

WTO RECOMMENDATIONS TO GOVERNMENT FOR SUPPORTING AND/OR ESTABLISHING NATIONAL CERTIFICATION SYSTEMS FOR SUSTAINABLE TOURISM

Certification systems for sustainable tourism play an increasing role in regulating tourism operations as voluntary instruments above legal frameworks. They usually address three main aspects, namely: 1) environmental performance of companies, operations and destinations; 2) product quality; and 3) corporate social responsibility of operations. They normally target tourism suppliers, such as accommodation, restaurants, sport and leisure facilities, tourist attractions, destinations, tour operators, (tourist) transport companies, tourist associations, etc.

Considering the growing number and importance of certification systems and other voluntary initiatives in tourism, and based on a recommendation made by the UN Commission on Sustainable Development, WTO undertook a comprehensive worldwide study on this topic. The results of this study were published in 2002, under the title "Voluntary Initiatives for Sustainable Tourism: Worldwide Inventory and Comparative Analysis of 104 Eco-labels, Awards And Self-commitments".

The WTO Committee on Sustainable Development of Tourism, at its 3rd Session held in Costa Rica, 25-26 September 2002 recommended the preparation of a set of guidelines for Governments on certification systems for sustainable tourism. Acting on this decision of the Committee, the present document aims at enhancing awareness among governments about the opportunities certification systems may provide as part of their sustainable development policy goals, and provides basic recommendations for supporting and/or establishing such systems at the national level. It is primarily based on the WTO study mentioned above. It also draws on the survey conducted among WTO Member States in November 2001-January 2002, considering the feasibility of a Sustainable Tourism Stewardship Council, on the experience gained in the area of certification through the International Year of Ecotourism 2002, on comments received from the Committee members, and on other relevant documents.

The Role of Governments in Present Certification Systems

The WTO study on voluntary initiatives for sustainable tourism revealed that governments have an important role in many of the certification systems presently operating. Twenty of the 59 certification schemes investigated are lead by government agencies. A further 18 have government involvement, either through direct financial support, marketing support, expert know-how in criteria setting, verification procedures, or surveillance of procedures followed by the certification body. Government financial support is crucial to half the schemes for which data is available. Government agencies involved generally include either environment ministries, national tourism authorities and tourist boards, and in fewer cases, standards institutes.

Certification systems can bring benefits to society, the environment, governments, private companies and consumers as well.

Potential benefits for society:

— Generally speaking, societies will benefit from certification systems that cover the three aspects of sustainability: social, environmental and economic. Certified companies are supposed to generate benefits in these three areas, while reducing their negative impacts. Therefore, the contribution of tourism activities to the sustainable development of host societies will be more evident, more measurable and more accountable.

— Furthermore, the level of awareness on sustainability issues will be stronger in the host society if the large majority of tourism companies and/or destinations are certified.

Potential benefits for the environment:

— It is evident that certification systems and ecolabels that include strict environmental criteria result in benefits for the local environment and, to the extent that some mass tourism activities can impact biodiversity and climate change, also the global environment.

— Furthermore, the widespread use of ecolabels and certification systems in the tourism industry helps to generate increased environmental awareness among both, tourists and host societies and should result in more caring attitudes with respect to the natural and built environments.

Potential benefits for governments:

— Providing an effective alternative to direct regulation, which could prove more difficult and time-consuming to implement;

— Enabling governments to adopt a flexible approach to monitoring the tourism industry, permitting organisations to proceed at the pace they feel most comfortable with, while encouraging them to develop innovative approaches to environmental and socio-cultural improvements;

— Giving tourism companies greater scope for making environmental and social improvements by exploiting opportunities specific to their individual circumstances, rather than governments having to control and inspect companies in order to check that they comply with general, industry-wide regulations;

- Allowing part of the costs of implementing and monitoring environmental protection measures to be transferred to the industry itself, thereby reducing the financial burden of regulation on the taxpayer;
- National programmes of tourism certification can enhance tourism's recognition in the country, national competitiveness and image in international markets.

Potential benefits for companies:

- Adherence to voluntary environmental initiatives can enable the company to market its products more effectively, and to improve their public image among consumers, business partners and with the host communities;
- Engaging in voluntary certification can help companies to signal their specific commitment to environmental, social and even economic improvements, which may in turn help to defer the need for further direct regulation by governments;
- Pursuing sound environmental management strategies can generate substantial cost savings for the company;
- Participation in a certification programme can provide better access to modern techniques, technology and know-how;
- Applying effective environmental management can help to protect the environmental and cultural assets upon which the tourism industry depends for its continued prosperity.

Finally, certification and ecolabels can of course benefit consumers by providing them with more information and guidance for their decisions on travel choices, as well as assurances for product and service quality.

Recommendations

Certification systems for sustainable tourism need to be developed and operated to fit geographical, political, socio-economic and sectoral characteristics of each country. For this reason, the following recommendations serve as general orientation and they need to be adapted to the economic, institutional, social and environmental conditions prevailing in each country.

1. Development of the Certification System

Governments can play a key role in the initiation and development of certification systems for sustainable tourism by creating the supportive legal and institutional structures. The following general recommendations can be made:

1. Consider a national certification system as an integral part of sustainable tourism development policies, strategies and objectives, and an effective tool to implement them.
2. Identify key stakeholders and potential target groups relevant to and interested in certification programmes.
3. Develop the certification system through multi-stakeholder consultation processes, involving all relevant interest groups, such us different government authorities (tourism, environment, transportation, finance, education, etc); tourism trade associations and other private groups; academic, education and research institutions; NGOs; consumer associations; etc. The development and the operation of a successful certification programme in many cases lays in the multi-stakeholder representation of the team awarding certificates and supporting the programme.
4. Coordinate an in-depth research on the conditions and feasibility of a certification system, including aspects such as:

- Existing legal and voluntary instruments affecting the tourism sector (e.g. laws, regulations, taxes, subsidies, local certification systems, codes of conduct, environmental awards, etc.);
- Experience of certification systems applied in other sectors in the country, like agriculture, forestry, and draw lessons from them for the tourism sector
- Certification criteria (see section 2 below);
- Operational mechanisms: application, verification, awarding, revision and inspection procedures; consulting and technical assistance for participants, marketing and communication; funding (see section 3).

5. Provide finance and/or seek partners for co-financing and providing technical contributions for the research, development and operational costs of certification programmes (e.g. different government departments, NGOs, academic institutions, international finance and development agencies, private foundations, etc).
6. Ensure transparency throughout all the stages of the development and operation of the certification system and establish an appeals process.
7. Make clear to the private sector the benefits, costs and other implications of certification systems.
8. Develop incentives to motivate and encourage tourism companies to become certified, e.g. marketing incentives by giving priority in trade shows and nationally sponsored publicity, or ensuring access to environmental technologies, etc.
9. Consider issues affecting the sustainability of destinations as a whole, involving all tourism product and service providers.

10. Pay special attention to equitable access to certification, especially by small and medium size firms, as they can have more difficulties in meeting the costs and technical requirements than bigger companies.
11. Conduct pilot projects for testing and demonstration of the certification system.
12. Prepare the market for certification, in order to reach a good demand level from tourism companies, and a critical mass at the initial phase to get the system running.

2. Certification Criteria

Developing certification criteria is a critical part of the certification system development process. The following general recommendations need to be considered:

1. Base criteria on existing legal standards and instruments and set them well above legal compliance.
2. Include the precondition of compliance by the applicant with these legislations.
3. Address the three dimensions of sustainability: environmental, socio-cultural and economic issues.
4. Define core criteria and supplementary criteria specific for different tourism product and service groups (e.g. hotels and other accommodations, transportation services, restaurants, tour operators and travel agents, attractions, etc.). By this way consider the implications to destinations as a whole, and not just certain tourism product and service groups.
5. In bigger countries, criteria can be adjusted to specific regional and local environmental and socio-economic conditions.
6. For each criterion, define indicators that are measurable and easy to understand by the different type of stakeholders involved in the certification process.

7. Base criteria and indicators on scientific research that evaluates the key environmental and socio-economic impacts of the sector.
8. Criteria should refer to attainable and realistic goals for private sector participants.
9. Criteria can be set in different levels of requirements: from more easily achievable to very demanding criteria. Thus, the certification system sets a framework for continuous improvement whereby applicants can achieve higher performance levels step by step.
10. Compliance with criteria can be measured through process and performance-based assessments. Indicators are essential tools for measuring environmental, social and economic impacts of tourism operations:

    Environmental indicators can relate to the following factors, among others:

    — Environmental impact assessment conducted for setting up the operation or construction of establishments;

    — Environmental management practices, company policies and technical measures (e.g. energy, water saving and waste treatment devices, environmental friendly transportation, etc.) in place;

    — Land use and property issues in destinations;

    — Health and safety;

    — Use of natural resources:

    - Energy (consumption, reduction, efficiency)
    - Water (consumption, reduction, quality)
    - Solid and liquid waste (reduction, reuse, recycling, treatment, disposal)
    - Appropriate building materials
    - Hazardous substances (reduction, handling,

use of nature friendly cleaning products)

- Noise (reduction)
- Air quality (quality, improvement)
- Habitat/eco-system/wildlife maintenance and enhancement;

— Environmental information/interpretation/education for customers;

— Transportation services (public transport, environmental friendly alternatives;

— Indicators and standards on the impacts at specific tourist use areas (e.g. beaches) and on the impacts caused by specific tourism activities and facilities (e.g. diving, golf, marinas etc.);

— Visual impacts of establishments and infrastructure; etc.

Social indicators can relate to the following factors, among others:

— Social impact assessment conducted for setting up the operation and the establishments;

— Staff policies and management (information, education, training, incentives, health, safety, etc.);

— Relationships with local communities (local employees, outreach and education programmes);

— Emphasis on, and conservation of local/regional culture, heritage and authenticity;

— Maintaining aesthetics of physical development/architecture;

— Community feedback systems, satisfaction of local population;

— Contribution to community development purposes (infrastructure improvement; social services, etc.);

— Information provided to guests on sustainability aspects;
— Guest feedback systems in place, customer satisfaction, etc.

Economic indicators can relate to the following factors, among others:

— Creation of local employment (number of employees from local communities and their level of skills);
— Supply chain management through green and sustainable purchasing policies;
— Creation of networks of environmentally friendly businesses within a given destination;
— Responsible marketing;
— Use of locally sourced and produced materials and food, etc.

In addition, certification criteria for ecotourism should specifically address the elements below, besides the general sustainability criteria:

— Financial and in-kind contributions to conservation of ecotourism sites by companies;
— Level of involvement of local communities and benefits accruing to them;
— Use of specialised guides and other interpretation techniques, information provided to tourists through ecotourism operations;
— Environmental education activities provided for tourists and local populations;
— Locally appropriate scale and design for lodging, infrastructure and tours;
— Minimal impact on and the appropriate presentation of local and indigenous culture.

11. Indicators to measure the success of certification systems can address:
    - The number of applications and certified companies (i.e. increase over time of the number of companies registered in a certain certification system);
    - The percentage of certified companies in the different tourism product and service groups;
    - Improvement in environmental and social performance in certified companies (e.g. changes in water and energy consumption, resource savings, etc.);
    - Environmental and social performance of certified companies as compared to non-certified ones (e.g. a current estimate is that environmental performance per certified accommodation enterprises can be taken as about 20 % better than the average performance at accommodation facilities in Europe).
12. Consider the whole product life cycle when setting product environmental criteria (from the manufacturing, transporting, through purchasing, consumption, to recycling, disposal, etc.).
13. Undertake periodic revision and update of criteria (e.g. every 2-3 years).

3. Operation of Certification Systems

The procedure is normally composed of the application, verification and certification processes. The funding mechanism for the above services and procedures is a crucial and critical element for the success of certification systems. Normally there is a funding, verification and certification body interacting in these processes. In many cases the funding and certification bodies coincide. Fundamental components of any certification system are the facilitation of consulting, advisory and technical assistance and marketing services. The following general recommendations can be made in relation to the operational processes:

3.1 Application

1. The system should be open to all potential applicants.
2. Provide clear and easily accessible information on the criteria, costs and benefits and other conditions of certification (e.g. through Internet, email, telephone, information kit).
3. Offer immediate sources for consultation services.
4. Show tangible benefits for applicants (e.g. costs savings, marketing advantage, access to technical assistance and modern technology and financial possibilities, etc.) and explain clearly the commitments and costs.
5. Application documents should be clear, easy to understand and fill in.
6. Conduct a pre-evaluation/assessment of the applicant in order to identify technical and technological aspects that need to be improved to meet the criteria. Provide assistance and financial incentives for these improvements.

3.2 Verification

7. Verification of compliance with criteria should be done by an independent or third-party organisation. In other words by a body which is independent from the parties being certified and of technical assessment or funding.
8. Verification is normally done through a combination of different activities: review of application documents and references, self-assessment by the

operation through questionnaire, on-site visit, fees to be paid by the applicant.

9. Verification audits should be conducted by suitably trained auditors.
10. The verification process can be also used to give recommendations to the applicants on how to improve their performance and achieve further progress.

3.3 Certification (awarding of certification)

The certification is basically the awarding of the certification to the applicant, granting a permit for using the logo, marketing and other services of the system.

11. Certification bodies can be composed of representatives of the mayor stakeholder groups participating in the development and operation of the system. Governments have a key role in certification bodies, by giving credibility and recognition of the system.
12. As it was also mentioned among the recommendations for criteria development, awarding of certification can be done at single-level or at multi-level. The latter one occurs if criteria are set on different scales with a view to ensure a framework of continuous improvement.
13. The certification, the use of a logo and related benefits should be granted for a pre-determined period, after which re-assessment and verification should be conducted to ensure continuous compliance with the same or higher criteria.
14. Follow up control can be conducted after certification. For example, the WTO study on voluntary initiatives demonstrated that more than 50% of the certification systems currently operating undertake some control visits after certification: 38% are announced, and 17% are surprise visits. Some eco-

labels either do phone checks, stimulating guests' feedback or sending "mystery guests" to the certified tourism service.

15. Procedures have to be in place for the cancellation and withdrawal of certification and the use of the corresponding logo in case of non-compliance.
16. The certification system can also include consumer and local community feedback mechanisms.

3.4 Consulting, Advisory and Technical Assistance Services

The facilitation of the following services represents important added value for tourism companies and can be decisive factors for joining the certification system.

17. Provide technical consultancy options from the initial expression of interest and through the application phases onward, and give guidance to the applicant at every stage of the process.
18. Facilitate technical assistance for applicants so that they can introduce advanced management techniques and technology to meet the certification criteria. Provide access to environmental technologies, equipments and techniques by creating alliances with other organisations that can provide assistance for this purpose.
19. Develop training and capacity building programmes in form of courses, workshops, distance learning, etc.
20. Organise regular meetings for certified companies to promote the exchange of experiences and the sense of group.
21. Constant assistance and advisory is especially important in certification systems where the criteria and awarding are set on different scales.

3.5 Marketing and Communication

Marketing is another fundamental element of certification programmes, representing perhaps the biggest attraction and the most tangible benefits for private companies. The following general recommendations can be made:

22. Develop a precise marketing strategy for the certification system targeting three groups in principle:
    - 22.1 Potential candidates: aiming at attracting companies to join the programme
    - 22.2 Applicants and certified companies: providing marketing and promotional support and market advantages for them
    - 22.3 Consumers: reaching recognition of the certification programmes, fostering responsible travel choices, and make effective the marketing advantage for certified companies.
23. Develop a well-distinguished and unequivocal logo design for the system. The logo can be accompanied by a motto, or slogan. Ensure legal protection of the logo.
24. The presentation of the system in media and communication should reflect a well recognised corporate image in the market for businesses and consumers as well. The system can represent a sort of brand.
25. Use all available forms and channels to publicise and provide information on the certification programme for companies and consumers (e.g. brochures, flyers, guide books, printed and electronic media, Internet, conferences, seminars, tourism and trade fairs, etc.)
26. Give good media coverage to the awarding ceremonies.

27. Provide marketing support and promotion for certified companies through national tourist boards or national tourism marketing organisations, e.g. presentation of these companies in national brochures, catalogues, listings, websites, support for presence at national stands at tourism fairs and exhibition, etc.
28. Give recommendations and examples to applicants and certified companies on how to include the certificate in their own marketing activities.
29. Demonstrate the distinction on environmental performance, economic and socio-cultural effects between certified and non-certified products/companies.
30. Communicate on a regular basis with certified members (e.g. through periodic meetings and events, newsletters, emails, exclusive access to information on Internet, etc.)
31. Provide clear and easily understandable information to consumers on the characteristics and added value that certification represents.
32. Develop consumer awareness raising and education campaigns on the certification system and certified products.
33. Involve consumer associations in these efforts

3.6 Fees and Funding

Governments have a key role in providing funding themselves, and/or in conceiving and developing alternative funding mechanisms with other partners for the operation of the certification system.

34. Establish the right balance between financial contributions of the public and private sectors.
35. Ensure that the sources of funding do not create a

conflict of interest, since undue influence by funding organisations should be avoided in the certification procedure.

36. Establish fees for participants to cover (at least part of) application and verification costs. Fees should be kept as low as possible in order to encourage participation.
37. Fees should be calculated proportionally to size of businesses (e.g. by number of beds or visitors, turnover, etc.).
38. Provide incentive measures and support the application of companies, especially of small and medium size enterprises that would otherwise be left out (e.g. by soft loans and subsidies to make the necessary improvements to meet the criteria).
39. Consider in-kind contributions by governments for the operation, e.g. providing facilities, office space and equipment.

Final Note: Governments are encouraged to convey to the World Tourism Organisation (WTO) their experience in connection with certification systems related to sustainability in tourism. This will allow WTO to periodically revise these guidelines, introduce any additional guidelines or modify those recommended above (Madrid, March 2003).

Select Bibliography

Amatya Jagdish M.S., (1970), *Pokhara Valley: Trekking in Annapurna-Dhaulagiri Area*, Kathmandu.

Anon, (1997), *Driving Through Malaysia*. Government of Malaysia brochure.

Archer, B.H. & Fletcher, J.E., (1990), Tourism: Its economic significance. In M. Quest (ed.), *Horwath Book of Tourism* (pp. 10-25). London: The MacMillan Press.

Armington, Stan, (1976), *Trekking in the Himalayas*, Lonely Planet Publications, Victoria.

Ashworth, G.J. and Turnbridge, J.E., (1990), *The Tourist-Historic City*, Belhaven Press, London.

Attix, Shelley, A., ed., (1993), *Ecotourism: A Directory of Marketing Resources*. Pearl City: University of Hawaii.

Bailey, N., (1996), Towards a research agenda for public-private partnerships in the 1990s, *Local Economy* 8(4), 292-306.

Bangs, R., (1993), Clean, green and meant to be seen the ethos of eco-tourism in *Proceedings of the 1993 World Congress an Adventure Travel and Eco-Tourism Manna*. The Adventure Travel Society 97-101.

Banister, D., (1995), Transport and the environment a review article. *Town Planning Review*, 66(4) 453-458.

Bari S.C., (1997), "What is tourism? Concepts and definitions." *Journal of Travel and Tourism*, Vol. 1, No. 1, March 1997 IITTM Gwalior.

Barnet, Richard J., and Ronald E. Muller, (1974), *Global Reach: The Power of the Multinational Corporation*. New York: Simon and Schuster.

Barry, Tom, (1984), *The Other Side of Paradise: Foreign Control in the Caribbean*. New York: Grove Press.

Beaver, Allen (1975), *Retail Travel Practice,* Beaver and Gordon Land Tour Ltd., London.

Becker, C., (1995), Tourism and the environment in A. Montanari and A.M. Williams (eds) *European Tourism Region: Spaces and Restructuring,* John Wiley, Chicenya 207-220.

Belk, R.W. and Costa. J.A., (1995), International tourism: An assessment and overview. *Journal of Macromarketing* 15(2), 33-48.

Belsky, Jill, (1999) 'Misrepresenting communities: the politics of community-based rural ecotourism in dales Point Manatee, Belize.' *Rural Sociology* 64 (4): 641-666.

Benjamin, Medea, and Andrea Freedman. *Bridging the Global Gap.* Cabin John, MD: Seven Locks Press, 1988.

Bernard, J., (1973), The sociology of community, in J. Reiss Jr and H.I. Wilenskv (eds) *Introduction to Modern Society Series,* Scott. Foresman and Co., Glenview.

Bezruchka, Stephen, (1974), *A Guide to Trekking in Nepal,* Sahayogi Prakashan, Kathmandu.

Bhauguan, H.H., (1972), *Public Sector Undertakings,* Vol. 4, No. 1, Feb., 1972.

Bhushan, Y.K., (1964), *Business Organisation and Management,* Sultan Chand and Sons, New Delhi.

Billimoria, R.P. and Singh, N.K., (1985), *Human Resource Development,* Vikas Publishing House, New Delhi.

Blamey, R.K. and Braithwaite. V.A., (1997), A social values segmentation of the potential ecotourism market, *Journal of Sustainable Tourism* 5(1), 29-45.

Blanchard, F., (1984), Seabird harvest and the importance of education in seabird management on the North Shore if the Gulf of St Lawrence, unpublished PhD thesis, Cornell University, Ithaca, NY.

Blazey, M., (1992), Travel and retirement Status. *Annals of Tourism Research* 19(4), 771-783.

Boniface, B.G. and Cooper, C.P., (1994), *The Geography of Travel and Tourism,* 2nd edn, Butterworth-Heinemann, Oxford.

Bosselman, F.P., (1978), In the Wake of Tourists; Managing Special Places in Eight Countries. *The Conservation Foundation,* Washington, D.C.

Boyle, Godfrey, (1996), "Solar Photovoltaics". In *Renewable Energy: Power for a Sustainable Future.* Ed Godfrey Boyle. Toronto: The Open University.

Brandon, Katrina, (1996), Ecotourism and Conservation: *A Review of Key Issues.* Washington, DC, World Bank.

Brause, Diane, (1996), *Directory of Alternative Travel Resources.* Dexter, OR:Lost Valley Educational Center.

Brent, J.R., and Echtnyer, (1995), "Tourism, Education and Human Resources Development," *Tourism Recreation Research,* Lucknow.

Breslin, P. and Chapin, M., (1984), Conservation Kuna-style, *Grassroots, Development* 8, 26-35.

Britton, S. and Clarke, W., (eds), (1987), *Ambiguous alternative: Tourism in Small Developing Countries,* University of the South Pacific, Suva.

Britton. S.G., (1991), Tourism, capital and place: towards a critical geography of tourism, *Environment and Planning D: Society and Space* 9, 451-478.

Broken Bud, 1765-D Le Roy, Berkeley, CA 94709; (310) 843-5506. Advocacy for antiprostitution tourism and child trafficking; newsletter.

Brown, L., (1981), *Building a Sustainable Society,* W.W. Norton, New York.

Bryden, J.M., (1973), *Tourism and Development: A Case Study of the Commonwealth Caribbean,* Cambridge University Press.

Buckley, P.J. and Witt, S.F., (1990), Tourism in the centrally-planned economies of Europe. *Annals of Tourism Research,* 17, 7-18.

Bureau of Tourism Research, (1992), *Tourism and the Environment.* Canberra, Australia: Bureau of Tourism Research.

Burkart, A.J. and S. Medlik, (1974), *Tourism: Past, Present and Future,* Heinemann, London.

Burns, Peter, (1995), *Tourism: A New Perspective.* Englewood

Cliffs, NJ: Prentice-Hall.

Bussolo and Lecomte, (1999), *Trade Liberalisation and Poverty.* ODI Poverty Briefing No. 6 (December). London, ODI.

Carncy, Diana, (1999), *Approaches to Sustainable Livelihoods for the Rural Poor.* ODI Poverty Briefing No. 2 (January). London, ODI.

Carr, M.I.L. (n.d.) Ecotourism, National Parks and Land use Planning in Costa Rica—Llanuras of Tortuguero: A Case Study. Unpublished.

Carrere, R., (1995), Loita Maasai endeavour to save sacred forest, *Shainan's Drum 37,* 17.

Carribbean Conference of Churches, PO Box 616 Bridgetown, Barbados, fax (809) 429-2075. The new address of the Ecumenical Coalition on Third World Tourism (ECT-WT).

Carter, F.W. and Turnock, D., (1993), Problems of the pollution scenario, in *Environmental Problems in Eastern Europe,* Routledge, London, 188-213.

Casey, John, (1995), "Here comes the sun." *Civil Engineering.* Vol. 65 No. 54-57.

Cater, E., (1991), Sustainable tourism in the Third World: problems and prospects, *University of Reading Department of Geography Discussion Paper 3.*

Cavanagh, James E., (1993), et al., "Ocean Energy Systems". In *Renewable Energy: Sources for Fuels and Electricity.* Ed. Thomas B. Johansson, et al. Washington D.C.: Island Press.

Chadwick, R.A., (1981), Some Notes on the Geography of Tourism; a comment, *Canadian Geographer,* 25.

Charlton, C.A., (1992), *Devon and Cornwall Branch Lines Passenger Survey,* Devon and Cornwall Rail Partnership, Plymouth.

Chib, S.N., (1989), *Essays on Tourism,* PATA India Chapter, New Delhi Cross Section Publications Pvt. Ltd.

Chopra, Suhita, (1991), *Tourism and Development in India.* London: Ashish Publishing House.

Christian Aid, (1995), *Abuse of Innocence: Tourism and Child*

Prostitution in the Third World. London: Christian Aid.

Clark, J.R., (1991), 'Carrying capacity and tourism in coastal and marine areas' *Parks* 2(3), pp 13-17.

Clark, W. and Munn, R.F., (eds) (1986), *Ecologically Sustainable Development of the Biosphere*, Cambridge University Press, New York.

Clarke, J., (1997), A framework of approaches to sustainable tourism, *Journal of Sustainable Tourism* 5(3) 224-253.

Cloke, P., Milbourne, P. and Thomas, C., (1995), *Lifestyles in Rural England*, Rural Development Commission, London.

Cohen, E., (1987), "Alternative Tourism : A Critique", *Tourism Recreation Research*, 12(2).

Colvin, J.G., (1994), Capirona: a model of indigenous ecotourism, *Journal of Sustainable Tourism*, 2(3), 174-177.

Coull, C., (1996), *A Traveller: Guide to Aboriginal BC.*, Beautiful British Columbia Magazine, Vancouver.

Danaher, Kevin, Beyond Safaris, (1991), *A Guide to Building People-on-People Ties with Africa.* Trenton, NJ: Africa World Press.

Daniels, A., (1995), Ahousat band's ecological walk business booms, *Vancouver Sun*, 27 January

Dartmoor National Park Authority, (1994), *Traffic Management Strategy*, Devon County Council and Dartmoor National Park Authority, Bovey Tracey.

Davies E., (1987), Planning in the New Zealand National Parks. *New Zealand Geographer* 43(2), 73-78.

Dawson, A.H., (1991), Poland, in Hall, D.R. (ed.) *Tourism and Economic Development in Eastern Europe and the Soviet Union*, Belhaven Press, London and Halstead. New York. 190-202.

Deepak, A., Regmi R. and Rimal, N. (1994), *Nepal District Profile A District Wide Socio-Techno-Economic Profile of Nepal.* National Research Associates, Kathmandu.

Devon and Cornwall Rail Partnership, (1996) *Annual Report 1995-1996.* Devon and Cornwall Rail Partnership, Plymouth.

Dex, S., (1985), *The Sexual Division of Labour*, Wheatsheaf Books, Brighton.

Din, K.H., (1992), The 'involvement stage' in the evolution of a tourist destination *Tourism and Recreation Research* 17(1), 10-20.

Dixon, J.A. and Sherman, P.B., (1990), *Economics of Protected Areas: A New Look at Benefits and Costs.* London: Earthscan.

Drake, S., (1991), Local participation in ecotourism projects, in T. Whelan (ed.) *Nature Tourism Managing for the Environment*, Island Press, Washington, 132-163.

Eaton, B. and Holding, D., (1996), The evaluation of public transport alternatives to the car in British national parks, *Journal of Transport Geography 4(1), 55-65.*

Eber, Shirley, ed *Beyond the Green Horizon: Principles of Sustainable Tourism.* London: Tourism Concern/World Wildlife Fund, 1992.

Ecumenical Coalition on Third World Tourism (ECTWT), (1992), *Caught in Modern Slavery.* Bangkok: ECTWT.

Edmonton Journal, (1991), Neighbours demand silence from fort, *Edmonton Journal*, 22, August, B2.

Ellis, J. (1994), Umorrduk Safaris, in *A Talent For Tourism: Stories about Indigenous People in Tourism*, Commonwealth Department of Tourism, Canberra, 31-33.

Enloe, C., (1989), *Bananas, Beaches and Bases: Making Feminist Sense of International Politics.* University of California Press, Berkeley, California.

Erbes, R., (1973), International tourism and the economy of developing countries. Paris: Organisation for Economic Cooperation and Development.

Escobar, A., (1995), *Encountering Development: The Making and Unmaking of the Third World*, Princeton University Press, Princeton, NJ.

Fennell, D.A. and Eagles, P.F., (1990), Ecotourism in Costa Rica: a conceptual frame work, *Journal of Park and Recre-*

ation Administration. 8(1), 23-34.

Fewings, J., (1995), A rural transport package for Dartmoor *Town and Country Planning* June, 180-182.

Flavin, Christopher and Nicholas Lenssen, (1990), *Beyond the Petroleum Age: Designing a Solar Economy.* World Watch Institute.

Foghorn Press, 555 De Haro Street, The Boiler Room #220, San Francisco, CA 94107; (415) 241-9550, fax (415) 241-9648. Outdoor and recreation books.

Forbes, B., (1993), *Tourism Development Plan, 1993-1998,* Brooking-Harbor Chamber of Commerce, Brookings.

Forsberg, P., Harvey, B. and Kelsay, D., (1996), *Curry County: Public Resources from Private Initiative,* Egret Communications, Port Orford, Oregon.

Forsyth, Timothy, (1995), 'Tourism and agricultural development in Thailand.' *Annals of Tourism Research* 22 (4): 877-900.

France, L., (ed.) (1997), *The Earthscan Reader in Sustainable Tourism,* Earthscan Publications, London.

France, Lesley (Ed), (19970, *The Earthscan Reader in Sustainable Tourism.* London, Earthscan.

French, H. Vanishing Borders, (2000), Protecting the Planet in the Age of Globalisation Washington, Worldwatch Institute.

Frenmont, P. (1983), *How to Open and Run a Money Making Travel Agency,* John Wiley and Sons, New York.

Garnham, H.L., (1985), *Maintaining the Spirit of Place,* PDA Publishers, Mesa.

Gascon, C., (1994), *Discover the Lower North Shore: Guide and Directory,* Coaster's Association, St. Paul's River.

Gayle, Dennis J., and Jonathan N. Goodrich, (eds.), (1993), *Tourism Marketing and Management in the Caribbean.* London: Routledge.

Gerald, M. Meier , (1975), *Leading Issues in Economic Development,* Oxford University Press.

Getz, D., (1986), Models in tourism planning towards integration of theory and practice, *Tourism Management* 7(1), 21-32.

Ghimire, Krishna, (19970, *Emerging Mass Tourism in the South.* UNRISD Discussion Paper no. 85. Geneva. UNRISD.

Gibbs, D., (1996), Integrating sustainable development and economic restructuring, a role for regulation theory, *Geoforum* 27(1), 1-10.

Gill, R., (1994), Manyallaluk, in *A Talent For Tourism: Stories about Indigenous People in Tourism.* Commonwealth Department of Tourism, Cariberra, 22-21.

Glacken, C., (1967), *Traces on the Rhodian Shore, Nature and Culture in Western Thought from Ancient Times to the End of the Enghteenth Century,* University of California Press, Berkeley.

Gollin, Jim, and Ron Mader, (1997), *Honduras: Adventures in Nature,* Santa Fe: John Muir Publications.

Gonsalves, Paul, (1987), *Alternative Tourism: An Operations Mannual for Third World Groups.* Bangalore: Equations.

Graphic Arts, *Culture Shock!series* Portland, OR: Graphic Arts Center Publishing, various years.

Gray, Matthew, (1998), 'Economic reform, privatisation and tourism in Egypt.' *Middle Eastern Studies* 34 (2): 91-112.

Great Barrier Reef Marine Park Authority, (1993), *Annual Report* 1992-1993. Townsville. Great Barrier Reef Marine Park Authority.

Greenpeace, (1992), *Impacts of Tourism Development in Pacific Islands.* San Francisco: Greenpeace Pacific Campaign.

Gregory A., (1983), *The Travel Agent: Dealer in Dreams,* 4th Ed., The Prentice Hall, London.

Grotta, (1992), Daniel, and Sally Wiener Grotta. *The Green Travel Sourcebook: A Guide for the Physically Active, the Intellectually Curious, or the Socially Aware.* New York: Wiley.

Gunn, C, (1994), *Tourism Planning Basics, Concepts, Gases,* Taylor & Francis, Washington.

Gurung, Harka, (1980), Vignettes of Nepal, Sajha Prakashan,

Kathmandu.

Hall, C.M. and Johnston, M. (eds), (1995), *Polar Tourism: Tourism in the Arctic and Antarctic Regions*, John Wiley, Chichester.

Hampton, Mark, (1998), 'Backpacker tourism and economic development.' *Annals of Tourism Research* 25 (3): 639-660.

Hanmer, Lucia, John Healey, and Felix Naschold. (2000), *Will Growth Halve Global Poverty By 2015?* ODI Poverty Briefing 8 (July. London: ODI).

Hardin, G., (1969), The tragedy of the commons. *Science* 162, 1243-1248.

Harman, W.W., (1993), Rethinking the central institutions of modern society: society and business, *Futures* 25 (December), 1063-1071.

Hart, A.J., (1992), Planning for tourism in Christchurch in comparative study, unpublished MA thesis, Department of Geography, University of Canterbury, New Zealand.

Harvey, B and Kelsay, D., (1994-96), *Various Progress Reports—Cury Country Sustainable Nature-Based Tourism Project*. Egret Communications, Port Oxford, Oregon.

Hayden, T., (1999), Tuberculosis is making a comeback *Newsweek* 8 November, p. 77.

Hayes, John L., (1976), Trekking North of Kathmandu, Peter Purna Banks Avalok, Kathmandu.

Hays, S.P., (1957), *The Response to Indusrialism, 1885-1914, University of Chicago Press, Chicago.*

Healy, R.G., (1996), Tourism, Ecotourism and Sustainable Development, unpublished mimeo, Duke University, Raleigh, NC.

Hewison, R., (1987), *The Heritage Industry: Britain in a Climate of Decline*, Muthuen, London, 160.

Heymann, D., (1995), Emerging infectious diseases. *World Health* 50(1), 4.

Hill, C., (1990), The paradox of tourism in Costa Rica, *Cultural Survival Quarterly* 14(1) 14-19.

Hinch, T.D. and Butler, R.W., (1996), Indigenous tourism a

common ground for discussion in R. Butler and T. Hinch (eds) *Tourism and Indigenous Peoples*, International Thomson Business Press. London, 3-19.

HMGN: (1994), Ministry of Tourism and Civil Aviation Department of Tourism, *Nepal Tourism Statistics 1993*, Rising Sun Printers, Kathmandu.

Hoffman, M.S. (ed.), (1991), *The World Almanac and Book of Facts 1992*, Pharos Books, New York.

Holing, Dwight, (1991), *Earthtrips: A Guide to Nature Travel on a Fragile Planet.* Los Angeles: Conservation International and Living Planet Press.

Howe, J., (1982), Kindling self-determination among the Kuna, *Cultural Survival Quarterly* 6(3), 15-17.

Hubbs Clay, (ed.) *Alternative Travel Directory.* Amherst. Transitions Abroad Publishing, annually.

Hughes, G., (1991), Are the costs of cleaning up Eastern Europe exaggerated? Economic reform and the environment, *Oxford Review of Economic Policy*, 7(4), 12-24.

Ise, L., (1961), *Our National Park Policy A Critical History* Published for Resources for the Future by The John Hopkins Press, Baltimore, Md.

Iwersen-Sioltsidis, Susanne, and Albrecht Iwersen, (1996), 'Tourism and developing countries.' *Intereconomics* 31 (6): 301-306.

Jacob, M., (1994), Toward a methodological critique of sustainable development, *Journal of Developing Areas* 28, 237-252.

Jansen-Verbeke, M., (1986), Inner city tourism: resources, tourists, and promoters *Annals of Tourism Research* 13(1), 79-100.

Jemo, I., (1996), *Experiences in the Postwar Reconstruction of the Historical Core of Dubrovnik.* Paper prepared for International Conference on Settlement Revitalisation in Postwar Reconstruction, Zagreb, April 26-27.

Jenner, P. and Smith, C., (1992), *The Tourism Industry and the Environment*, E.I.U. Publications. London.

John Muir Publications PO, Box 613, Santa Fe, NM 87504; (505) 982-4078. "Adventures in Nature" travel guide series.

Johnston, C.R., (ed.), (1990), Breaking out of the tourist trap. *Cultural Survival Quarterly* 14(1 & 2).

Johnston, R.J., (1991), *Geopgraphy and Geographers: Anglo-American Human Geography Since* 1945, 6th edn., Edward Arnold, London.

Jones, P., (1993), Wildlife viewing in Atlantic Canada: A case study of constraints and opportunities, unpublished Master's project, Simon Fraser University, Burnaby.

Jones, S.B., (1933), Mining tourist towns in the Canadian Rockies, *Economic Geography* 9, 368-378.

Khandwalla, N.P., (1995), *Organisational Designs for Excellence,* Tata McGraw Hill, New Delhi.

Killick, Tony, (1999) Making Adjustment Work for the Poor. ODI Poverty Briefing 5 (May). London.

Kincaid, Jamaica, (1988), *A Small Place,* New York: PLUME/ Penguin Books,

Kinnaird, Vivian, and Derek Hall, (eds.), (1994), *Tourism: A Gender Analysis.* New York; Wiley.

Kirkby, S.J., (1995), Introduction, in J.Kirkby, P.O.keefe, and I.Timberlake (eds) *The Earthscan Reader in Sustainable Development,* Earthscan Publications, London.

Kleinhenz, C. and Hallitzky, E., (1991), *Costs and Benefits of the Sumava National Park. Management Plan for the WWF,* University of Passau. Passau.

Kotler, P., (1980), *Marketing Management: Analysis, Planning, Implementation and Control,* Englewood Cliffs, Prentice Hall.

Lawson, F., and M. Baud-Bovy (1977), *Tourism and Recreation Development,* London: Architectural Press.

Lea, John, (1988), *Tourism and Development in the Third World.* London: Routledge,

Leheny, D., (1995), A political economy of Asian sex tourism. *Annals of Tourism Research* 22(2), 367-384.

Leiper, N., (1990), Tourist attraction systems, *Annals of Tour-*

ism Research 17(3), 367-384.

Lemons, J. and Brown, D.A., (1995), *Sustainable Development, Science, Ethics and Public Policy,* Kluwer Academic Publishers, London.

Lew, A.A and van Otten, G.A., (eds), (1998), *Tourism and Gaming on American Indian Lands,* Cognizant Communications Corporations, New York.

Lew, A.A and Yu, L., (eds), (1995), *Tourism in China. Geographic, Political and Economics Perspective,* Westview Press, Boulder, Colorado.

Lewand, Alan A., and Lawrence Yu, (eds.), (1995), *Tourism in China.* Boulder, CO. Westview Press.

Lindberg, K., (1991), *Policies for Maximising Nature Tourism's Ecological and Economic Benefits,* World Resources Institute, Washington.

Lipietz, A., (1992), *Towards a New Economic Order: Postfordism, Ecology and Democracy,* Polity Press, Cambridge.

Liu, Juanita, (1991), *Pacific Islands Ecotourism: A Public Policy and Planning Guide.* Honolulu: Pacific Business Center Program, University of Hawaii.

Long, V.H., (1990), Tourism development, conservation and anthropology, *Practicing Anthropology* 14(2), 14-17.

Loomis, J.B.; and Walsh, R.G., (1996), *Recreation Economic Decisions: Comparing Benefits and Costs* (2nd Edition) Venture Publishing, Inc. State College Pennsylvania.

Lowenthal, D., (1958), *George Perkins Marsh: Versatile Vermonter,* Columbia University Press, New York.

Lowndes, V., Nanton, P., McCabe, A. and Skelcher, C., (1997), Networks, partnerships and urban regeneration, *Local Economy* 11(4), 333-342.

Lozawa, Tomoya, (1980), Trekking in the Himalayas, Yama-Kei, Publishers, Tokyo.

Lujan, C.C., (1993), A sociological view of tourism in an American Indian community maintaining cultural integrity at Taos Pueblo, *American Indian Culture and Research Journal* 17(3), 101-120.

Mak, A., (1981), The Montagnais. In *The Lower North Shore.*

Ministere des Affaires Culturelles du Quebec, Quebec, 86-99.

Mallari, A.A. and Enote, J.A., (1996), Maintaining control: culture and tourism in the Pueblo of Zuni, New Mexico, in M.F. Price (ed.) *People and Tourism in Fragile Environments,* John Wiley & Sons, Chichester, 19-31.

Mander, Jerry, and Edward Goldsmith, (eds.), (1996) *The Case Against the Global Economy.* San Francisco: Sierra Club Books.

Manidis Roberts Consultants, (1995), *Determining an Environmental and Social Carrying Capacity for Jenolan Caves Reserve,* Manidis Roberts, Sydney.

Mather, Sue. *Tourism in the Caribbean.* New York: Economist Intelligence Unit, n.d.

Mattson, V.E., (1985), *Frederick Jackson Turner: A Reference Guide* G.K. Hall, Boston.

Maxwell, Simon, (1999), *The Meaning And Measurement Of Poverty.* ODI Poverty Briefing 3 (February). London, ODI.

Mercer, D.C., (1970), The geography of leisure: a contemporary growth point, *Geography* 55(3), 261-273.

Metz, J.J., (1991), A reassessment of the cause and severity of Nepal's environmental crisis. *World Development* 19, 805-820.

Mieczkowski, Zbigniew, (1995), *Environmental Issues of Tourism and Recreation.* Lanham, MD. University Press of America.

Milne, S. and Pohlmann, C. (forthcoming) The evolving hotel industry: evidence from Montreal, in K. Debbage and D. laonnides (eds) *The Economic Geography of Tourism,* Routledge, London.

Milne, S. and Wenzel, G., (1991), Tourism and economic development in the Baffin Region of Canada's Northwest Territories, unpublished paper, McGill University, Montreal.

Milne, S., (1997), Tourism, dependency and South Pacific

microstates, beyond the vicious cycle? in D.G. Lockhart and D. Drakakis-Smith (eds) *Island Tourism: Trends and Prospects*, Pinter, London 281-301.

Mings, R.C., (1978), Tourism Industry Development : at the Cross roads, *Tourist Review* 33(3) : 2-9.

Ministere des Transports du Quebec, (1988), *Statistiques de transports maritime* Government du Qucbec, Quebec.

Mulchand, S., (1993), Northern exposure, *Asia Travel Trade*, September, 26-27.

Murphy, P.E., (1985), *Tourism: a community approach*, Methuen. London.

Mutchell, England Murphy, P. (1991) Geography and tourism, *Annals of Tourism Research* 18, 57-70.

Myers, N. and Gaia Ltd staff, (1984), *Gaia: An Atlas of Planet Management*, Anchor/Doubleday, New York.

Nelson, J.G., (1973), Canada's national parks—past, present and future, *Candadian Geographical Journal* 86(3), 68-89.

Nicholson- Lord, D., (1994), Hitting- and obliterating- the trail, *World Press Review* January, 48.

Nicholson, M.H., (1962), *Mountain Gloom and Mountain Glory*, Norton, New York.

Nickerson, N.P. (1996), Foundations of Tourism, Simon and Schuster International, England.

Pannell Kerr Forster Management Consultants, (1990), *Fort Edmonton Park: Opportunities for a Major Tourist Attraction*, Pannell Kerr Forster Management Consultants, Edmonton.

Pareek, V. and T.V. Rao, (1981), *Designing and Managing Human Resources Systems*. Oxford Publications, New Delhi.

Parks Canada, (1999), *Parks Canada—Guiding Principles and Operating Policies*. Ministry of Supply and Services, Ottawa.

Partners for Livable Places, (1981), *Tourism and Communities: Process, Problems, and Solutions*, Washington, DC: Partners for Livable Places.

Pattullo, Polly, (1996), *Last Resorts: The Cost of Tourism in the Caribbean*. London: Cassell.

Patty, A., (1999), Australian sex tourists find their laws back home don't take a vacation. *The World Paper* January-February, p. 16.

Pearce, D.G., (1979), Towards a geography of tourism, *Annals of Tourism Research* 6(3), 243-272.

Pelton, R.Y., Aral, C. and Dulles, W., (1998), *Fielding's The World's Most Dangerous Places*, 3rd edn. Fielding, Inc., Redondo Beach, California.

Peppet, D., (1984), *The Roots of Modern Environmentalism* Croom Helm, London.

Perrottet, T., (1996), Grace & fervour, *The Weekend Australian, The Weekend Review: Travel*, 14-15 December, 16.

Pilarski, Michael, (1997), *Friends of Trees Guide to Hawaii*. Bellingham, WA: Friends of the Trees.

Pilgrim, J., (1983), *Outdoor Recreation Resource Management*. Croom Helm, Kent.

Pinchot, G., (1968), Ends and means, in R. Nash (ed.) *The American Environment: Readings in the History of Conservation*, Addison-Wesley, Reading, Mass., 59-64.

Pizam, A. and Knowles, T., (1994), The European hotel industry, in C.P. Cooper and A. Lockwood (eds) *Progress in Tourism, Recreation and Hospitality Management, Vol, 5* John Wiley, Chichester, 135-152.

Pleumarom, A., (1999), "Tourism, globalisation and sustainable development" in Third World Network Dossier for CSD 7, Third World Network, Malaysia.

Plummer, J.T., (1989), Changing values. *The Futurist* 23(1), 8-13.

Pollock, A. and Benjamin, L., (2001), Shifting Sands: The Tourism Ecosystem in Transformation, DestiCorp Limited.

Poynter, J.M., (1993), *Tour design, marketing and management*, Prentice Hall, New York.

Prentice, Richard, (1993), *Tourism and Heritage Attractions*. London: Routledge.

Price, M.F., (ed.), (1996), *People and Tourism in Fragile Environ-*

ment, John Wiley & Sons, Chichester.

Pridham, G., (1996), *Tourism Policy in Mediterranean Europe: Towards Sustainable Development?* Occasional Paper 15, University of Bristol, Centre of Mediterranean Studies, Bristol.

Priestley, G.K., Edwards, J.A. and Coccossis, H., (1996), *Sustainable Tourism? European Experiences*, CAB International, Wallingford.

Priestly, Gerda K.J. Arwel Edwards, and Harry Coccossis, (eds.), (1996), *Sustainable Development? A European Experience.* Wallingford, Oxford: CAB International.

Prior, D., (1996), 'Working the network': local authority strategy in the reticulated local state. *Local Government Studies* 22(2), 92-104.

Rames, K.T., (1995), *Structural Adjustment, World Trade and Third World Tourism: An Introduction to the Issues.* Bangkok: ECTWT.

Ramsar, (1992), New opportunities for cooperation in Europe, *Ramsar Newsletter*, 13. 2-7.

Rao, T.V. and Pereira, (1986), *Recent Experiences in Human Resource Development*, Oxford Publications, New Delhi.

Redclift, M. and Benton, T., (1994), *Social Theory and the Global Environment*, Routledge, London.

Redclift, M., (1987), Sustainable Development and the market a framework for analysis *Futures* 20(6), 638.

Reed, D., (1990), *The European Bank for Reconstruction and Development: an Environmental Opportunity*, World Wide Fund for Nature, Washington.

Renshaw M., (1989), Tour Operations in Collaghan (Eds.), *Travel and Tourism*, Business Education Publishers, Durham.

Richter, L.K., (1988), Indonesian tourism: the good, the bad and the ugly. *Contours* 14(1), 29-30.

Richter, Linda K., (1989), *The Politics of Tourism in Asia.* Honolulu: University of Hawaii Press,

Rieffel, Rober, (1978), Nepal Namaste, Sahayogi Prakashan,

Kathmandu.

Robert and Charles, (1990), Tourism principles, practice, and philosophies, John Wiley and Sons Inc., New York.

Roberts, J., (1996), Green Consumers in the 1990s; Profile and Implications for Advertising, *Journal of Business Research*, 36, 217-231.

Robinson, H., (1976), *A Geography of Tourism*, London, Macdonald and Evans, London.

Robinson, H., (1976), *A Geography of Tourism*, MacDonald and Evans, London.

Roe, D and Urquhart, P., (2001), Pro-Poor Tourism: Harnessing the World's Largest Industry (or the World's Poor, IED, UK and Khanya, South Africa.

Rohter, Ira, (1992), *Envisioning a Green Hawaii: Two Futures.* Honolulu: Hawaii Green Party.

Rossel, Pierre, (ed.), (1988), *Tourism: Manufacturing the Exotic* Copenhagen: International Work Group for Indigenous Affairs.

Rovinski, Y., (1991), 'Private reserves, parks and ecotourism in Costa Rica'. pp. 39-57 in Whelan. T (ed) *Mature Tourism Managing for the Environment.* Island Press. Washington, DC.

Ruitenbeek, H.J., (1991), *Indicators of Ecologically Sustainable Development: Towards New Fundamentals.* Canadian Environmental Advisory Council, Ottawa.

Sayet; A and Waler. R., (1992), *The New Social Economy*, Blackwell, Oxford.

Schneider, D.M., Godschalk, D.R. and Axler, N., (1978), *The Carrying Capacity Concepts as a Planning Tool*, Planning Advisory Service Report No. 338, American Planning Association, Chicago.

Scottish Tourist Board, (1994), *Tourism and the Environment*, Scottish Tourist Board, Edinburgh.

Sen, Amartya, (1981), *Poverty and Famines: An Essay on Entitlement and Deprivation.* Oxford. Clarendon Press.

Sheldon, P., (2002), Information Technology Contributions

to Biodiversity in Tourism, in Tourism, Biodiversity and Information, di Castri, F. and Balaji, V., (eds.), Backhuys, Leiden. The Netherlands, pp. 449-456.

Sheldon, P.J., (1989), Tour Wholesaling, in Witt S., and Moutinho L., (Eds.) *Tourism, Marketing and Management Handbook*, Prentice Hall, U.K.

Sheldon, Pauline, (1997), *Tourism Information Systems*. Wallingford, Oxford: CAB International.

Sierra Club Adventure Travel Guides, Sierra Club Books, 730 Polk Street, San Francisco, CA 94109; (805) 965-3452. For "Adventuring In...."travel guide series.

Simpson, Pally, and Geoffrey Wall, (1999), 'Consequences of resort development: a comparative study.' *Tourism Management* 20: 283-296.

Singh, Tej Vir, H. Leon Theuns, and Frank M. Co. (1989), *Towards Appropriate Tourism: The Case of Developing Countries*. New York: Peter Lang.

Smith, Stephen L. J., (1995), *Tourism Analysis. A Handbook.* Essex: Longman Scientific & Technical.

Smith, V. (ed.), (1977), *Hosts and Guests: The Anthropology of Tourism*, University of Pennsylvania Press, Philadelphia.

Spaho, E., (1992), Tourism: promising contracts, *Albanian Economic Tribune*, 6(10). 17-19.

Standring, K., (1991), Eastern bloc-buster, *Birds Illustrated*, 1(1), 76-81.

Stanfield, C.A. and Rickert, J.E., (1970), The recreational business district, *Journal of Leisure Research* 2(3), 213-225.

Stratford, A.H., (1993), *Air Transport Economics in the Supersonic Era*, The Macmillan.

Thompson, J., (1991), East Europe's dark dawn. *National Geographic*, 179(5), 37-69.

Timothy, Dallen J., and Geoffrey Wall, (1997), "Selling to tourists: Indonesian street vendors.' *Annals of Tourism Research* 24 (2): 322-340.

Turnock, D., (1979), Water management resources in Romania, *GeoJournal*, 3,609-622.

Waller, M., (1989), The ecology issue in Eastern Europe: protest and movements. *Journal of Communist Studies, S.* 303-328.

Wells, M., Brandon, K. and Hannah, L., (1992), *People and parks: Linking Protected Area Management with Local Communities,* The World Bank/World Wildlife Fund/ US Agency for International Development, Washington.

Williams, P., (1990), "Tourism Technology and Environment" *Journal of Travel Research,* Vol. XXIX, No.2, pp. 55-56.

Index

●●●